# THE OHIO RIVER

## IN AMERICAN HISTORY

Courtesy Dock, Mount Vernon, Indiana

Captain Rick and pocket trawler, 'Free State'

## COVER PHOTOS:

**Front:**

'Pittsburgh's Point' and confluence of Allegheny and Monongahela Rivers....upper left

Sunset on the lower Ohio, near Brandenburg Kentucky...lower left

That notorious lair –Cave-In-Rock, Illinois ...upper right

**Back:**

Cincinnati Ohio, seen from across the Ohio River in Covington Kentucky...upper third

Along the upper Ohio River near Wellsburg, West Virginia...middle left

The Allegheny and Kiskiminetas Rivers, near Schenley, Pennsylvania...middle right

Vibrant Audubon Park, in Henderson Kentucky...lower left

Six miles from the head of navigation on the Kanawha River, Smithers, WV...lower right

# THE OHIO RIVER

## IN AMERICAN HISTORY

### Along with the Allegheny, Monongahela, Kanawha, Muskingum, Kentucky, Green and Wabash Rivers

By Captain Rick Rhodes

Photographs and Sketches by Rick Rhodes
Edited by Bill Byrnes

Published 2008 by **Heron Island Guides**
# 305, 2560 62nd Avenue North
St. Petersburg, Florida, 33702
www.heronislandguides.com

Published by: Heron Island Guides
# 305, 2560 62nd Avenue North
St. Petersburg, Florida 33702

Fax: 727-527-8287
Phones: 727-459-5992
        888-459-5992
Website: www.heronislandguides.com.

Quantity discounts are available on bulk purchases of this book.  For
more information, please contact the publisher.  An order form can
also be found on the second-to-last page of this book.

River details in this book are based on authoritative data at the time of
research.  The river sketches should not be used for navigating a
vessel on these rivers.  US Army Corps of Engineer Charts should be
used for river navigation.  The author has made utmost efforts to
ensure the accuracy and completeness of information contained in this
work.  Heron Island Guides and the author will not accept any liability
for damages caused by a reader following information in this book.

This book is printed and bound in the United States of America

Library of Congress Card Number:  2008926171

ISBN (13): 978-0-9665866-4-0
ISBN (10): 0-9665866-4-6

# CONTENTS:

## SECTION I
## THE OHIO RIVER IN AMERICAN HISTORY

**CHAPTER:**

## SECTION II
## SPECIFIC REGIONS AND HIGHLIGHTS

# APPENDICES:

# SKETCHES:

# AMERICAN HISTORY (ONLY) VERSION:

In the spring of 2007, Heron Island Guides came out with a softbound title that took two years to research, "The Ohio River – In American History and Voyaging on Today's River." This book attempted to do two things: 1) Provide historical information and an appreciation of these great rivers to local river buffs and anyone else traveling along the Ohio River or on one of its main tributaries, and 2) Provide up-to-date information on the many facilities useful to recreational boating interests. Not totally unexpected, the 'boating segment' did not adequately support that book. Within the 'local history segment,' many conveyed that our fact-filled 320-page, $36 book was too pricey. Hence, this 2008 version removed the boating information –96 pages –from the 2007 book. Thus, we hope that this hardbound title will be a more appealing book for you river historians and river travelers –as well as a book priced $6 less.

# BOOK ORGANIZATION:

The Ohio River Watershed drains more than half the states east of the Mississippi River –New York, Pennsylvania, Maryland, West Virginia, Virginia, Kentucky, Ohio, Indiana, Illinois, Tennessee, Mississippi, Alabama, Georgia, and North Carolina. Where the Ohio River ends, at its confluence on the Mississippi River, the Ohio contributes about 60 percent of the water flowing into the lower Mississippi.

For our young nation, the Ohio River was the first major artery encountered that flowed westward, and greatly aided our country's growth west. Today, 25 million people, almost 10 percent of the US population, reside in the Ohio River basin. This history-loaded book will primarily focus on the six river states directly bordering on the Ohio River. This 2008 work is divided into two sections: 1) The Ohio River in American History, and 2) The Regional Section containing many riverside particulars as they pertain to one of our eleven regional Ohio River chapters.

Section I explores the Native Americans living in the Ohio River region before the Colonists arrived, the French and Indian War, the American Revolution, the Development of the Northwest Territories, the Underground Railroad, the Civil War, Early River Transportation, the Steamboat Era, the Development of the Locks and Dams, and the growth and the decline of the industries seen along the Ohio River today.

Section II –our Regional Section – geographically divides the Ohio River and its navigable tributaries into eleven distinct regions. Local historical anecdotes are contained in each of these eleven chapters. In this section, we start in Pittsburgh, with the three rivers that converge at 'The Point.' Afterward, we travel from northeast to southwest, and divide the Ohio River itself into seven chapters. Four major tributaries – the Allegheny, Monongahela, Muskingum, and Kanawha Rivers –all have their own dedicated chapter. Discussions of smaller tributaries (e.g., the Green, Kentucky, Little Kanawha, Beaver, Hocking, Licking, Wabash, and Big Sandy Rivers, as well as others) are addressed in their relevant Ohio River chapter. There is also a chapter on the significance of the current commercial traffic seen on the river today.

We've included 23 river sketches throughout the book. There is an overall sketch and three small-scale sketches that divide the entire area into three sub-regions, plus 19 larger-scale sketches. Eighty-six black and white photographs are interspersed throughout this book.

We also have incorporated five appendices that present lists of locks and dams, connecting highways on both sides of the Ohio River, a list of major regional hospitals, a list of major universities, and a list of some annual festivals held along these rivers.

# Sketch 1-A: The Ohio River Region –from Western PA to Southern IL

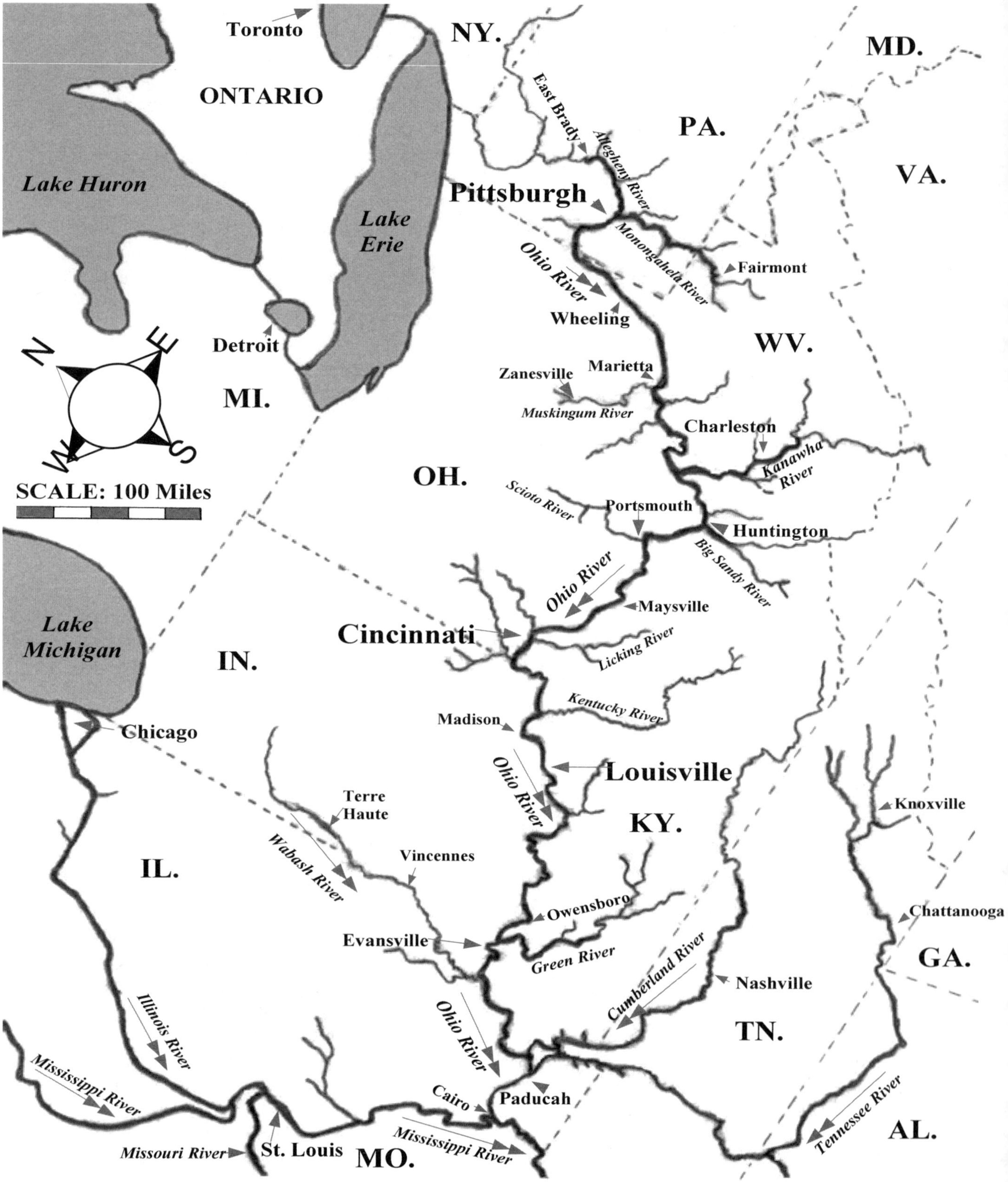

Toronto

ONTARIO

NY.

MD.

East Brady

PA.

Allegheny River

VA.

Lake Huron

Lake Erie

Pittsburgh

Monongahela River

Fairmont

Ohio River

N
E
W
S

Detroit

Wheeling

WV.

MI.

Zanesville

Marietta

Charleston

Muskingum River

Kanawha River

SCALE: 100 Miles

OH.

Scioto River

Portsmouth

Huntington

Big Sandy River

Ohio River

Lake Michigan

Maysville

IN.

Cincinnati

Licking River

Chicago

Kentucky River

Madison

Knoxville

Terre Haute

Ohio River

Louisville

Wabash River

Vincennes

KY.

Chattanooga

IL.

Owensboro

GA.

Illinois River

Evansville

Green River

Cumberland River

Nashville

Mississippi River

Ohio River

TN.

Missouri River

St. Louis

MO.

Cairo

Paducah

Mississippi River

Tennessee River

AL.

8

# SECTION I
# THE OHIO RIVER IN AMERICAN HISTORY

## CHAPTER 1
## Native Americans and the French and Indian War

Native Americans had been living in the Ohio River region for thousands of years. The Iroquois Indians, the ones who named the river "Oyo," were centered in what is now New York and near the upper reaches of the present-day Allegheny River. In those days, the Iroquois considered the Allegheny an extension of the Ohio River.

Less than a hundred years after the white man arrived on the scene, the Iroquois formed a confederation or league, 'The Five Nations.' These five groups were the Mohawk –the most dominant, Cayuga, Oneida, Onondaga and Seneca people. A sixth nation, the Tuscaroras, joined the Iroquois confederation in 1726. The Iroquois used this union to better bargain with the newcomer European Dutch, as well as to develop a strengthened position when fighting other Native American, especially those tribes to their southwest in the Ohio River region. The Iroquois were especially savvy and cunning when crafting allegiances with the white newcomers.

The Native American Delawares, Mingos, and Shawnees lived southwest of the Iroquois and in the heart of the present-day Ohio River region. These 'Ohio River Indians' were part of a broader group, the Algonquin, tied together by a linguistic commonality. The Iroquois, allied and armed with help from the Dutch, positioned themselves to either eradicate or remove these Algonquin tribes to their west and south. With the help of European weaponry, the aggressive Iroquois attacked, and more often than not expanded into nearly every direction, including to the south and west. Even by standards of their day, Iroquois warriors were extremely brutal when it came to inflicting pain on their vanquished.

West of the new Iroquois lands, the French had been forging alliances, based on fur trade, with the Hurons, Ottawas, Miamis and other Algonquins for about 150 years. By the mid-1600s, the Iroquois had driven-out the Miamis and Hurons from the eastern Great Lakes region as well as driven-out the Shawnees from their Ohio River country. Before long, the Iroquois were attacking the French. The French responded with a small but effective force of regular troops. In 1664, this Iroquois miscalculation was compounded when the Iroquois' major ally, the Dutch, lost their position of strength in the East to the British. New Amsterdam became New York.

The series of wars between the French and their Algonquin Indian allies against the Iroquois was also known as the Beaver Wars. The Beaver Wars subsided as the 17th Century drew to a close. Most of the displaced Shawnees, who survived and fled west and south, were returning to their original lands in the Ohio River region. The clever Iroquois, having lost their Dutch benefactor, were soon currying favor with the British. The early British were less astute in Indian affairs than the Dutch. Realizing this, the Iroquois were not above striking conflicting accords with the British's traditional enemy –the French. Before long, the Iroquois were often playing-off the British and French against each other.

In 1668, Frenchman Rene Robert Cavalier Sieur de LaSalle had heard Iroquois stories that there was a great river to the south that flowed westward. In 1669, an intrigued LaSalle departed Montreal to find and to explore this great river that supposedly flowed toward China. When his party reached the western shore of Lake Ontario, they proceeded overland and southwestward. LaSalle claimed to have reached the Ohio River and then followed it as far as present-day Louisville. There is some speculation about this claim. Nonetheless, LaSalle is typically credited as being the first European to see the Ohio River. More than ten years later, in 1682, and after the Ohio had been explored by many white men, LaSalle sailed the length of the Mississippi River. He proclaimed this entire Mississippi and Ohio River region for the king of France. In 1684, LaSalle tried to establish a French Colony near the mouth of the Mississippi River. But in 1687, arrogant LaSalle was murdered by his own Frenchmen.

Nonetheless, French traders and trappers soon began scattering along the two major river routes (i.e., the Mississippi and Ohio) on the western side of the Allegheny (i.e., present-day Appalachian) Mountains. These French fur traders shipped their pelts out of the interior of the continent in either one of two ways – 1) through mostly water routes along the Great Lakes, often through Fort Detroit, and then on to the St. Lawrence River, or 2) down the Mississippi River to New Orleans. The undermanned French needed to retain this rich interior land of the Ohio River valley, and realized that they would need Indian allies against the encroaching waves of British settlers. By the 1720s, British colonists, particularly in Pennsylvania and Virginia, were rapidly moving westward.

In Pennsylvania, the Six Nation Iroquois Confederation positioned itself to negotiate away Native American lands that weren't even theirs to begin with. The Iroquois granted the British land in western Pennsylvania that belonged to the Delaware, Shawnee and Conestoga Indians. Once again, displaced Ohio River Indians became refugees, and were forced west and south. The Shawnees and Delawares moved deeper into the Ohio country and west of the 'Forks of the Ohio' (i.e., present-day Pittsburgh). Here, at least for a while, some Native Americans felt that they were beyond the

reach of the conniving Iroquois and intruding colonial settlers. By the mid 1740s, no less than 2,500 Indians were again living in the bountiful Ohio River Valley.

Native Americans, all over the continent, were also being decimated by white mans' diseases, for which they had little natural immunity. As Native American villages became depleted, many tried to replenish their lost numbers by way of bereavement rituals. These bereavement rituals involved raiding parties that would attack white settlements as well as other Indians communities, in order to take women and children as hostages. During these warring raids, adult men –all perceived as warriors –were considered impossible to assimilate, and were typically slain during the raid. After the hostages returned to the village of the attacking Indians, they had to successfully pass the scrutiny of the 'new tribe' by running through a gauntlet. If the hostages didn't panic, they would be assimilated into their new tribe to help repopulate lost numbers.

Nevertheless, new settlers continued to arrive and to occupy Native American lands. Furthermore, enterprising British and Colonial traders, looking westward from Pennsylvania and Virginia, were making commercial inroads. These new traders were competing directly with the French for Indian pelts and furs, in exchange for firearms and other goods.

In 1749, a small group of Virginia Planters formed the Ohio Company. The Ohio Company's purpose was to explore and survey the land west of the Alleghenies, establish and nurture trade with the local Indians, and eventually start moving settlers into that region. The Ohio Company established an outpost at Wills Creek (present-day Cumberland Maryland). About that same time, in French territory, the governor of Canada sent Celoron de Bienville on an expedition to stake out this same land for France. Celoron's expedition, departed southward from Lake Erie to the headwaters of the present-day Allegheny River. The Celoron expedition followed the Ohio River as far as the Great Miami River (i.e., near present-day Cincinnati), before returning overland to Lake Erie.

In 1752, confrontational French Governor Marquis Duquesne took a strong-armed tactic to stop British westward encroachment. In western Pennsylvania, Duquesne began building and fortifying outposts. His plan called for moving southward from Lake Erie to the 'Forks of the Ohio' –where a new French fort would become Fort Duquesne. When the governor of Colonial Virginia, Robert Dinwiddie, got wind of this French move, he sent 21-year old Major George Washington on a reconnaissance mission. Washington was a good choice because he had already surveyed some of this land for the Ohio Company. In 1754, Washington's report to Dinwiddie was alarming. Indeed, the French were beefing up their presence with forts in western Pennsylvania. Dinwiddie immediately authorized a stockade to be built at the 'Forks of the Ohio,' before the French, coming down the Allegheny River from the north, could do so. Most of the forty or so men building this fort, Fort Prince George, came from Redstone Old Fort (i.e., today's Brownsville Pennsylvania) –56 miles up the Monongahela River from the 'Forks of the Ohio.' But as soon as the Virginia fort-builders saw the superior French flotilla sailing down the Allegheny, they fled.

Within seven weeks, a French contingent of 35 soldiers was heading southwest from the Forks to meet the nearby Virginians. Their 'diplomatic mission' was to give a message to Lieutenant Colonel George Washington advising him to evacuate this land belonging to the French King. Not knowledgeable of the French's 'diplomatic intent,' Washington's men and his Indian allies, intercepted, surrounded, and surprised the French contingent near present-day Uniontown Pennsylvania. As the day dawned, confused fighting broke out. The ambushed French suffered fourteen casualties while the Virginians suffered only four. Later both sides claimed the other side shot first. After tensions subsided and calmer heads prevailed, the wounded French commander delivered his message to Washington explaining his firm but non-hostile mission. Before the French ensign could finish, an Iroquois chief –one of Washington's allies, Tanaghrisson, raised his hatchet and crushed the young ensign's skull. Washington was dumbfounded. This was a calculated move by Tanaghrisson. After earlier being rebuffed by the French, this Iroquois Chief had planned to draw the Virginians into a much deeper hostility, and position himself as a powerbroker to be reckoned. Washington was now caught-up in a series of events whirling out of his control.

Washington decided to take the offensive and attack Fort Duquesne. Once again, treacherous Tanaghrisson deceived Washington. As Washington's Virginians were marching on Fort Duquesne, their Iroquois 'allies' abandoned them. At Redstone Old Fort, Washington realized that his mission was now suicidal. Washington smartly decided to start a retreat with his four hundred Virginians. After two days of retreating, his men reached Fort Necessity (near Uniontown Pennsylvania) –a fort hastily constructed the prior year. Soon, six hundred regular French militiamen along with about a hundred French-allied Indians appeared. The French and Indians started what would likely be an all-out slaughter, as small inadequate Fort Necessity couldn't hold-out. The French commander was also the older brother of the young French ensign whose head had been split open by Washington's Iroquois ally just a month earlier. But the judicious French commander, realizing his ammunition was dwindling, and trying to abide by the 'Rules of War,' knew he was in a tenuous position to take prisoners, since no stated formal war was declared. The French commander ordered a cease fire, and offered Washington a chance to sign articles of capitulation, if his

Site of the *Battle of Point Pleasant*, Tu-Endie-Wei State Park, West Virginia

Prickett's Fort –first built in 1774, near Fairmont, West Virginia

Virginians would leave the Ohio River watershed immediately.

The British apparently learned nothing from the failed Virginias encounter with French and Indians near the 'Forks of the Ohio.' About one year later, pompous British Major General Edward Braddock was again marching toward the Forks. Braddock even rebuffed friendly overtures and aid from anti-French Indians. Braddock's thousands of men and heavy artillery departed Wills Creek (Cumberland Maryland), and soon had a column that could stretch for more than two miles. In early July 1755, as this massive force was approaching Fort Duquesne, Braddock forded the Monongahela River for a second time. After that second ford, and near Frazier's Cabin (present-day Braddock Pennsylvania), when the British were about ten miles from Fort Duquesne, they encountered their enemy. The French side – a force of about 150 Canadian militiamen and French regulars, plus a few hundred Indian allies –rather than flee, as Braddock had expected, split their force in order to intercept and attack Braddock's. But the Indians and French didn't have time to set-up an ambush. Nonetheless, the encounter was still a rout. The scarlet-coated British occupying the road were easy pickings for the Indians hiding in the brush. British heavy artillery was useless. Furthermore, some of Braddock's troops were shot in the back by inept friendly fire. Within a few hours, the British force was totally demoralized. Braddock was mortally wounded after being shot through a lung. The British had just suffered their worst defeat on the continent.

George Washington, one of Braddock's aides-de-camp, was the only one of three aides not wounded. Not wanting to have Braddock's dead body exhumed and mutilated by the Indians, Washington decided to bury him in the middle of the road, at the forward end of the retreating British column –thereby obliterating any trace of a new grave. Twenty-one year old

Daniel Boone was another lucky survivor of Braddock's failed advance. The joyous Indians could have further decimated the retreating British army, but were sidetracked when they discovered the British's cache of rum hidden in the spoils of the battle. The Indians didn't even go back to Fort Duquesne. During this *Battle of Monongahela*, nearly 900 of Braddock's soldiers were killed or injured, while fewer than 50 French and Indians were killed or injured. Despite the heavy losses, when the retreating British force reunited with their detached advancing rear guard, they still had about 2,000 soldiers. However, in spite of their superior numbers, the British kept hightailing. After the victory, with the Indians celebrating and then abandoning their French allies, the few Frenchmen remaining at Fort Duquesne could not have held the fort if there were even a minor British counterattack. To this point, the British and Colonist failures were marked by pomposity, ineptitude, and gross miscalculations.

For three more years, the over-confident Indians had their way on this Pennsylvania and Virginia frontier. Skirmishes and bereavement raids on white settlers were commonplace. Colonel George Washington had the unenviable task of trying to keep the frontier Virginia settlers safeguarded. Some estimates have the western frontier counties of Pennsylvania, Virginia, and Maryland losing as much as one-half of their populations between 1755 and 1758. Many settlers moved back to the relative safety of the East. But a few stayed. In 1755, in southwestern Virginia, Mary Draper Ingles was likely the first white woman to ever see Kentucky. Pregnant Mary Ingles, her two young boys, and her sister-in-law were kidnapped by Shawnee Indians. They were victims of an Indian bereavement raid. Months later, Mary and an elderly Dutch woman, Frau Stumf, escaped [when in the custody of two Frenchman] while on a salt finding expedition to Big Bone Lick Kentucky. Mary and Frau Stumf, foraging for food fruits and vegetables as the winter was settling-in, successfully retraced Mary's route back along the Ohio, Kanawha, and New Rivers to southwestern Virginia and to her husband. Today, Mary Ingles' epic escape is retold in the outdoor drama play, 'The Long Way Home,' occasionally produced during the summers in Radford Virginia.

In 1756, despite its inept campaigns in North America, Great Britain declared war on France. The turmoil that began with skirmishes near the Forks of the Ohio was to become a major war waged on five continents. Many historians say that this was the first really 'global war.' In the bigger picture, the French and Indian War was a part of a French and English conflict known as the Seven Years War. And the British had another bad year in 1757.

French Fort Duquesne was a vital re-supply and rearming point for Indians harassing the settlers. But by 1758, the tide of war was starting to change. Overwhelming British forces were victorious in laying siege to Louisbourg (in present-day far eastern Nova Scotia) and overrunning Fort Frontenac (near present-day Kingston Ontario). Fort Frontenac was a pivotal supply port on northeastern Lake Ontario. Furthermore, the far-sighted policies of the new British Secretary of State, William Pitt, started to empower the Colonists, giving them a larger stake in the continent's future, should the outcome of the French and Indian War be favorable.

By late 1758 in Philadelphia, ailing British General John Forbes was resolved to dislodge the French from Fort Duquesne. Forbes planned to clear a road, and build a series of forts nearly all of the way to the Forks of the Ohio. In September, 750 men departed Fort Ligonier, the last British outpost before Fort Duquesne. Once again the British were defeated near the Forks of the Ohio. About 300 were killed, wounded, or captured by the Indians based at or near Fort Duquesne. However, unlike

Braddock's men three years prior, the remaining British needed only to retreat to nearby Fort Ligonier. The French and Indians soon attacked Fort Ligonier, but failed. Two months later, as winter was arriving, General Forbes again marched with his 5,000 men from Fort Ligonier to Fort Duquesne. When Forbes was only 10 miles away from Fort Duquesne, the 300 Frenchmen there blew-up and abandoned their own fort, and retreated up the Allegheny River. After the British arrived at the leveled fort, they rebuilt it to ten times its previous size, and named the area Pittsburgh, after the British Secretary of State William Pitt.

Perhaps the biggest factor thwarting the French's ability to hold onto Fort Duquesne was the *Treaty of Easton,* just signed in October 1758. This compact, between the British and most of the Ohio River Indians –the Delawares, Shawnees, and a few others –was essential for General Forbes' success. Basically, the British promised the Indians that there would be no more new settlements west of the Allegheny Mountains if, in turn, the Indians would refrain from supporting the French. The Indians complied, and the British 'promised' to control their settlements. Less than three years after the *Treaty of Easton* and after the arrogant British had won the war, the Indians realized that they had been misled. Instead of small outposts, like the French had, the British started building huge forts that needed large supporting communities just to maintain those garrisons.

By July 1759, in the Great Lakes area, overwhelming British forces had secured Fort Oswego and Fort Niagara. In the summer of that year, the French forces consolidated just about all they had remaining under Marquis de Montcalm at Quebec City. After a battle on the *Plains of Abraham,* Quebec fell to General James Wolfe and the British. Both commanders were mortally wounded during this epic battle. After that great battle on the *Plains of Abraham,* there were two more battles to be fought. In early 1760, the French, who had retreated to Montreal, counterattacked Quebec at the *Battle of Sainte Foy*. However, the French were unable to retake Quebec due to timely British reinforcements arriving on the St. Lawrence River. Later that same year, the British successfully took Montreal.

The War officially ended with the Treaty of Paris in February 1763. 'New France' became 'British Canada.' With the British victory in North America, the Colonists were feeling empowered. They believed that the land from the Atlantic to the Mississippi River was now theirs.

By mid-1763, the Ohio Country Indians realized that they had been duped by the *Treaty of Easton*. Soon Ottawa Chief Pontiac was fighting back. *Pontiac's Rebellion* was a short-lived but an extremely brutal conflict. Prisoners were typically slain, and smallpox tainted blankets were deliberately left behind for the Indians. Pontiac was successfully able to consolidate and rally many Native American groups throughout the region. Pontiac and his allies killed hundreds of settlers, and destroyed eight British forts in the Ohio River region, including Fort Venago on the Allegheny River. Only Fort Detroit, Fort Niagara, and Fort Pitt remained tenuously intact.

In August 1763, Fort Pitt with its 700 soldiers and settlers might have fallen, had not a timely reinforcement from the East arrived. In a situation similar to the one from 1755 to 1758, the white settlers were justifiably panicked. In October 1763, this conflict subsided when British King George III re-affirmed the tenets of the *Treaty of Easton* –reserving the land west of the Allegheny River for the Native Americans. But King George III, likely motivated by idealism and honor, was out of touch with the political reality occurring across the Atlantic.

The Colonists helped the British defeat the French and Indians. The Colonists felt their blood rightfully entitled them to a bigger piece of the pie, and a larger stake in the direction that North America was to take. The Colonists basically ignored the *Treaty of Easton*, and King George's 1763 Proclamation, reaffirming it. Even George Washington stated, "[the Proclamation of 1763 was] a temporary expedient 'to quiet the minds' of the Indians…and must fall off course in a few years." With this in mind, George Washington planned to position himself to benefit [not if, but] when settlers returned to the Ohio River region.

In 1770, Washington made another trip to the Ohio River exploring from Pittsburgh to the Kanawha River (i.e., present-day Point Pleasant West Virginia), and then another 200 miles down the Ohio River. In 1773, Washington had planned another such trip to escort Virginia's new governor, Lord Dunmore, through the Ohio River region. However, a death in the family forced Washington to cancel this trip at the last minute. Nonetheless, Lord Dunmore still visited the area without Washington. When Virginia's Lord Dunmore saw the many thousands of [Pennsylvania] settlers illegally living in the vicinity of Pittsburgh, he thought that his Virginians also ought to be getting a bigger piece of this [unlawful] 'Ohio River' Land Grab.

**Lord Dunmore's War**

In December 1773, about 50 Massachusetts Colonists dressed up as Mohawk Indians raided three British ships, and dumped 342 crates of British tea into Boston Harbor. This action was prompted by a perceived unfair tax on the Colonist by the British Crown. Back in Virginia, Lord Dunmore was a passionate supporter of the Crown. Dunmore thought that he could defuse Colonial-British tensions by getting the Colonists to focus on a 'new enemy' – the Native Americans living in the Ohio River frontier region. By early 1774, spoiling for a fight with the Indians, Dunmore readied 2,400 Virginia militiamen.

A few historians have speculated that Dunmore, seeing Revolutionary War clouds on the horizon, concocted an Indian War, known as Lord Dunmore's War, to deplete the numbers of the Virginia militia who might later be able to take up arms against the British Crown.

Tensions in the Ohio River region between white settlers and Native Americans had been brewing for years. Nonetheless, the main spark that lighted the conflagration occurred near Yellow Creek (i.e., near present-day Wellsville Ohio) on the Ohio River. A hunting party of Mingos, from Chief Logan's family, was in a local tavern celebrating after a successful hunting trip. Prior to this, Chief Logan had been more than cordial to the white newcomers. As the inebriated Indians departed the tavern, a small band of white settlers, laying in wait outside, gunned them down. After the slaughter at Yellow Creek, Chief Logan and his allies justifiably retaliated on other white settlers. But now, Lord Dunmore had 'his excuse' to wage a war on the Indians of the Ohio Region.

Advancing on the Native Americans in the Ohio River Valley, Dunmore planned to split his force into two groups. One body of men, led by Dunmore himself, would leave from Fort Pitt, travel down the Ohio River for a hundred or so miles, and then proceed overland into present-day Ohio toward the large Shawnee village on the Scioto River. The other group, lead by Colonel Andrew Lewis, would start beyond the headwaters of the Kanawha River, on the New River (the same route Mary Ingles had taken, and then retraced nineteen years prior) and work its way to the Ohio River along the banks of the Kanawha. Not long after Lewis' force of about 1,100 reached the junction of the Ohio and Kanawha Rivers (now present-day Point Pleasant West Virginia), Lewis' men were attacked by a group of about 500 Mingos and Shawnees, led by Chief Cornstalk. The *Battle of Point Pleasant* ensued. After a day of brutal fighting, some of it hand-to-hand, Cornstalk and his outnumbered Indians had to retreat back across the Ohio River. This battle was another victory for the white settlers. After Point Pleasant, Lewis marched southwest to link-up with Dunmore's force about eight miles from that Shawnee Village on the Scioto River.

The Native Americans were becoming more and more pragmatic over their overwhelming prospects of driving away the new white settlers. Lord Dunmore's War ended when the Native Americans accepted peace terms of the *Treaty of Camp Charlotte*. The Indians had to cede all their land claims on the south side of the Ohio River (i.e., present-day West Virginia and Kentucky) to the Virginians. Lord Dunmore was proclaimed a hero, and the settlement of Kentucky was about to begin in earnest. Some claim that the *Battle of Point Pleasant* was the last battle of the French and Indian War; others state that it was the first battle of the American Revolution.

During the early stages of the American Revolution, Native Americans, including Cornstalk, tried to remain neutral. Cornstalk had developed reasonably amicable relations with the newcomers, and became an eloquent spokesman for the Indians. However by about 1778, most of the Native Americans had sided with the British, hoping that a British victory would keep the colonists' unregulated rapid westward expansion in check. In 1777, Cornstalk had retuned to the American fort at Point Pleasant. He was on a diplomatic mission to inform the fort's commander that his Shawnees soon would be supporting the British. Nonetheless, he was promptly imprisoned, but was treated reasonably well. However, not long afterward, Cornstalk and his son were murdered by the Americans.

# CHAPTER 2
## The American Revolution and the Northwest Territories

After the Colonists had endured, and been victorious in the French and Indian War, they felt they that were owed a larger stake in the affairs on the continent, including westward expansion. After his victory over the Ohio River Native Americans, egotistical Virginia governor, Lord Dunmore, overplayed his hero's hand. Dunmore's goodwill soon was lost, and the Virginia colonists were becoming less empathic to their overbearing loyalist governor, and more in tuned to the plight of their fellow colonists in New England.

During the French and Indian War, George Washington also learned some invaluable lessons. He likely developed a fondness for his former enemies, the French whose officers especially in warfare, conducted themselves more honorably than most. After having survived many 'life and death experiences,' Washington developed a sense that 'divine providence' had been sparing him for some grand future mission. Then treacherous and double-dealing (i.e., by offering the Native Americans and the Virginia Colonist conflicting rationales for his actions) Lord Dunmore affronted Washington on several matters. After that, it was not difficult for the most experienced military leader in the Colonies to accept command of the new Continental Army.

Twenty-six years earlier, in 1750, explorer-physician Thomas Walker found the Cumberland Gap near where present-day Virginia, Kentucky and Tennessee meet. The gap is a major break in the Appalachian Mountain chain. Walker named it after King George's II son, the Duke of Cumberland.

Around 1767, Daniel Boone had been the primary force behind blazing the Wilderness Road through this Cumberland Gap to the fertile land of Kentucky. Three times, Daniel was captured by Indians; three times, he escaped. Daniel Boone was also an agent for the Transylvania Company. The Transylvania Company, founded in 1775, was to buy Native American lands for future western settlements –similar to the Ohio Company's plan, 26 years earlier. Daniel Boone established the Transylvania Company's first settlement at Boonesborough on the Kentucky River. The prior year, 1774, about 40 miles southwest of Boonesborough, Harrodsburg –Kentucky's first settlement –was established on the Salt River. For a time, Kentucky was often called the 'Colony of Transylvania.'

By 1775, and encouraged by the *Treaty of Camp Charlotte*, there may have been close to 300 white settlers on the south side of the Ohio River. Some of these Kentucky settlers came via the Cumberland Gap, while others entered the area via the Ohio River. At that time, Virginia's western boundary extended all of the way to the Mississippi River. 'Kentucky County' was that part of Virginia west of the Appalachian Mountains. The Cherokee Indian word, 'Kentucky' means 'Dark and Bloody Ground.' In 1792, Kentucky became our nation's fifteenth state and was the first state admitted to the Union west of the Appalachian Mountains.

During the American Revolution, Boonesborough was besieged by Indians allied with the British no less than three times. By 1777, the Kentucky settlements were reeling from British-supported Indian raids. These settlements were in peril of being completely wiped-out. With help from Daniel Boone and others, Virginia militia Major George Rogers Clark became the prime protector of the Kentucky settlements of Harrodsburg and Boonesborough.

Clark was a 22-year old Captain in the Virginia militia when Lord Dunmore marched from Pittsburgh to southern Ohio. After several more trips to the area, Clark visited Kentucky County as a surveyor for the Ohio Company. The rich countryside stole his heart.

By 1778, George Rogers Clark was planning to rescue Kentucky by taking the offensive and fighting the British on a western frontier. He believed this was the best way to insure the survival of Kentucky's two tenuous settlements. Clark persuaded Patrick Henry, Virginia's great orator and first post-colonial governor, to support the 'Kentucky County' of Virginia. The Kentuckians prime need was for gunpowder to fend-off Indian attacks. From Patrick Henry's point of view, it was a smart strategy to help Clark and to have a 'buffer zone' west of Virginia's population centers.

In early May 1778, Clark had hoped to assemble 500 men. But he departed Redstone Old Fort on the Monongahela River with a detachment of barely 150 men. Going down the Ohio River, Clark re-provisioned at Fort Pitt and Fort Henry (i.e., present-day Wheeling West Virginia), and stopped at Point Pleasant (West Virginia). After building a fort on Corn Island on the Ohio River (i.e., near present-day Louisville), Clark and his men continued down the Ohio in late June. Soon they reached the abandoned Fort Massac (near present-day Metropolis Illinois). Clark's objective was the British Fort at Kaskaskia, near the Kaskaskia River's confluence on the Mississippi River. After arriving at Fort Massac, instead of taking the more probable water route –further down the Ohio and then turning north up the Mississippi River toward Kaskaskia –Clark decided to go overland through the Illinois territory. There were at least two reasons for this. The British may have had an outpost at the junction of the Ohio and Mississippi Rivers, and that outpost could have compromised Clark's mission. Secondly, Clark's men wouldn't need to fight the current paddling up the Mississippi River. In Kaskaskia, the British assumed if they were attacked, it would come from the

Mississippi River. Clark's overland element of surprise worked. On the Fourth of July in 1778, Clark captured the British Fort at Kaskaskia. It was only fifteen years prior, that the British had defeated the French and commandeered that fort. To Clark's pleasant surprise, most of the 1,000 or so French inhabitants of the town at Kaskaskia were not hostile to his Virginians –who were now fighting France's old enemy, the British.

After taking Kaskaskia, Clark's men easily took command of a few other nearby British outposts in the Illinois Territory – Prairie du Rocher, St. Phillips, and Cahokia. Soon after taking Kaskaskia, with the crucial help of a French priest, Father Pierre Gibault, the French settlement at Vincennes pledged its allegiance to the Americans. But that didn't last long. The British commander from Detroit retook the fort, Fort Sackville at Vincennes. In February 1779, Clark and about 170 of his men, including some new French recruits, departed Kaskaskia for Vincennes. It was a miserable soaking wet march through the southern Illinois marshes and sloughs overflowing from cold winter runoff. The men's clothing stayed water-logged. As Clark neared Vincennes, and before confronting the two dozen or so British defenders at Fort Sackville, Clark was able to make contact with the French citizenry in the town of Vincennes. The British commander, realizing that he had lost the locals' support before the pitched fighting began, smartly surrendered to Clark. Vincennes was Clark's greatest victory –and with little bloodshed. Afterward, Clark had hoped to march on the British stronghold at Detroit. This goal eluded Clark because he never received needed reinforcements from the East. Clark's funding was chaotic, at best. He personally financed the greater part of his many campaigns in the West, hoping to get repaid later. This never happened, and Clark's funds were depleted by the end of the war.

The British and their Indian allies, primarily based out of Detroit, continued to make minor attacks into Kentucky. But

Clark was typically able to thwart most of these advances. By the summer of 1780, encouraged by Clark's military successes, the new town of Louisville, near Clark's old fort on Corn Island, had grown to about 20,000.

In October 1781, British General Cornwallis, surrendered to General Washington in Yorktown Virginia. Washington's success at Yorktown was in no small part due to French Admiral de Grasse and his fleet of 28 ships successfully blockading the mouth of the Chesapeake Bay, thereby thwarting the needed British reinforcements destined for Cornwallis. The war in the East was winding down. But 1782 would be a rough year in the West. This was highlighted by a horrible ambush and defeat in which one-third of the Kentuckians were killed at the hands of about 1,000 Indians and British at Blue Licks. Clark was not at Blue Licks, but he was blamed by many for having been unable to prevent it. After Blue Licks, Clark led a few retaliatory raids into southern Ohio

Indomitable Clark was a master at psychology, theatrics, suspense, and playing on his opponent's perceived fears. But as tough as Clark was, he was fair and evenhanded when it came to dealing with civil matters. This won him points among local French inhabitants. Clark was also able to convert many Indians who had been loyal to the British. Some historians say this is where Clark's real success lay. Indians have said about Clark, "This Chief of the Big Knives did not speak like any other white man they had ever heard." In late 1778, Clark concluded no less than ten Indian treaties. Historian Van Every states, "Clark's great achievement was not the uncontested occupation of the Illinois territory, but his success at neutralizing a considerable segment of military power upon which England depended." By going on the offensive, and with a severely undermanned force, Clark was able to neutralize the British and their Indian allies on the western frontier.

Clark won the American Revolution in the West, and he justifiably earned the status of 'Savior of Kentucky.' To use a more modern expression, 'Clark talked *the talk*, and walked *the walk*.' In his later years Clark was hounded by creditors and near financial ruin due to the personal debt he incurred while fighting for our new country. After the war, and despite his military successes, Clark had many jealous detractors, especially in the more comfortable East. They accused him of being a drunk, which did become a reality. In 1818, George Rogers Clark died a broken man. At that time, all but a few of his closest friends realized the debt that our young nation owed this nearly forgotten hero.

After the Revolutionary War, Daniel Boone didn't fare much better than Clark. In 1779, he was robbed while carrying $20,000 in cash to purchase land for other Kentucky settlers. Later, Boone lost all of his own Kentucky land claims, due to legal technicality with the titles. Further problems with creditors, prompted Boone to leave Kentucky, and eventually settle in present-day Missouri. After the Louisiana Purchase in 1803, Boone once again lost all of his Missouri land titles. Unfortunately, two of Kentucky's greatest patriots, Daniel Boone and George Rogers Clark fell as victims to some lesser-minded nameless money-grubbers of yesteryear.

Ebenezer Zane was another local pioneer and trailblazer. In 1769, Zane established a fort on the Ohio River. This fort soon became Wheeling Virginia. In 1796-97, after the Revolutionary War, Zane blazed 'Zane's Trace,' a crucial 230-mile route through southeastern Ohio stretching from Wheeling to present-day Maysville Kentucky (also on the Ohio River). Zane's Trace remained the only major road in Ohio until the War of 1812. Zanesville Ohio, near the navigable head of the Muskingum River, was named after Zane.

Fort Boonesborough, near the Kentucky River

Fort Massac, on the Lower Ohio River

## The Northwest Territories

When the Colonists won the war and signed the *Treaty of Paris* in 1783, the British ceded a vast amount of Indian land to the newly-formed United States without the Native American's consent. A few within the United States government wished to purchase Indian lands via legitimate means. However, it was only a minority who were prone to such niceties. Most preferred moving outright onto Indian lands.

In 1784, the new Congress passed an ordinance stating that the land north of the Ohio River, west of the Appalachians, and east of the Mississippi River be divided into ten new states –with no further thought on the matter. A year later, Congress addressed more of the 'nuts and bolts,' and passed the *Land Ordinance of 1785*. This 1785 ordinance provided a framework how this land was to be surveyed –using the township system that we still use today. That measure was followed by the *Northwest Ordinance of 1787*. This ordinance created the 'Northwest Territories,' out of the region described in the *1785 Ordinance*. The *Northwest Ordinance* set up a mechanism how the United States would expand westward, by the admission of new states –versus the expansion of existing states. The *Northwest Ordinance of 1787* created the first organized US territory. The states of Ohio, Indiana, Illinois, Michigan, Wisconsin and a part of Minnesota were eventually carved out of the Northwest Territory. The *Ordinance of 1787*, created during the time of the Articles of Confederation (i.e., before the currently accepted US Constitution), also strengthened the hand of the federal bureaucracy while weakening the hand of the existing state bureaucracies, and at a time when the power of federal government was often undermined by the state governments.

The process for the creation of a new state could start once a territory's population reached 60,000. In 1803, Ohio was the first such state created, and became our nation's 17th. The formal banning of slavery in these new territories had the effect of making the Ohio River a dividing line between the North and the South. Nonetheless, in these early years there were still conditions of 'forced servitude' in many parts north of the Ohio River.

After the American Revolution, thousands of military men were promised land in return for their valued military service during the war. The financially strapped Continental Congress allocated these men bounty land grants, should the colonists win the war. The amount of a land grant was based on rank. These federal government land grants were to be in the newly-created Northwest Territories, which the United States didn't officially own until the passage of the *Ordinance of 1787*. To this day, and due to this phenomenon, a disproportionate number of Ohioans are descendents of Revolutionary War veterans.

Earlier in 1785, an Indian treaty, the *Treaty of Fort McIntosh* was signed at the Beaver River's confluence on the Ohio River. Going well beyond the *Treaty of Camp Charlotte*, this treaty stated that the Indians had to vacate their lands in eastern Ohio. From the Native American's point of view, this treaty was untenable and white settlers were often attacked.

In 1787, Scottish-born Arthur St. Clair was the first appointed governor of the Northwest Territories and was tasked to bring order to the region. St. Clair, like George Washington, distinguished himself as a capable military officer during the French and Indian War. By the mid-1770s, also like Washington, St. Clair felt more like an American patriot than a British subject. He rose to Brigadier General in the Continental Army, and was a factor in Washington's victories at Trenton, Princeton, and Yorktown. St. Clair also served as the ninth President under the Articles of Confederation (i.e., before the US Constitution and before Washington became president in 1789).

In 1788, the first permanent settlement in the Northwest Territories, Marietta, was started near the Muskingum River's confluence on the Ohio River. Earlier, during the early 1770s, while passing through the area, George Washington was most impressed. Washington relayed his enthusiasm about the site to fellow Revolutionary War General Rufus Putnam. Putnam was also a veteran of the French and Indian War and fought in upstate New York during the Revolution. By late 1788, with Putnam spearheading, the new settlement of Marietta had over 100 inhabitants. A military outpost, Fort Harmar, on the opposite and south side of the Muskingum River had been constructed three years prior.

In 1789, with Arthur St. Clair's efforts, the Ohio Indians agreed to the *Treaty of Fort Harmar*. But like the *Treaty of Fort McIntosh,* it too was a farce and didn't offer the Native Americans anything substantial. Hence, most of the Indians kept up their hostilities along the Ohio River frontier and harassed white settlers. This violence escalated into the *Northwest Indian War*.

In 1790, General Josiah Harmar, another Revolutionary War veteran, with a force of about 1500, was selected for a punitive expedition against the Ohio Indians. After some initial success, Harmar marched against Miami Chief Little Turtle, on the Maumee River, in Northwestern Ohio. Harmar's force was defeated by Little Turtle. In 1791, Harmar was replaced by St. Clair who led an even larger force. Chief Little Turtle and Shawnee Chief Blue Jacket, recollecting their humiliation at *Camp Charlotte* –that ended Lord Dunmore's War, also defeated St. Clair's force. On the banks of the Wabash River, St. Clair lost 600 men. This American defeat was the Army's greatest loss to any Native American force thus far in history. After the debacle, St. Clair resigned from the Army, but continued to serve as the territorial governor.

President Washington then sought out yet another successful Revolutionary War veteran, Major General 'Mad' Anthony Wayne. After putting his troops through a most rigorous training program, Wayne then planned his assault on Chief Blue Jacket. In 1793, Wayne's force departed Cincinnati, and proceeded to build a line of forts, as General Forbes had successfully done when tackling Fort Duquesne, 35 years earlier. South of present-day Toledo, the *Battle of Fallen Timbers* ensued. This time, Wayne's 3,000 Americans were able to defeat Blue Jacket's and Little Turtle's 1,500 Shawnees, Miamis, and several other Indian allies. One of Wayne's aides-de-camp was an aggressive officer –William Henry Harrison. In 1795, the defeated Indians had to sign the *Treaty of Greenville*, which moved them farther west, and required them to abdicate much of the present-day states of Ohio and Indiana. Ten years later, the Indians had to sign the *Treaty of Fort Industry* which pushed them yet even farther west. In 1809, there was another treaty –another massive land grab, the *Treaty of Fort Wayne* pushing the Native Americans even farther west. This last treaty was negotiated by the new governor of the Indiana territory, William Henry Harrison.

Shawnee Chief Tecumseh was becoming outraged, and started forming a large Indian Confederation that would be necessary to oppose the ever encroaching Americans. In 1811, William Henry Harrison, with more than 1,000 troops marched up the Wabash River against an Indian force less than half his size. But perhaps more importantly for Harrison, the Native American's new charismatic leader, Tecumseh, was absent on a recruiting mission three states away. Near present-day Lafayette Indiana, the *Battle of Tippecanoe* began. The outnumbered Indians were defeated, and in the aftermath, Harrison burned down their village. Even in our 21$^{st}$ Century, genocide and ethnic cleansing continues. Civilized nations, like the United States, should do everything in their power to prevent it. But let's not forget, that from 120 to 220 years ago, a young United States is not without this awful stain.

From about the end of the Revolutionary War to the War of 1812, the Indians in the Northwest Territory had been receiving aid from the British –primarily through Canada. In 1812, the United States declared war on Britain for a variety of reason. One justification for war was this British aid to the Indians in the Northwest Territory.

In 1813, the British and their Indian allies suffered a crushing defeat at the *Battle of the Thames* (near Detroit, in present-day southern Ontario). During the battle, William Henry Harrison with a force of 3,500 attacked about 1,300 British and Indian allies who were lead by an infuriated Tecumseh. In the fog of the battle, the British retreated, leaving Tecumseh and his warriors to face an even more disproportionate force of Americans. Tecumseh was killed, and future Indian resistance in the Northwest Territories soon dissolved. In 1815, the War of 1812 ended in a stalemate. Nonetheless, the future of 'British Canada' was assured (and not to be 'United States' Canada'). This was also the last time that the Americans and British have fought against each other.

## Lewis and Clark on the Ohio

In May 1804, more than ten years before the end of the War of 1812, George Rogers Clark's younger brother, William Clark, and his companion, Meriwether Lewis were about to make history. They departed the eastern banks of the Mississippi River near the confluence of the Missouri River (near present-day Wood River Illinois). A group of around four dozen men led by Co-captains Lewis and Clark came to be known as the 'Corps of Discovery.' From Wood River, the Lewis and Clark expedition was about to travel over 8,000 miles in 28 months (1804-1806), using river routes as much as possible.

In 1803, the year before the 'Corps' left the Mississippi River, US President Thomas Jefferson doubled the size of the United States with the Louisiana Purchase. President Jefferson's priority was for the Corps to find and map a water route across the continent. One day after the news of the Louisiana Purchase was made public, Lewis was on his way to Pittsburgh. During the summer of 1803 in Pittsburgh, Lewis oversaw construction of the 55-foot keelboat that would be needed for going upstream on the Mississippi and Missouri Rivers.

On August 31, 1803, one month behind schedule, Meriwether Lewis, 11 men, his keelboat, a pirogue, and at least one canoe departed Pittsburgh and started down the Ohio River. The two and a half months that they would be spending on the Ohio would be their shakedown for the next two plus years. On September 7th, Lewis arrived in Wheeling, took two days off, did his laundry, and re-provisioned. Even 200 years later in today's high tech world, some things –boating needs (i.e., doing laundry) –never change!

Heading down the Ohio, they stopped in Maysville Kentucky. On September 28th, they began a one week layover in Cincinnati. Lewis then stopped at Big Bone Lick Kentucky to obtain fossils for President Jefferson. Lewis's contingent arrived in Louisville (i.e., at the 'Falls of the Ohio') on October 14th. William Clark, with more men, was already there. Clark had been in Louisville for most of the summer making preparations and waiting for Lewis' arrival.

On November 11th, a larger compliment – Lewis, Clark, with more men – arrived at Fort Massac (i.e., present-day Metropolis Illinois). During a two-day layover at Fort Massac, The Corps was able to pick up a few more critical recruits. On November 14th, the flotilla arrived at the confluence of the Ohio on the Mississippi Rivers close to 1,000 miles downstream from Pittsburgh. They spent six days at the confluence, where Meriwether Lewis taught William Clark how to use a sextant –a skill that would be invaluable during the next two and a half years. After leaving the confluence, they headed north up the Mississippi River to their winter encampment near Wood River. In May of 1804, their epic journey starting up the Missouri River was about to begin. In 1806, after successfully crossing the continent and back, they returned to the Ohio River.

Ripley Ohio Riverfront –the John Rankin House is high atop the hill

The National Underground Railroad
Freedom Center, Cincinnati Ohio

# CHAPTER 3
# The Underground Railroad, the River Jordan, and the Civil War

In 1776, Thomas Jefferson penned this line into the Declaration of Independence, "We hold these truths to be self-evident, that all men are created equal, that they are endowed by their creator with certain unalienable rights that among these are Life, Liberty, and the Pursuit of Happiness." When Jefferson said "all men," he really didn't mean "all men." Women, certain minorities, and especially African American slaves were excluded. For more than eighty years after that statement, our country had one major hypocritical stain on this ideal –slavery. Slavery was most eloquently defended on biblical grounds by southerners like John Calhoun and others. Until, Mr. Abraham Lincoln, just about every major northern politician including Daniel Webster put aside our Declaration's ideals. Any political move that went toward rectifying the brutality of slavery was brushed aside, for the expediency of the day –keeping the slave-holding white southerner contented.

By the first part of the 19th Century, our former colonial occupiers had already abolished slavery. Slavery was gone in Spain and its colonies, the British Empire, and the French Empire, Canada, Mexico, and all South America (except Brazil). But slavery was yet to be abolished in the southern United States. In the 1850s, America shared this shrunken world stage with such moral heavyweights as Burma, China, Ethiopia, Mauritania, and Saudi Arabia as countries that still permitted slavery within their borders.

Both former early Presidents George Washington and Thomas Jefferson personally grappled over the issue of slavery. Upon his death, George Washington freed his slaves; Thomas Jefferson did not. Our seventh president, Andrew Jackson, vilified the abolitionist movement as "unconstitutional and wicked." and demanded that the northern states outlaw all abolitionist activity. Andrew Jackson's Vice President, Martin Van Buren, (and soon to be our eighth president) cast a tie-breaking vote in the US Senate, that prohibited the Post Office Department from delivering abolitionist literature. William Henry Harrison, as well as many others in Congress at that time, believed that 'Freedom of the Press' should not apply to abolitionists. Our eleventh President James K Polk, and a Tennessee slave holder, placed a gag rule on Congress forbidding that body to even discuss the slavery issue. Polk also came down especially hard on abolitionists. Our thirteenth President Millard Fillmore was outraged when he learned that escaped slaves were not always being returned to their southern owners. Fourteenth and fifteenth presidents, Franklin Pierce and James Buchanan were both pro-slavery Democrats from the North (New Hampshire and Pennsylvania, respectively). In 1861, Abraham Lincoln finally came onto the national scene as our sixteenth president.

Some estimates say that 25 percent of the slave cargo perished during the Atlantic crossing, and another 25 percent perished shortly after arriving in America. By the early 1800s, 17 percent of America's total population was in bondage; there were nearly 1 million slaves. Between 1800 and 1830, the US slave population more than doubled to just about 3.5 million. The slave population peaked at about 4 million by the time of our Civil War. The North was not immune to the evils of slavery, but the last northern state outlawed slavery well before anything started to happen in the South. Rhode Island had abolished slavery before the Declaration of Independence. By 1830, all the states north of Maryland had abolished slavery.

A great demand for cotton in the British Empire and Europe, along with advancements in cultivation influenced the demand for slave labor. By 1830, the value of cotton exceeded the combined value of all other exports. In the South, there were about 350,000 white slave holders. However, the real slave wealth was concentrated in the top 3,000 to 4,000, who owned about two-thirds of all the South's slaves. Furthermore, this southern aristocracy received about three-quarters of all the revenues from the South's exports. By many accounts, the owners of large cotton plantations in the Deep South were the wealthiest people in the entire world. Slaves and cotton were the two pillars of this wealth. As often occurs, especially in the United States, economic wealth translates to political clout.

In 1820, Kentucky had about 15,000 slaves, close to one-quarter of its total population. Kentucky slave owners were generally small land owners, and Kentucky slaves were often used for breeding and auction purposes. The major slave-workforce states, those with large plantations, were found in the Deep South. During the forthcoming Civil War, Kentucky along with Maryland, Delaware, and Missouri –states with significant slave populations, did not join the Confederacy. But there was a star on the Confederate Flag for Kentucky, and a 'Confederate Capital' was established in Bowling Green. Nonetheless, the sympathies of these four states' white populations remained with the South. In 1863, when President Lincoln's Emancipation Proclamation was issued, these four states were in a bit of a conundrum. That proclamation only freed the slaves in the rebelling Confederate States.

The *Northwest Ordinance of 1787* banned slavery in the new territory. Nonetheless, there were still a handful of slave holders in this territory. In 1816 and 1818, Indiana and Illinois entered the Union as the nineteenth and twenty-first states, respectively. But in Illinois, both the governor and lieutenant governor owned slaves. There are more than a few stories of slaves who had crossed the Ohio River into

Gallatin County Illinois (i.e., southeastern Illinois), only to be recaptured there, shackled, and put back into bondage working in the nearby Illinois salt mines.

In 1793, Congress overwhelmingly passed the first Fugitive Slave Act, signed by President George Washington. This act arose from yet another border dispute between Pennsylvania and Virginia. Three Virginians had kidnapped a Negro in Pennsylvania, and sent him into bondage in Virginia. The Pennsylvania governor fought back in the legal arena …and lost. The end result was this Fugitive Slave Act. This act allowed slave catchers autonomy to hunt for runaway slaves anywhere in the North. It further denied Negro captives any legal recourse, and made a Negro's offspring a fugitive for life. Furthermore, this act made it a federal crime for anyone to assist runaways. A whole new 'slave catching' industry developed. The act had a chilling effect on about one-fifth of the US population –all of the Negroes. African Americans were now not safe even in the Northern States. Hence, many started fleeing to British Canada.

The *Fugitive Slave act of 1850* went well beyond the one of 1793. The 1850 Act stated that a federal marshal or any other federal official who did not arrest a runaway would be fined $1,000. Now, besides the slave catchers, official law enforcement in the North (as well as the South), had 'the duty' to arrest runaways, even if personal moral convictions were opposed. And this could be based on no more than a slave owner's hearsay claim that the runaway was 'his property.' Again, the suspected runaway, or even a framed free black, had no rights, whatsoever. The Act of 1850 made northerners responsible for enforcing southern slavery. It also further heightened the black migration to Canada. By 1852, there were believed to be around 25,000 runaways in Canada.

Individual states also had their own laws. In 1835, Georgia imposed the death penalty on any person publishing something that might be construed to insight slaves to rebellion. In Kentucky, it was a crime to teach slaves how to read. Kentucky slaves were sometimes not permitted to congregate or conduct worship services. They were also not allowed to have formal marriages …nonetheless many slave men and slave women still had their families. Slave catchers operated freely in Ohio, Indiana, and Illinois, and often traveled as far as Canada to hunt quarry. In Ohio, fugitives were plucked from black churches. Freed blacks were not safe. There are many instances of a freed black being unlawfully taken by a slave catcher, and sent back into bondage –usually in the Deep South. Upon being accosted as a runway, a freed black was supposed to produce 'a certificate of freedom.' However, these papers were often deliberately destroyed by their capturers.

Nonetheless, at any point in history, there are always those rare few who are ahead of their time. In the early 1800s those few believed that slavery was a horrible abomination, and that divine providence would want it eliminated. In the United States, leading this unpopular vanguard movement, were freed blacks (who had to be especially careful …having very much to lose), Quakers, and some Presbyterians, and certain Methodists sects. Most, but not all, of these brave folks lived in the North. There were also a few (braver) who lived in the South. Some had first hand experiences with the atrocities of Southern slavery, and fled north hoping to find a more welcoming audience. Many of these people became the forerunner and conductors of the Underground Railroad.

There are several books on this fascinating subject, and I thought the best one was *"Bound for Canaan…The Underground Railroad"* by Fergus M. Bordewich. "The National Underground Railroad Freedom Center" in Cincinnati, barely a couple blocks from the Ohio River is a 'must visit.' The Freedom Center's address is: 50 East Freedom Way, Cincinnati, OH, 45202; their phone is ☎ 513-333-7500; and their website is:' www.freedomcenter.org. The Center is open six days week (i.e., closed on Mondays) from 11AM to 5PM.

Inside the National Underground Railroad Freedom Center

In 1775, and about the same time as the American Revolution, a small Abolitionist movement started to form in America. The Abolitionist's supporters included Thomas Paine, Ben Franklin, John Jay and Alexander Hamilton. As US laws became more capricious, the abolitionist movement grew. However, by the 1830s, the abolitionist movement was also feeling a severe backlash. Even up North, some of the more vocal abolitionists were being heckled, pilloried, tarred and feathered, egged, stoned, and sometimes severely beaten. In Ann Hagedorn's book, *Beyond the River,"* she states that many abolitionists had a price on their head, and that in 1841, abolitionist John Rankin was said to be worth $3,000, dead or alive. In 1835, William Lloyd Garrison produced an abolitionist newspaper, *The Liberator.* On one occasion an angry New England mob nearly killed him as they were clamoring, "Kill him! Lynch Him! Hang the abolitionist!"

As I travel along the Ohio River today, I find many associating themselves (i.e., through their great, great …great grandfather, etc) with the heroic efforts of the Underground Railroad. No doubt this [Underground Railroad] awareness is good. Nonetheless, the Underground Railroad was an unpopular minority movement, especially in its early days. In many instances, it took a lot of guts to go against mainstream grain and be a conductor for the Underground Railroad. I just wonder how many of those who espouse the virtues of the Underground Railroad today, would really have been willing to put up with the ignominies and personal sacrifices that the Underground Railroad supporters faced 180 years ago?

The Underground Railroad did move many abolitionists from the lecture circuit to the front lines. The Railroad became a 'driving wedge' behind the abolitionist movement. By the early 1800s, the railroad was starting to take its shape. The Underground Railroad operated across a border 2,000 miles long –from Kansas to the Delmarva (i.e., the Delaware-Maryland-Virginia Peninsula), and from the Deep South to Canada. Nonetheless, more routes and more escaping slaves made their perilous journey north to freedom across the Ohio River than anywhere else along this frontier. And the Ohio River's busiest region for crossings was between eastern Ohio and central Indiana. East of the Ohio River, (i.e., Pennsylvania and New York) the valleys between ridgelines kept runaways from being able to fan out, and thus made the probability of recapture higher. But in Ohio, Indiana, and Illinois, escapees could fan out along a web of roads leading northward to Ontario. Once a runaway reached Cincinnati or Marietta, Ohio, it was less than 300 miles to Canada. It was only 90 miles to Canada from the Ohio River at Wellsville Ohio.

No one knows for sure how many slaves made it to freedom …and how many more got caught trying. Between 1800 and 1830, there are no good estimates of runaways. During the Underground Railroad's heyday, 1830-1860, it's estimated that 70,000 to 100,000 escaping slaves were able to make their way to eventual freedom. Estimates have at least 30,000 runaways ending-up in Canada. Windsor Canada (in southern Ontario across from Detroit) was seen as 'British Liberty.' Canada had abolished slavery in 1793, four decades before Britain formally abolished it in 1833. Soon after Canada abolished slavery, African Americans became British subjects, were treated accordingly, and had the right to vote.

In the Underground Railroad, everything had to be clandestine. If a suspected 'slave helpers' home was raided by the one of the thousands of slave catchers, that Underground Railroad operator didn't want to have any evidence or records laying around. Hence, no records were kept. Some have guessed that 9,000 to 13,000 or upwards, were involved in Underground Railroad activities. Very many of the quieter heroes of the Underground Railroad were nameless freed blacks, and we'll never know who they were.

In 1831, an irate slave catcher, in hot pursuit, first coined the term "Underground Railroad" in Ripley Ohio. When his quarry apparently 'just vanished,' he said something like, "He must have gone off in an Underground Railroad." In the 1840s, railroads hadn't been around that long, and the lingo stuck …as did the railroads. Escaping slaves were passed from one safe house to the next, steadily making their way north. Routes and safe houses were passed along by word of mouth; no 'paper trail' was left behind. Present-day US Route 68 was one strategic northbound route for the Railroad. US Route 68 was also the first stone paved road west of the Alleghenies, and it eventually ran from southern Kentucky to Lake Erie. US 68 crossed the Ohio River near Maysville Kentucky, traveled along the river to Ripley Ohio, before again turning north. In Kentucky, US Route 68 was once an old Indian trail, and before that –a buffalo trail.

Runaways primarily traveled at night toward the North Star, but if it were cloudy, they'd have problems. An escape could typically take two months or much longer. Besides trying to avoid the slave catchers and bloodhounds, runaways endured many privations –separation from family and friends, cold, hunger, hiding in cramped confines, inadequate footwear, remaining soaked in bad weather, lack of sleep …just to name a few.

In Kentucky, there were enslaved blacks, who never escaped. Instead they choose to remain enslaved. Knowing the bottom lands along the Ohio River, they would be able to escort other blacks fleeing across the river …sometimes providing many years of valuable service to the Railroad. Oftentimes, successful young male escapees would get viable paying jobs up North, and later try to purchase the rest of their family still in bondage. Sometimes this worked, and sometimes it didn't.

By the 1820s, the Ohio River was the most important interstate highway of its day.

Slaves, upon reaching the southern banks of the Ohio, saw it as their symbolic River Jordan, and across it lay their promised land of freedom. Fergus Bordewich states "…the Ohio [River] would be in the dreams of countless slaves the River Jordan, the threshold of Canaan, and the front line of a battle in the moral conflict that would define America for the next three-quarters of a century." Based on a rough frequency of the Ohio River town names that came up, here is a list of some of those crossings most active during the Underground Railroad's heyday: Ripley-Aberdeen OH, Cincinnati OH, Madison IN, Portsmouth OH, Ironton OH, Leavenworth IN, Marietta OH, Martins Ferry OH, Jeffersonville IN, New Albany IN, Belpre OH, Wellsville OH, New Richmond OH, Evansville IN, Cairo IL, Rising Sun IN, Gallipolis OH, and Moscow OH. And I'm sure that we've missed many other Underground Railroad Ohio River crossings.

There is unproven African-American lore that slaves were stitching quilts in 'patterns' that had hidden meanings for those on the Railroad. Nevertheless, many of the African-American spiritual songs of that time are still known today. These deeply moving passionate songs reflect a slave's yearning for freedom along with Christian beliefs. Oftentimes a secret code or message was veiled in the lyrics. Here are just a very few that you may have heard: 1) from *Swing Lo Sweet Chariot*, "Swing Lo Sweet Chariot, Coming for to carry me home, I looked over Jordan, and what did I see? Coming for to carry me home;" 2) from *Oh Freedom*, "Oh freedom, Oh freedom, Oh freedom over me! And before I'd be a slave, I'll be buried in my grave, and go home to my Lord and be free;" 3) from *Steal Away*, "Steal away, steal away to Jesus! Steal away, steal away home, I ain't got long to stay here," 4) from *Deep River*, "Deep river, my home is over Jordan, deep river, Lord, I want to cross over into campground," and from 5) *Follow the Drinking Gourd*, "Where the great big river meets the little river, follow the drinking gourd, for the old man is a-waiting to carry you to freedom, if you follow the drinking gourd." Three of these five songs make a direct reference to the Ohio River –as the River Jordan in two, and as the 'great big river" in *Follow the Drinking Gourd*. The other two songs express a deep desire for freedom and escape.

Ohio, the first state carved from the Northwest Territory in 1803, was also the first state without legalized slavery on its soil. By 1820, fast-growing Ohio was the fifth largest state, and by 1850, it was the third largest state. There were more Underground Railroad stations in Ohio than any other state. John Brown, the martyr of Harper's Ferry fame, started out as an Underground Railroad conductor in Ohio. In Cincinnati and southeastern Indiana, Quaker Levi Coffin and his wife Catherine aided thousands. Coffin also started a store which sold goods made by Negroes. Levi Coffin has often been anointed as the President of the Underground Railroad. In 1852, when Harriet Beecher Stowe wrote, *Uncle Tom's Cabin*, she lived in Cincinnati. Stowe's book created a new awareness in the North as to the horrors of slavery, fueling the abolitionist cause. In 1862, when Stowe met President Abraham Lincoln, he greeted her, "So you're the little woman who wrote the book that started this great war." That book was the second best seller in the 19th Century behind only the Bible.

Some of the most fierce struggles and gunfights between slave catchers and those helping runaways were fought in Madison Indiana. By 1840, Madison was the second largest city in Indiana. In Madison, much of the Underground Railroad's aid was conducted by freed blacks, who were especially threatened by the slave catchers. One Madison barber, George De Baptiste, and a former Virginia slave himself, probably aided over a 100 runaways fleeing north.

In Portsmouth Ohio, another African-American barber, James Poindexter, regularly rowed his boat near the Kentucky shore to pick up runaways trying to flee across the Ohio. Once in Portsmouth,

Poindexter passed off his north-fleeing refugees through primarily a network of other African Americans. Captain William McClain ran a steamboat route between Cincinnati and Portsmouth, skirting the Kentucky shore, and welcoming runaways aboard. After McClain's steamboat arrived in Portsmouth, he handed-off his refugees to the local Underground Railroad network. But slave catchers also operated with impunity on the north side of the river.

The character "Eliza" in Harriet Beecher Stowe's novel is based on a true story of a soaking wet woman who escaped crossing the Ohio River in Ripley Ohio one cold winter night. In 1838, Eliza Harris crossed the river with her baby, throwing the child and herself from one shifting ice floe to the next. She lost her shoes in the icy river, and her feet were bloodied on the sharp ice. Unfortunately, awaiting her on the Ripley shore was a notorious slave catcher. But even this hardened man, who had captured many a runaway, was so moved by her valiant effort, that he had a momentary change of heart. When Eliza finally reached Ripley, this slave catcher said something like, "Ma'am, you have won your freedom, now get out of here." Ripley was also the setting for *"Uncle Tom's Cabin."*

The small creeks near Ripley, Ohio (e.g., Red Oak, White Oak, Eagle and Straight Creeks) were good conduits for escaping slaves to throw off pursuers and bloodhounds. Abolitionist's John Rankin's house sat high atop a hill overlooking the Ohio River in Ripley. His house became the single most famous landmark of the Underground Railroad. At night, the Rankin home had a light on in a window to guide runaways to their door. To the runaways, John Rankin's code named was 'north star.'

In the early 1800s, Ripley was a fairly busy port with a small ship building industry and a few packing houses. Steamboat service linked Ripley to Pittsburgh upriver, and St. Louis and New Orleans downriver. But soon after John

Rankin's arrival, Ripley became known as a hotbed of Underground Railroad activity. In the 1840s, some Kentuckians, from across the river, called Ripley, "that black, dirty abolitionist hellhole."

John Rankin of Ripley was likely the most effective Underground Railroad man in the entire Ohio Valley Region. He was a 'moral entrepreneur' who had a brilliant way of leading folks to his abolitionist way of thinking. In Ripley alone, he probably swayed over 150 to be Underground Railroad supporters. He used his rhetoric, his actions, and his power of persuasion. Rankin started developing his abolitionist views while witnessing first hand, the evils of slavery while growing up in Tennessee. He became an activist Presbyterian Minister, saying what was on his mind. He was chased out of Tennessee, and later Kentucky, before eventually settling in Ripley. There, he first settled defiantly close to the river to help runaways. Later he moved his family about a mile away, and to a home high atop a hill that could be seen from well into Kentucky. Rankin's entire family –wife, nine sons and four daughters, were all involved in the Underground Railroad.

The Rankin house and farm were often under surveillance by slave catchers. At least one time, Kentuckians attacked the Rankin home. A gunfight ensued. During the melee, John Rankin thought that two of his sons had been killed. Luckily (or perhaps it was divine providence), all of Rankin's family survived this attack.

Rankin adeptly used the Bible to renounce slavery. Other Rankin messages also resonated, "Every man desires to be free … All were designed for freedom; else man was created for disappointment and misery …All the feelings of humanity are strongly opposed to being enslaved, and nothing but the strong arm of power can make man submit to the yoke of bondage …God made of one blood all nations of men …Every man ought either to do his own work or pay the man who does it for him …Let us be willing to go down and do the lowest service in Christ's Kingdom, and labor to elevate the lowest of our [human] race, that they may become the sons and daughters of the Almighty."

Rankin also had a pragmatic side. He proposed that the federal government compensate slave owners if they would release their slaves. This idea evoked ridicule from other abolitionists. By the time the Civil War started in 1861, John Rankin had been denouncing slavery for 45 years. But Rankin had long hoped that it would never have to come down to a Civil War.

If Rankin was Ripley's conscience, John Parker was Ripley's backbone. Parker worked the front lines typically handing-off his runaways to Rankin and company. In 1827, Parker was born into slavery. He grew-up as a defiant young slave near Mobile Alabama. He escaped and was captured several times. At a young age, he taught himself to read and write. Somehow at 18 years of age, he was able to raise money, and purchase his own freedom. For a while, he lived in Cincinnati, and worked in a foundry. He moved to Ripley, not because of foundry work, but because he thought the whites and the blacks worked more efficiently in the local Underground Railroad –his real passion. In Ripley, Parker led a double life: iron-worker, by day; Underground Railroad ferryboat operator, by night. Sometimes Parker went deep into Kentucky to bring runaways out. During one of his many forays into Kentucky, he noticed small papers posted on trees. Upon closer inspection, they all stated the same thing. It was a poster of him, soliciting a $1,000 reward, dead or alive. Parker was barely fazed. In Ripley, he was often stalked by bounty hunters. It is said, that he'd often ambush them. Parker likely helped more than 900 runaways find freedom. Bold, fearless, courageous, in-your-face, and inventive all describe John Parker. John Parker is also one of only a very few African Americans to obtain US patents during the 19th Century –for a soil pulverizer and a tobacco screw press. Thanks to Parker, Rankin and others, no less than 2,000 runaways passed through Ripley Ohio.

In 1830, across the Ohio River near Owensboro Kentucky, Josiah Henson and his family made their escape. Most runaways were single men, who oftentimes had to make the horrible choice between leaving their family, or a chance at freedom. Bringing along an entire family was cumbersome, and greatly decreased the odds of a successful escape. But Henson was one who beat those odds.

Henson was born a slave in Maryland. He was exceptionally bright, excelled at just about everything he did, and won the favor of his master. He even bought into his master's idea of slavery. For his first forty years, he stayed extremely loyal to his master. In 1825, he was in charge of escorting a boatload of slaves down the Ohio River to his master's second plantation near Owensboro Kentucky. When he was near Cincinnati, blacks ashore as well as his human charges were pleading with him to let his human cargo make a break for freedom. His loyalty to his master won out, and down the Ohio River they proceeded. At his master's Owensboro plantation, he was again supervising more slaves. But after decades of loyal service, he was beginning to feel something gnaw inside him. He decided to work even harder, and purchase his freedom. When he came up with the pre-arrangement amount, his master wouldn't let him go. His master had deceived him, and then he realized that his master had been deceiving him many times in the past. After forty years, he finally realized that he would never be anything more than another piece of property in the eyes of his master.

With the help of a small boat rowed by another black man, Henson and his family crossed the Ohio River near Grandview Indiana. He was escaping with his wife and two sons. His family's trip to Canada is loaded with suspense, endurance, persistence, and luck. After he reached southern Ontario,

he founded a settlement aimed at schooling other fugitives in the skills that they would need as productive free men. Henson was soon an Underground Railroad conductor working between Ontario and Tennessee. Henson was often making daring trips into the South to help others escape. He also served as a Canadian military officer. Josiah Henson's story was the role model for the 'Uncle Tom' character (i.e., that loyal slave) in Harriet Beecher Stowe's *Uncle Tom's Cabin*. In 1909, Henson's great grand nephew, Mathew Henson, accompanied Robert E. Peary on his expedition to the North Pole.

In 1863, when Abraham Lincoln issued the 'Emancipation Proclamation' – freeing the slaves in the southern rebellion states, this was an invitation for those slaves to flee from the South. What was a crime before this proclamation was now accepted government policy. Those two heinous Fugitive Slave Acts were finally dead. In 1865, the Thirteenth Amendment finished-off Abraham Lincoln's Emancipation Proclamation by finally abolishing slavery. The Underground Railroad's work was done! The Railroad was a great humanitarian, moral, ecumenical and social endeavor that proved to be the greatest civil disobedience movement since the American Revolution. It was the first movement requiring interracial cooperation in America. In many instances, blacks played a more pivotal role operating the Railroad than whites.

I often have heard it said, "…because It's The Law." And yes, thankfully we are a nation of laws. But I do not have to reflect long and hard on American History, to come up with scores of examples of 'immoral laws,' including the two Fugitive Slave Acts addressed in this chapter. Soon after our country was founded, some Americans felt that a few laws of the United States were downright immoral. These Americans chose to follow a higher law rather than the laws passed by our 'politically correct' Congress. Thankfully for us, these people turned out to be right, while the majority of us were downright wrong. From the Underground Railroad days to the present, there have been numerous instances where a small devoted minority, guided by higher ideals, has been morally right, while the vast majority of us have been either complacent or just plain morally wrong. Thankfully, one of America's inherent strengths seems to be its ability to recognize, over time [sometimes very much time] our past errors, admit to them, and do some things that ameliorate a part of the transgressions inflicted by past immoral laws. We should all remember the words of Bernard Malamud, "The purpose of freedom is to create it for others."

**The Civil War**

Both Civil War Presidents, Abraham Lincoln and Jefferson Davis, were born poor less than a year apart in the border state of Kentucky. Lincoln slowly moved northwestward, living for a while in Indiana, before becoming a somewhat successful lawyer in central Illinois. Davis moved southward to Mississippi, where he made fortunes in the cotton business.

During the war, the last of our six 'Ohio River' states, West Virginia, entered the Union. The northwestern part of Virginia consisted of many small farms, and next-to-no slaveholding plantations. On the other hand, the tidewater and piedmont parts of Virginia had many large slave plantations. During the framing of the US Constitution, the three-fifths clause was established to keep white southern plantation owners happy. So a slave was counted as three-fifth of a person for federal representation and appropriation purposes. This didn't benefit the non-represented slaves; it only provided a disproportionate representation for the rich southern whites. Some historians have even suggested that Virginian Thomas Jefferson would not have been elected president in 1800, had it not been for this three-fifths clause.

By the 1850s, those non-slave owning small farmers in the western part of Virginia were caring less and less about the over represented rich planters in their own state to the east. Nonetheless, at the onset of the Civil War, there was somewhat divided sentiment between North and South in the mountainous counties of this northwestern part of Virginia. The present-day state of West Virginia provided about 36,000 soldiers for the Union Army and less than 20,000 for Confederate Forces. The only sister of famed Confederate (and 'West' Virginian) General Stonewall Jackson staunchly supported the Union. The government of Virginia, dominated by wealthy tidewater planters, was over-represented in the state legislature. On the other side of the state, the smaller 'western' Virginia mountain farmers, mostly of German and Scotch-Irish descent, felt an inequitable representation and taxation.

Since these 'western' Virginians were unable to stop Virginia's secession from the Union, they soon made plans to secede from Virginia. In 1861, a 'Restored Government of Virginia' was created in Wheeling to replace the 'vacated government' in Richmond. Francis Pierpont of Fairmont was chosen as 'the Governor of Restored Virginia.' In effect there were now two Virginias –one based in Wheeling, and one based in Richmond. Four months later, at a second Wheeling convention, the creation of a new state was overwhelming approved and another governor for that new state was inaugurated. This new state was to be called 'Kanawha,' but the name was later changed to 'West Virginia.' In June 1863, Abraham Lincoln proclaimed the new state of West Virginia as the 35th state admitted to the Union. In 1885, the state capital permanently moved from Wheeling on the Ohio River to Charleston on the Kanawha River. Today, West Virginia's seven largest cities are all situated on the Kanawha, Ohio, or Monongahela Rivers.

During the Civil War, the Ohio River Valley was spared from much of the horrific fighting that occurred further south. Nonetheless, there were a few minor north-south skirmishes along the Ohio and Kanawha Rivers –in Charleston and

Guyandotte, West Virginia, in Buffington Island Ohio, in Newburgh, Leavenworth, Mauckport and Corydon Indiana, and in Paducah, Owensboro, and Augusta in Kentucky.

In the early years of the war, Illinois civilian, Ulysses S. Grant offered his services to the Union. Before being a pre-Civil War civilian, Grant was a West Point graduate, a veteran of the Mexican War, a very good cavalry man, and an unpretentious and unassuming leader. In 1861, Grant was given a command of a regiment of unruly Midwestern farm boys to be trained at Fort Defiance in Cairo Illinois. Not much was expected of Grant. But Grant and his troops were soon fighting their way down some of America's great rivers. Grant understood that if you controlled the rivers, you controlled a supply line and about everything else that goes with that. By the fall of 1862, the Union Army and Navy, working together, had gained control of about 1,000 miles of southern rivers.

In February 1862, not far from Cairo, Grant launched his first attack –on *Fort Henry* on the nearby Tennessee River, 25 miles south of Paducah. This was an early Union success. Ten days later, Grant attacked nearby *Fort Donelson* on the Cumberland River. Some historians consider *Fort Donelson* to be the first decisive battle of the Civil War. Many Confederates who escaped from *Fort Henry* had made their way to *Fort Donelson*. When that 12,000-man Confederate garrison was overwhelmed, Grant coined a new term, demanding 'Unconditional Surrender.' The Confederate General, Simon Bolivar Buckner was a former West Point classmate of Grant. Buckner thought Grant's term was quite unchivalrous. But it was vintage Grant, and complimented his persona as 'US' Grant. When Bucker surrendered to Grant at *Fort Donelson*, Grant generously offered Buckner his purse to cover expenses. After the Civil War, Grant truly befriended many of his former Confederate adversaries. Grant's four pallbearers were all Civil War generals; two

of which were Confederates, including General Simon Bolivar Buckner. With the Union successes at *Fort Henry* and *Fort Donelson*, the blue troops had access to the Tennessee River as far as Muscle Shoals Alabama as well as the Cumberland River. These two early Grant victories all but insured that Kentucky would not be joining the Confederacy.

After *Forts Henry and Donelson*, Grant started an offensive south up the Tennessee River, against the Confederate Forces of General Sidney Johnston. In April 1862, Union and Confederate forces met near Pittsburg Landing on the Tennessee River, and the *Battle of Shiloh* ensued. The *Battle of Shiloh* lasted for two days, and the tide of battle ebbed and flowed for both sides. In the end, the Confederates had to retreat. After the first day at *Shiloh*, General William Tecumseh Sherman remarked to Grant, "Well, Grant, we've had the devil's own day, haven't we?" Grant puffed on his cigar, looked up at his good friend and said, "Yup, but we'll lick them tomorrow." The *Battle of Shiloh* was extremely costly –24,000 lives (about 13,000 Union and 11,000 Confederate). In just two days, America had lost more men at *Shiloh* than in all of its prior conflicts combined...and this was just the beginning of the Civil War. *Shiloh* dispelled a popularly held notion that this war would soon be won with 'one more romantic battle.' Before *Shiloh*, Grant and Sherman, along with Confederate General Robert E. Lee were ridiculed, when they –in the vast minority –predicted that the forthcoming struggle between the North and South would be dreadfully costly. Sherman had spent time as the superintendent of a Louisiana military academy, developed a genuine affection for southerners, but also understood the mentality of the forces at play in the burgeoning conflict. After *Shiloh*, a horrified northern populace was incensed at the casualty count, and pressed that Grant be relived of command. Later that same year, with the war going badly for the North, President Lincoln restored Grant to command, saying something like "at least

General Grant fights," –unlike so many of Lincoln's other early generals. In March of 1864, Lincoln placed Grant in charge of the entire Union Army, and 13 months later, this terrible war was finally over.

In the summer of 1862, Union General George W. Morgan controlled the pivotal Cumberland Gap in southern Kentucky. But soon General George Morgan's supply lines were cut-off, and he found himself surrounded by Confederates. He and about 8,000 Union troops decided to make a northbound 'run for it,' and attempted a withdrawal to the relative safety of the Ohio River. He and his men made their retreat covering more than 200 miles in 16 days to Greenup Kentucky. During this retreat, Union General George Morgan's was being harassed by the Confederates. Another General Morgan, Confederate General John Hunt Morgan and his raiders, known as Morgan's (Confederate) Raiders periodically hassled Union General George W. Morgan during this 'masterful retreat.'

In early July 1863, Confederate General John Hunt Morgan, disobeying his superior's orders, crossed the Ohio River, and went on a raid throughout southern Indiana and southern Ohio. When his depleted troops reached Salineville Ohio, this marked the furthest north penetration of any significant Confederate force. Morgan and about 2,000 men crossed the Ohio River at Brandenburg Kentucky, aboard two commandeered steamships. The militia in Indiana was no match for Morgan's Cavalry. Morgan looted Mauckport Indiana, and within days his force captured about 350 home guards in Corydon Indiana. From there, Morgan's troops continued on a northeast route, plundering, horse stealing, destroying bridges, railroads, telegraph lines, and supply depots. But Morgan never strayed too far from the Ohio River, because he knew that sooner or later, he'd need to make his way back across that river to return south.

Near Pomeroy Ohio, Union forces were becoming better organized and coordinated, and Morgan's noose was tightening. About ten days after Corydon, Morgan attempted to re-cross the Ohio River near Buffington Island. About 300 of his men made it across the river, before the *Battle of Buffington Island* ensued. About 900 of Morgan's Confederates were captured or killed by Union forces. Three future US Presidents, and all Ohioans –Rutherford B. Hayes, James Garfield, and William McKinley –fought with the Union at *Buffington Island*. Morgan and his depleted force escaped annihilation, but were still stranded in Ohio. About 20 miles north of *Buffington Island*, near Belleville West Virginia, Morgan again tried to cross the Ohio. About 300 more of his troops got across, before Union forces, in hot pursuit, arrived. Morgan, now with a contingent of only about 400 Confederates, regrouped and continued heading northeast –but deeper into enemy territory. They were desperately trying to get back to the Ohio River and cross it. But the Union force knew this too. About 10 miles from the Ohio River (near Wellsville) in Columbiana County Ohio, Union troops again caught-up with Morgan and his 400 Confederates. The skirmish of Salineville ensued. Morgan's men were either killed or captured and Morgan himself soon surrendered. Morgan was sent to a prison in Columbus Ohio. But a year later, Morgan and six other Confederates escaped and returned to the South.

Less than a year after Morgan had been routed in eastern Ohio, Confederate Cavalry General Nathan Bedford Forrest attacked with about 3,000 men at Union-held Paducah Kentucky. Earlier, Forrest had served with distinction at *Fort Donelson* and *Shiloh*. His objective in Paducah was to plunder and wreak havoc. While Forrest was occupying Paducah, the 650 union troops were holed-up in a garrison west of town. Forrest's command took supplies, horses and mules, and destroyed much property. Within weeks, one of Forrest's subordinates returned to Paducah to seize some prized horses that were missed during the first raid.

35

Old time sailing ship underway, near Wheeling, West Virginia

Old Lock House # 34 turned into a River Museum, Chilo, Ohio

# CHAPTER 4
## The Steamboat Era and Taming the River for Navigation

Before the Steamboat Era, pirogues, flatboats, and keelboats were the primary means of transportation on the Ohio River and its tributaries. A pirogue wasn't much more than a large dugout canoe. Some pirogues could be as long as 50 feet, as wide as five feet, and could hold a score of people and tons of freight. A flatboat was not much more than a raft with an interior cabin. Flatboats could only go downstream, and had limited steering ability, but some flatboats could be quite large. When flatboats reached their downstream destination, they were dismantled for their lumber.

Keelboats, looking more like 'real boats,' with a bow and stern, were more durable and functional …and they could go upstream. But this was strenuous work. Going upstream, keelboats often times had to hug the shallower waters near shore, so they could be poled, pulled along using tree branches, or pushed/pulled with men in waist deep water making upstream headway of only a few feet at a time. Both flatboats and keelboats could also be sailed. As arduous as this was, it was still easier to move cargo on rivers and streams than overland. As early as 1793, Cincinnati and Pittsburgh were connected by a weekly keelboat service. By 1811, keelboats were making roundtrips between Cincinnati and New Orleans.

Heading-only-downstream flatboats still had a niche after the arrival of the steamboats. The tonnage carried on flatboats didn't peak until 1847, when an estimated 2,200 flatboats found their way to New Orleans …the natural terminus for 'one-way' flatboats. In the early 19th Century, industrial ports like New Orleans, Pittsburgh, Cincinnati, and New York were well on their way. The era was ripe for steamboats.

In 1803, Thomas Jefferson concluded the Louisiana Purchase. In 1804-1806, Lewis and Clark's Corps of Discovery explored these new lands that doubled the size of the United States. America now had the land on both sides of the massive Mississippi River system with its virgin forests and abundant wood supply (i.e., fuel for steam boilers). Steamboats started to come onto the scene after the War of 1812, and slowly started replacing keelboats. Early steamboat travel was unreliable and dangerous. In these early years, wary folks felt safer putting themselves and their cargo on vessels other than steamboats. In 1815, about 15,000 men were still employed in the 'keelboat and flatboat industry.'

Successful inventor, Robert Fulton was encouraged to design a boat that could be propelled by steam produced in boilers fueled by wood fires. In 1807, Robert Fulton's Folly, the *Clermont*, made a successful 150-mile upstream trip on the Hudson River, from New York to Albany. Witnesses along shore figured the 142-foot long, mechanical noise-making, smoke-belching *Clermont* would explode at any minute. But the side-paddlewheeler didn't explode. Fulton tweaked his basic design, and soon had a commercially profitable boat. And later, he nearly developed a business monopoly.

Four years later in October 1811, another Fulton side-wheeler, about 120 feet long the *New Orleans*, started a nightmarish one-way downstream trip from Pittsburgh arriving in New Orleans four months later. The *New Orleans* was able to travel as fast as 8 MPH with the current. The pilot of the *New Orleans* was Nicholas Roosevelt – President Theodore Roosevelt's grandfather's brother. After that trip, the *New Orleans* was placed in packet service between Natchez and New Orleans. Packet boats were steamships working a route between two or more river cities while carrying passengers, freight and mail. Two years after the *New Orleans* started packet service, she was lost. The ship went up to a riverbank to retrieve firewood for her boilers, got hung-up on a stump, was holed, and sank.

In 1816, the *Washington* made a trip from Wheeling, where she was built, to New Orleans. The *Washington* was the fastest steamboat to date, and made the 1,500-mile trip to New Orleans in 24 days. The *Enterprise* was the first steamboat to go down the river to New Orleans and then to return to Pittsburgh in 1819. The *Enterprise* was built in Brownsville Pennsylvania (formerly Redstone Old Fort), and played a small role in the 1815 *Battle of New Orleans*.

Both the *Washington* and the *Enterprise* had a stern wheel (i.e., the paddle boards were fixed to a wheel at the stern of the boat). Sternwheelers would become the mainstay on the Mississippi and Ohio Rivers. Side-wheelers were more maneuverable, especially if there was a wheel on each side. With two wheels, a side-wheeler could basically pivot in place with the two big wheels going in opposite directions. Large side-wheelers were faster and could handle more cargo, but they also required a larger crew. Side-wheelers were better suited for wide expanses of open water. Advancements in the propulsion mechanisms and the rudder designs made the sternwheelers more economical on the Mississippi and Ohio Rivers. The paddle boards on the sternwheelers were better protected from notorious Mississippi and Ohio River snags and other debris. A shallow draft, flat bottom, and a less beamy vessel, were other attributes favored on Mississippi and Ohio River steamboats.

Widely-known Robert Fulton was not the only one who made contributions to early steamboats. In 1791, Connecticut-born John Fitch was granted the patent after a successful trial of a steam powered boat on the Delaware River. Fitch also received a similar patent from France. In Europe, Fitch was more widely regarded as the inventor of the steamboat. Decades later, Fulton turned Fitch's idea into something very profitable.

Henry Shreve was another early American steamboat pioneer. Shreve designed the steamboats *Enterprise* and *Washington,* and captained the latter. Shreve is credited with opening-up the Ohio and Mississippi Rivers to commercial steamboat traffic due to several structural and mechanical modifications. As an active steamboat captain, Shreve was quite aware of the many dangers lurking in these western rivers. In the 1820s, Shreve started work on designing small 'sang-removing' boats or 'snag boats.' These vessels had a split hull, could straddle, and then hoist a large snag out of the river. Shreve's snag boats very much enhanced the safety for the larger passenger-carrying steamboats. In 1834, one of Shreve's snag boats was able to successfully remove a notorious raft of snags clogging-up the Red River. This 'Great Red River Raft' consisted of intertwined trees, limbs and debris that extended intermittently for about 150 miles. A location along this stretch of the Red River was later named after Shreve – Shreveport Louisiana.

Before steamboats, a dangerous river trip from Louisville to New Orleans typically took four months. In 1820, with the advent of steamboats, that same trip had been cut to three weeks. Twenty years later, that same steamboat trip was shortened to less than a week. In 1814, the *New Orleans* made the 268-mile trip from New Orleans to Natchez in just less than seven days. But by 1880, the *Robert E. Lee* could make that same trip in less than 18 hours. In 1814, only about twenty steamboats were docking in New Orleans. Five years later, close to 200 steamboats had landed there. By 1834, the Crescent City had more than 1,200 steamboat landings. In 1817, fourteen boats were regularly plying the rivers between New Orleans and Louisville. Two years later, there were thirty-one boats on that long route.

In 1811, when the *New Orleans* passed by Henderson Kentucky, John James Audubon was so impressed that he contracted for the construction of the *General*

*Pike.* Before becoming a famous naturalist, Audubon had failed at several business ventures around Henderson. After failing again trying to make steamship transport profitable, Audubon's first profitable deal was 'selling' the *Pike.* Nevertheless, by 1820, the *Pike* was one of the first regular packet boats on the Ohio River, operating between Cincinnati and Louisville. Ten years later, packet boats had become reliable enough to carry mail on the Ohio River. By the 1850s, three million passengers were annually taking packet boats on the Ohio River. In the 1840s, steamboats had reached the upper Mississippi River, and there was regular packet service between St. Louis and present-day St. Paul Minnesota. Just before the Civil War, steamboat traffic peaked. However, after the Civil War, steamboat traffic started its decline, in large part due to the very rapid growth of the railroads. Nonetheless, packet boats continued to be a viable means of transportation on the Mississippi River into the late 19th Century.

By the 1830s and 1840s, coal was replacing wood as the preferred fuel for steam boilers. In the 1850s, coal became the more prevalent fuel on most of the inland rivers. Early steamboats had to stop along the river banks to retrieve wood, usually from prearranged local farmers, about every five-to-six hours. The earliest use of coal fired-boilers was more practical for steamers operating nearer to Pittsburgh.

Of the 6,000 or so inland river steamships constructed between 1820 and 1880, about three-quarters of them were built in the Ohio River Valley. The upper valley was an especially important center for steamboat building. Well before the 1820s, a handful of noteworthy steamships had already been constructed in Pittsburgh, Brownsville, and Wheeling. Pittsburgh, Cincinnati, and Louisville were becoming major ship building centers. By the 1830s, more than 300 steamboats had been constructed around Pittsburgh. By 1834, 221 steamships had been built in the Cincinnati area. During the Civil War years, Cincinnati

shipyards started manufacturing ironclad gunboats. The Louisville area had built about 100 steamboats by 1830. Smaller, custom-made steamboats were made for travel on the Muskingum, Kanawha, Little Kanawha, Guyandotte, and Big Sandy Rivers. Even today, if you have a chance to travel up the Kanawha or the Muskingum Rivers, you will still see many of these smaller paddle wheelers.

Before long, steamboats were racing each other. Competition between companies was intense, and packet boats were often pushing each other to break time records. The wood or coal-fueled steam boilers were often severely pushed to the limit, and sometimes to the point of failure. Excess steam in the boilers, that could have been vented, was often not released. Instead it continued to be captured in the strained boilers with the intent of trying to make the machinery turn faster and faster. In 1870, possibly the most famous steamboat race ever held was between the *Robert E. Lee* and the *Natchez.* These were likely the two fastest steamships on the Mississippi River. The race was from New Orleans to St. Louis. The *Lee* was able to easily outdistance the *Natchez,* and was also aided by having a fuel tender boat lashed to it somewhere in mid-route, while a fuel transfer took place, and the *Lee* remained underway. Meanwhile, the *Natchez* stopped to take-on fuel, as well as to load and offload cargo and passengers. The *Lee* covered the almost 1,300 miles in less than four days, and averaged 13.8 miles per hour. The *Natchez* arrived in St. Louis six hours behind the *Lee.*

Steamboat races were unregulated and an invitation for disaster. Poorly maintained and overly strained boilers caused many deadly explosions. Only five years before the famed *Robert E. Lee-Natchez* race, and on that same stretch of Mississippi River, the worst military maritime disaster in US history occurred. In April 1865, at the end of the Civil War and days after President Lincoln's assassination, the extremely overcrowded 260-foot long steamboat

*Sultana* was transporting recently liberated Union Prisoners of War held by Confederates at Andersonville and Cahaba camps. These Union ex-POWs were aboard the *Sultana* heading to Cairo Illinois, and eventually home. There were about 2,400 folks aboard a steamer with a rated capacity of 376. Just upstream from Memphis, and not far from the Ohio River, there was a terrific blast aboard the *Sultana* as a steam boiler exploded. At around 2:00 AM, hundreds were instantly killed. Before long, the *Sultana* was a raging inferno. About 1,900 died in either the initial explosion, or by being trapped and burned in the inferno, or by drowning. Of the 500 initial survivors, about another 200 soon died of the horrible burns they received that night. The vessel was overcrowded, in large part, due to the greed of the vessel owners. The boiler exploded, in all likelihood, due to the failure of a temporary boiler patch that was hastily fitted three days before in Vicksburg Mississippi.

Before the Civil War and the *Sultana* disaster, there had been many other steamboat accidents on the Ohio River. In 1838, only 25 days after the *Moselle* was launched, she exploded. This fast and sleek steamer had just departed Cincinnati for Louisville. Still close to the shore, a likely overly-exerted boiler exploded. There has been some speculation that the captain, wishing to impress bystanders with the *Moselle's* speed, had the boilers overly-stoked. What-was-left of the *Moselle* after that explosion, sank within minutes. No less than 130 were killed or missing in this disaster. In 1852, the steamer *Redstone*, operated a packet route between Cincinnati and Madison Indiana. In the early afternoon, as the *Redstone* was backing away from a Scott's Landing in Carrolton Kentucky, a boiler exploded, and she sank within three minutes. Of the 80 to 100 aboard the *Redstone*, it's believed that about three-quarters of them perished in the immense blast. The force of that blast sent boat and body parts flying and landing more than a half-mile away.

After the Civil War, Ohio River Steamboat accidents continued. In 1866, the *General Lytle* exploded about 18 miles downstream from Madison Indiana and about 20 were either killed or seriously injured. Later that same year, the *Pine Bluff* caught fire and sank near the mouth of the Licking River across from Cincinnati. Two years later, in December 1868, just before midnight, two steamers collided with each other a couple of miles above Warsaw Kentucky. The *United States* was heading downriver to Louisville, and the *America* was heading upriver to Newport Kentucky. The *America* rammed into the *United States*. After the collision, an ignition of barreled coal oil on the deck of the *United States* set both steamers ablaze. They both tried to make it to the Indiana shore. The *America* made it, but the *United States* didn't. Both steamers burned to the waterline, and another 162 lives were lost. In 1874, and only several miles upriver from the *America-United States* disaster, in nearby Boone County Kentucky, the *Pat Rogers* caught fire and sank, and an estimated another dozen folks lost their lives.

In 1892, The Cincinnati-New Orleans packet boat *Golden Rule* was tied to a wharf in Cincinnati. It caught fire, possibly because a barrel of gasoline had been placed too close to a steam boiler. Two other close-by moored vessels were also set ablaze. About a dozen folks perished –mostly passengers that couldn't get out of the burning *Golden Rule*. Less than three years later, another steamboat from Cincinnati was heading to New Orleans. It was a March morning, and foggy. The *Longfellow* was behind schedule, and packet company officials ordered the captain to leave, in spite of the fog. The *Longfellow* struck the pier of the C&O Railroad Bridge in Cincinnati, broke-up, and eleven lives were lost. Years before the *Longfellow* accident, the *Polander*, leaving the Cincinnati wharf, and the *Hornet*, coming in to that same wharf, slammed into each other in the fog. The Captain of the *Hornet* was crushed to death. In 1927, on another Cincinnati fog-bound day, the towboat *GW McBride* slammed into the L&N Railroad Bridge. The wooden *GW McBride* was nearly split down the middle, and at least ten lives were lost. In the winter of 1905, the steam-powered towboat *Defender*, en route from Cincinnati to Pittsburgh, exploded near the wharf in Huntington West Virginia. A dozen lives were lost, but a half-dozen survived this explosion in the icy river.

As early as 1850, and well before the *Sultana* disaster, steamboat accidents had already claimed about 4,000 lives, not to mention the thousands more permanently maimed or missing. It was estimated that about 500 steamboats had been lost due to accidents. A survey, made after the Civil War, tallied 129 individual sunken hulks on the Ohio River alone. The average lifespan of a steamboat was estimated to be between four and six years, due to explosions, fires, sinkings, and groundings. Iron-hulled steamboats had been around since the early 1830s, but they were not widely accepted. Most of the few iron-hull boats were built in Pittsburgh. An iron-hulled steamer could outlive a wooden-hull steamer by five times. Nonetheless, the economics of the day, and the availability of raw materials favored wood construction. It wasn't until the 1880s that iron and steel hulls started gaining economic acceptance. The steel hulls of some of the old surviving steamboat might still be found on these rivers today – supporting floating restaurants, marinas or other floating structures.

In 1910, one of the more colorful non-fatal steamboat accidents occurred on the Ohio River. The 235-foot steamboat *Virginia* ended-up in a cornfield, and was made famous by a ballad and a book by John Hartford, "*Steamboat in a Cornfield.*" After an exceedingly dry 1909, the following year had a very wet spring, and the Ohio River overflowed its banks. In a bend near current-day Willow Grove West Virginia the downriver bound *Virginia* lost the channel, and ended-up aground near river mile 228. Soon, the river receded, and the *Virginia* was high and dry in a West Virginia cornfield,

600 feet away from the Ohio River. She stayed there for six months. The nearly bankrupt owners, the Pittsburgh and Cincinnati Packet Line, contracted a 'house mover.' As the contractor was making slow progress towards river, rain began to fall and the river began to rise. Before long, the Ohio was again out of its banks and the *Virginia* refloated. The Packet Line figured they didn't have to pay the moving contractor, saying the boat was refloated due to an 'Act of God.' The moving contractor took the Packet Line to court. The judge did agree that the final floating was an 'Act of God,' nonetheless the contractor had put the boat within 'God's Reach,' and 'must be paid.' And John Hartford had the story for his colorful steamboat ballad. There's a replica of the *Virginia* on these waters today; you'll typically find the steamboat *Natchez* plying somewhere between New Orleans and Pittsburgh.

By the mid 1850s, steamboats were also becoming heavily involved in cargo shipments. In 1866, about 90 steamboats were pushing Ohio River coal tows. Steamboat tows were the first vessels to economically transport large quantities of cargo upriver. Even to this day, it is far less expensive, per ton mile, to move bulk commodities, such as coal, gravel, sand, petroleum, and grains on the winding rivers than via any other inland transportation mode (i.e., rail or truck). By the 1880s, the passenger steamboats were in sharp decline. However, commercial, and especially coal-carrying, vessels were on the rise. In 1902, the *Sprague*, perhaps the largest inland river steam-powered towboats ever –at almost 1,500 tons and 318 feet, was built on the Mississippi River near Dubuque Iowa. The paddle-wheeler *Sprague* held many cargo records and provided useful service as late as the 1940s.

In the 1890s, internal combustion engines, primarily feed by gasoline, started replacing coal-fired steam boilers. By the early 1900s, propeller-driven vessels started replacing paddle-wheel driven. Around

1890, German Rudolf Diesel had developed a much safer compression industrial engine – the diesel. In the United States, diesel technology started taking off in the 1920s. By the 1950s, diesel engines had made commercial steam-powered, and even gasoline-powered, vessels obsolete.

About the time of the Civil War, the rapid growth of the railroads hastened the end of the Steamboat Era. Early locomotives also used stream propulsion technology, and by the 1870s trains began seriously supplanting steamboats as the main transporter of passengers and freight. By the early 1900s, all but a few of the packet boat companies had succumbed. One notable exception was Cincinnati's Greene Line. Nearly all of the packet companies that survived the early 1900s, later fell during the Great Depression. By the 1930s steamboat passenger and freight service was all but over. Nonetheless, the Steamboats Era gave an impetus for a large part of the industrial development that was soon to follow in the Ohio River Valley.

Today on the Ohio River, you might see a few historical paddlewheelers –the *Delta Queen*, the *Belle of Louisville*, and the *Spirit of Jefferson*. 'The Belle' and the *Spirit of Jefferson* are based in Louisville, and the *Delta Queen's* homeport is Cincinnati. The *Spirit of Jefferson*, so named in 1996, was built in 1963, and was previously named the *Mark Twain* and the *Huck Finn*. She and the *Belle of Louisville* are operated by the local Louisville metropolitan government. The *Belle of Louisville* was sturdily constructed in 1914 on the Allegheny River and was first named the *Idlewild*. In her early years she was a ferry on the Mississippi River connecting Memphis Tennessee and Arkansas. During World War II, her bow was fitted with tow knees to push barges. Later she was a tramp steamer on the Mississippi, Missouri, Illinois, and Ohio Rivers. Tramp steamers went wherever they could make a buck. In 1947, she was renamed the *Avalon* and continued her tramping ways on all the Midwestern rivers.

But by 1962, she was a mess, and a business interest in Louisville purchased her at auction for $34,000. In 1963, the newly refurbished (and no doubt at a cost many times more than her purchase price) *Belle of Louisville* had a new home at the downtown Louisville waterfront, and was soon ready to race Cincinnati's *Delta Queen*. At the time that *the Belle* was purchased and refurbished it was not a unanimously popular decision to sink so much money into an old boat. But *The Belle* endeared herself to the folks of Louisville. In 1989, *the Belle*, was designated as a National Historic Landmark, and in 2004, she celebrated her 90th birthday. *The Belle* and the *Delta Queen* still square off in an old time steamboat race on the Wednesday before the Kentucky Derby.

From 1924-27, the *Delta Queen* was fabricated in Glasgow Scotland, and then shipped to and assembled piecemeal in California. From 1927 to 1940, both the *Delta Queen* and the *Delta King* worked from San Francisco to Sacramento in the Sacramento-San Joaquin River deltas, and hence the 'Delta' in their names. The *Delta Queen* served as a hospital transport during World War II. After the War, she was purchased by Captain Tom Greene of Cincinnati's celebrated Greene Line Steamers. As the 19th Century drew to a close, the Greene Line Steamer Company was able to hang-on much longer than most other lines. Captain Greene's mother, Mary Becker Greene earned her pilots license, and captained more than a few of the Greene Line Steamers during the late 19th and early 20th Centuries. In 1947, the *Delta Queen* was prepared for an ocean transit and a passage through the Panama Canal. This operation was supervised by legendary Captain Fred Way. The towed *Delta Queen* arrived in New Orleans after being out at sea for about a month. She soon made her way to Pittsburgh and was further refurbished at Neville Island for about seventeen times her most recent purchase price. In 1949, aboard the *Delta Queen*, Captain Mary, mother of the Greene Line, died in her cabin after nearly 60 years of working aboard steamboats –52 years as a captain or pilot. In 1973, the Greene Line became the Delta Queen Steamboat Company. During the past thirty years, ownership of that company has changed hands several times. Today, the *Delta Queen* is the only operating steamboat with staterooms and she can carry 174 passengers. The *Queen* makes it a point to return to Cincinnati for her homecoming every spring. But her future is uncertain, at best, because enforced federal regulations may soon make her uneconomical to operate.

Besides *the Belle* in Louisville, historic paddleboats are making a comeback as tourist attractions. Cincinnati and Pittsburgh have several large paddleboat landings serving today's tourists who wish to take a jaunt down the river in a 19th Century boat. Several stationery casinos as well as restaurants along the river are dressed-up to look like old time steamboats. Every three or four years, the Port of Cincinnati hosts its 'Tall Stacks Festival' in October. The *Delta Queen,* the *Belle of Louisville*, as well as no less than another dozen large paddle wheelers never miss this five-day gala event on the Cincinnati waterfront.

Besides in Cincinnati, Pittsburgh, and Louisville, a surprising number of smaller paddle wheelers can be found on today's Muskingum and Kanawha Rivers. I've also seen small ones way up the Monongahela and Little Kanawha Rivers. Marietta, Pomeroy, and Malta (on the Muskingum River) in Ohio, and Parkersburg, Point Pleasant (on the Ohio) and Charleston and St. Albans (on the Kanawha River) in West Virginia, as well as tiny Augusta Kentucky all have their lively annual steamboat festivals, hosting a wide array of old time boats. The Steamboat Era may be a thing of the past, but colorful vestiges of that era have and will continue to endure.

Part of a Wicket Dam on display, Hannibal, Ohio

## The Evolution of Our Locks and Dams on the Ohio River

During the earliest days of steamboat navigation, it was obvious that 'The Falls of the Ohio' near Louisville was the most significant natural obstacle to navigation on the entire Ohio River. 'The Falls' practically cuts Ohio River navigation into two pieces. 'The Falls' is actually a series of rapids that dropped the river level by about 26 feet in a two-mile stretch. Steamboats could navigate over 'the falls' during times of high water, but high water levels were anything but consistent. Often, it was more prudent to offload steamboat passengers and freight at one end of 'the falls,' and make an overland trip through the area to another steamboat near the opposite end of 'the falls.' The Louisville area became a natural terminus for northbound vessels coming from as far away as New Orleans, and for southbound vessels coming from Cincinnati and Pittsburgh.

Soon after Louisville was founded in 1778, 'falls pilots' found a market niche guiding flatboats over 'the falls.' At high water, there were three routes, or chutes, that vessels could take over 'the falls.' The one nearest the Right Descending Bank (RDB), or closest to Indiana, was the most preferred route. If a steamboat wished to make the run from Pittsburgh to New Orleans, without having to delay for needed high water levels at 'the falls,' a canal and lock system was needed for bypassing 'the falls.'

In 1825 construction on that canal began. By 1830, the privately-funded Louisville and Portland Canal was completed. This canal was constructed on the Left Descending Bank (LDB) –the Kentucky side, using hand tools, wheelbarrows, ox-drawn plows, horse-drawn carts and scrappers. The finished two-mile canal had three locking chambers, a 26-foot total lift, and a controlling depth of about three feet. During the canal's first three months of operation, around 800 vessels, including about 400 steamboats, had locked-through. But soon, the locking chambers of the original Louisville and Portland Canal needed enlarging to accommodate larger steamboats. By 1872, the locking chambers

were lengthened and widened from 183'X49' to 325'X80.' Further improvements increased the controlling depth from three to six feet, and reduced the number of locking chambers from three to two. In 1921, the Louisville and Portland Canal was replaced by Lock & Dam 41. And by 1960, Lock & Dam 41 was replaced by the present-day McAlpine Lock and Dam.

After solving the navigation problem around 'the falls,' the next two most pressing navigation concerns were the low water levels typically encountered on the upper Ohio River near Pittsburgh, and the removal of boat-damaging snags found all along the river. In the 1850s Congress approved five snag-removing boats. These were critical. In 1888, one snag-boat, the *E.A. Woodruff*, traveled about 2,100 miles up and down the Ohio River, and removed 1,225 snags, 127 large rocks, 46 new wrecks, and 13 old wrecks. The *Woodruff* was able to remove one snag that weighed 164 tons.

Before, the 20th Century, water levels on the Ohio River could be as low as one foot between Pittsburgh and Cincinnati, and as low as two feet between Cincinnati and Cairo Illinois. Near St. Marys West Virginia, horses and wagons could sometimes be seen fording across the river. In the late 19th Century, it was a common sight for coal tows to beach themselves on the banks of the Monongahela and upper Ohio River while waiting for higher water. Around Pittsburgh, beached coal tows sometimes had to wait six months before they had enough water depth to proceed. Then, when the water levels rose, all the tows proceeded all at once!

In 1877, the first wing dams were constructed in the Ohio River. A wing dam is a two-part submerged barrier placed on the sides of the riverbed angling downstream and partway into the river channel. The purpose of a submerged wing dam is to direct faster-moving water closer toward the center of the river, thus creating a natural 'self-scouring effect' that would keep the river channel deeper and less prone to sedimentation than areas outside of the wing dam and the channel. Wing dams were not a panacea, but they did help maintain a deeper river channel.

Near the late 19<sup>th</sup> Century, the Ohio River was not 'twenty-four/seven,' as we know it today. Even with the Louisville and Portland Canal, snag boats, and wing dams, a boat with any sort of draft might have to wait days, weeks, months, or longer before being able to negotiate certain sections of the Ohio. As early as the 1830s, many were addressing this problem. By the 1870s, a system of creating locks and dams, and associated river pools was being seriously considered. Pools, as the name implies, are slack water areas that are backed-up by a particular dam, and named for that dam holding back that pool. The length of a pool usually extends from one lock and dam to the next.

Coal towboats on the Monongahela River were seriously pushing for a lock and dam below Pittsburgh. In 1877, construction of a lock and dam near Davis Island, about five miles below 'the Point' in Pittsburgh, had begun. In 1885, the first lock and dam, Lock and Dam #1 (also known as the Davis Island Lock and Dam) above the Louisville and Portland Canal was completed. The Davis Island Lock and Dam was the first of many to be 110 feet wide by 600 feet long –a standard that lasted well beyond the 19<sup>th</sup> Century. By the 1890s, more federal funding for Ohio River navigation was becoming a reality. By 1908, five more locks and dams were completed below Pittsburgh. This was the beginning of the first comprehensive 50-lock and dam system on the Ohio River. By 1906, the prescribed six-foot controlling channel depth had been increased to nine feet, thereby permitting even deeper draft vessels the ability to navigate. Today, there are many more locks and dams, per river mile, on the upper Ohio than on the lower Ohio. This is due to the naturally shallower and faster-flowing state of the natural river in its uppermost reaches. This 'steeper slope on the upper river' phenomenon will likely hold true for any long river.

Commercial navigational interests, especially the coal towboats, were pushing for a way to bypass the time-consuming locking-though process when the river stage had a high enough water level. Earlier in 1852, on the Seine River, the French Corps of Engineers came up with a dam made up of individual moveable wickets. During times of high water, these wickets could lay flat on a masonry foundation placed at the bottom of the riverbed. In times of low water, the individual two-position wickets could pivot and be raised off the riverbed creating a 'moveable' dam as well as a deep water pool upstream from that dam. Individual wickets were about four feet wide and anywhere from 15 to 20 feet high when in their raised or 'damming position.' On the Seine River, the French lowered and raised individual wickets using cables extending from a low stationary bridge over the river. The Ohio River had a modification, whereby a wicket boat, or a maneuver boat, was able to raise and lower individual dam wickets. These maneuver boats had a boom and a hook to raise and lower single wickets. Upright wickets could be erected in a navigable pass from 600 to over 1,200 feet wide using about 100 to 330 individual wickets across that pass. An efficient boat crew could lower or raise the dam wickets in about three or four hours. Today, there is an informative actual-sized 'high and dry' display of a section of a wicket dam and a maneuver boat at the Hannibal Lock and Dam Visitors' Center, at river mile 126, on the Ohio side of the river.

In 1929, fifty-two years after the ground was broken for Lock and Dam #1 at Davis Island, Pennsylvania, the Ohio River canalization project, for the first time in the river's history, was completed. The entire river now had a nine foot controlling depth with 50 locks and dams. Individual locking chambers were 600 feet long by 110 feet wide. The fruition of this dream was celebrated by a great boat parade from Pittsburgh to Cairo Illinois. US President Herbert Hoover had always taken a keen interest in Ohio River navigation. Riding a lighthouse tender from Cincinnati to Louisville, Hoover presided over ceremonies. However, Black Tuesday and the great stock market crash of October 1929 was just days away. The table on the next page depicts the location, as well as important construction and 'open for navigation' dates of these early Ohio River locks and dams.

| Dam No | Miles below Pittsburgh | Approximate Location | Construction Started | Open for Navigation |
|---|---|---|---|---|
| - | 6.1 | Emsworth, PA  (replaced #1 and #2) | 1919 | 1921 |
| 3 | 10.9 | Glenosborne, PA | 1899 | 1908 |
| 4 | 18.6 | Legionville, PA | 1898 | 1908 |
| 5 | 23.9 | Freedom, PA | 1898 | 1907 |
| 6 * | 28.8 | Beaver, PA | 1892 | 1904 |
| 7 | 36.9 | Midland, PA | 1910 | 1914 |
| 8 ** | 46.1 | Newell, WV | 1904 | 1911 |
| 9 | 55.6 | New Cumberland, WV | 1910 | 1914 |
| 10 ** | 65.7 | Steubenville, OH | 1912 | 1915 |
| 11 | 76.3 | 2.3 miles below Wellsburg, WV | 1904 | 1911 |
| 12 | 87.0 | 2 miles above Wheeling, WV | 1911 | 1917 |
| 13 | 95.8 | McMeechan, WV | 1901 | 1911 |
| 14 | 113.8 | Woodland, WV | 1911 | 1917 |
| 15 ** | 128.9 | New Martinsville, WV | 1911 | 1916 |
| 16 | 146.4 | Ben's Run, WV | 1913 | 1917 |
| 17 ** | 167.4 | 4 miles above Marietta, OH | 1913 | 1918 |
| 18 | 179.3 | 4.5 miles above Parkersburg, WV | 1902 | 1910 |
| 19 | 191.4 | Little Hocking, OH | 1908 | 1916 |
| 20 | 201.7 | Belleville, WV | 1911 | 1917 |
| 21 | 213.8 | Portland, OH | 1915 | 1919 |
| 22 | 220.1 | Ravenswood, WV | 1915 | 1919 |
| 23 | 230.6 | Millwood, WV | 1917 | 1921 |
| 24 ** | 242.0 | Graham, WV | 1913 | 1919 |
| 25 | 260.0 | 5 miles above Point Pleasant, WV | 1917 | 1922 |
| 26 | 278.0 | Hogsett, WV | 1908 | 1912 |
| 27 | 300.3 | 4 miles above Guyandotte, WV | 1918 | 1923 |
| 28 ** | 310.9 | Huntington, WV | 1911 | 1915 |
| 29 | 319.4 | 3 miles below Catlettsburg, KY | 1911 | 1916 |
| 30 | 338.9 | 3 miles below Greenup, KY | 1919 | 1923 |
| 31 | 358.4 | 3 miles below Portsmouth, OH | 1912 | 1920 |
| 32 | 381.7 | 1 mile above Rome, OH | 1919 | 1925 |
| 33 | 404.0 | 3 miles above Maysville, KY | 1915 | 1921 |
| 34*** | 432.8 | Chilo, OH | 1919 | 1925 |
| 35 # | 449.7 | 1 mile below new Richmond, OH | 1913 | 1919 |
| 36 | 459.2 | 10 miles above Cincinnati, OH | 1920 | 1925 |
| 37 | 481.3 | Fernbank, OH | 1905 | 1911 |
| 38 ** | 501.3 | McVile, KY | 1920 | 1924 |
| 39 | 529.6 | 1 mile above Markland, IN | 1914 | 1922 |
| 41 | 604.0 | Louisville, KY | 1911 | 1921 |
| - | - | New Power Navigation Dam | 1925 | 1927 |
| 43 | 630.2 | 3 miles below West Point, KY | 1914 | 1921 |
| 44 | 660.3 | Leavenworth, IN | 1920 | 1926 |
| 45 | 699.7 | Addison, KY | 1920 | 1927 |
| 46 | 752.9 | Owensboro, KY | 1923 | 1928 |
| 47 | 772.5 | Newburg, IN | 1923 | 1927 |
| 48 | 804.1 | 6 miles below Henderson, KY | 1912 | 1921 |
| 49 | 838.0 | 2.5 miles below Uniontown, KY | 1924 | 1927 |
| 50 | 867.7 | Ford's Ferry, KY | 1924 | 1929 |
| 51 ** | 903.1 | Golconda, IL | 1925 | 1929 |
| 52 + | 928.0 | Brookport, IL | 1924 | 1929 |
| 53 + | 951.2 | Foot of Grand Chain | 1925 | 1929 |

*Restaurant, **Camp/Marina/Ramp/or Wall,  ***Museum,  # Research Center,  + Still Operating

Of the 54 locks and dams originally contemplated for the Ohio River, locks and dams #40, #42, and #54 were scratched before construction. Modifications to other nearby locks and dams deemed these three unnecessary. The Emsworth Lock and Dam (completed in 1921) replaced #1 (completed in 1885) and #2 (completed in 1906). The Emsworth Lock and Dam was also the first one with two locking chambers on the Ohio River. When the last of these locks and dams was completed in 1929, all but two had navigable high water passages (i.e., individual wickets that could also be lowered). If you go boating on the Ohio today, look for those old lock walls along the sides of the river, as well as other evidence of these earlier locks. One old lock house has been converted into a restaurant and another into a river museum. Several others have been turned into riverside campgrounds. Over the VHF radio, many towboat captains still report their vessel's 'position,' relative to these earlier locks and dams.

The 'lock and dam' or canalization project that was completed in 1929 lessened the continued need for river dredging, but it did not eliminate that need. New river shoals and bars, and shifting channels, especially after a flood, kept the dredge boats busy. A needed second round of Ohio River modernization projects was started in 1954. The original fifty locks that were constructed between 1892 and 1929 were outdated, too small, and drained too slowly.

Bigger tows, more river traffic, and greater cargo volume necessitated a major upgrade on the Ohio River. The 1954 plan was to replace the fifty old locks and wicket dams with nineteen higher lift and quicker draining locks and dams. The old lock lifts were between five and eleven feet high, and the pool lengths created behind these dams averaged less than 20 miles. The newer locks and dams were to be from 16 to 35 feet high, with an average pool length of 51 miles. Instead of a boat having to negotiate

through 'another lock' about every nineteen miles, that boat could now go two and a half times farther, before going through that time-consuming locking-through procedure.

The old wicket dams were replaced by non-navigable sections of moveable gates –roller gates, vertical lift gates, or tainter gates. Gated dams were constructed to permit increased control over the water level in the navigation pool upriver of the dam. Machinery mounted on tall concrete piers moved large chains which lifted gates that were hinged to the body of the piers. The gates were raised or lowered to control the amount of water flowing under them, and the upstream pool was maintained at a relatively constant level for an authorized depth of at least nine feet throughout the pool's length. This system using tainter gates would become the most prevalent. Tainter gates are radial steel gates with a convex surface facing upstream. These massive gates can be raised and lowered, due to their arced upstream surface with only minimal mechanical effort.

The vast majority of the old locks and dams were going to be completely removed, but a few of the former structures were going to be rebuilt and improved. Emsworth, Dashields, Montgomery, Gallipolis, and McAlpine Locks and Dams fell into this rebuild category. The Emsworth project consists of two gated dams. In 1959, the Greenup Lock and Dam was the first one built as a brand-new structure. All of the new locks would have two locking chambers, further hastening the river traffic. Furthermore, the locking chambers were lengthened from 600 to 1200 feet. The dams were not designed for nor operated for flood control. But an incidental benefit derived from the pool formed by the dam is the availability of a source of municipal and industrial water. The table on the next page depicts the location, the pool length, the lift and the 'open for navigation' dates for our current Ohio River lock and dam system.

| Lock and Dam Name | Miles below Pittsburgh | Nearby Town | Pool (miles) | Lift (feet) | Opened/Re-opened for Navigation |
|---|---|---|---|---|---|
| Emsworth | 6.2 | Pittsburgh, PA | 17.4 | 18.0 | 1921, 1938, 1986 |
| Dashields | 13.3 | Glenwillard, PA | 7.1 | 10.0 | 1929, 1989 |
| Montgomery | 31.7 | Monaca, PA | 18.4 | 17.5 | 1936, 1989 |
| New Cumberland | 54.4 | Stratton, OH | 22.7 | 20.5 | 1959 |
| Pike Island | 84.2 | Warwood, WV | 29.8 | 21.0 | 1963 |
| Hannibal * | 126.4 | Hannibal, OH | 42.2 | 21.0 | 1972 |
| Willow Island | 161.7 | Reno, OH | 35.3 | 20.0 | 1972 |
| Belleville | 203.9 | Reedsville, OH | 42.2 | 22.0 | 1967 |
| Racine | 237.5 | Letart, WV | 33.6 | 22.0 | 1967 |
| Robert Byrd | 279.2 | Gallipolis Ferry, WV | 41.7 | 23.0 | 1937, 1993 |
| Greenup | 341.0 | Greenup, KY | 61.8 | 30.0 | 1959 |
| Meldahl | 436.2 | Chilo, OH | 95.2 | 30.0 | 1962 |
| Markland | 531.5 | Warsaw, KY | 95.3 | 35.0 | 1963 |
| McAlpine | 604.4 | Louisville, KY | 72.9 | 37.0 | 1921, 1930, 1961, 1965,  ** |
| Cannelton | 720.7 | Cannelton, IN | 116.3 | 25.0 | 1975 |
| Newburgh | 776.1 | Newburgh, IN | 55.4 | 33.0 | 1969 |
| John T. Myers | 846.0 | Mount Vernon, IN | 69.9 | 22.0 | 1975 |
| Smithland | 918.5 | Hamletsburg, IL | 72.5 | 22.0 | 1979 |
| 52 | 938.9 | Brookport, IL | 20.4 | 12.0 | 1928, 1969 |
| 53 | 962.6 | Grand Chain, IL | 23.7 | 13.4 | 1929, 1980 |
| Olmstead ** | 964.4 | Olmsted, IL | 45.9 + | 26.0 | Future Date |

\* Has Visitor's Center, ** Under Construction, + Distance after removal L &Dams # 52 and # 53.

The next four sketches depict the current drop/lift on the Ohio, and three of its navigable tributaries at the locks and dams. Today, the Ohio River drops about 437 feet in its 981 miles. The Allegheny lifts 112 feet in 55 miles, through eight locks. The Monongahela lifts 147 feet in 104 miles through nine locks, while the Kanawha River lifts 76 ft through three locks in 54 miles.

Maneuver or Wicket Boat, Hannibal, Ohio

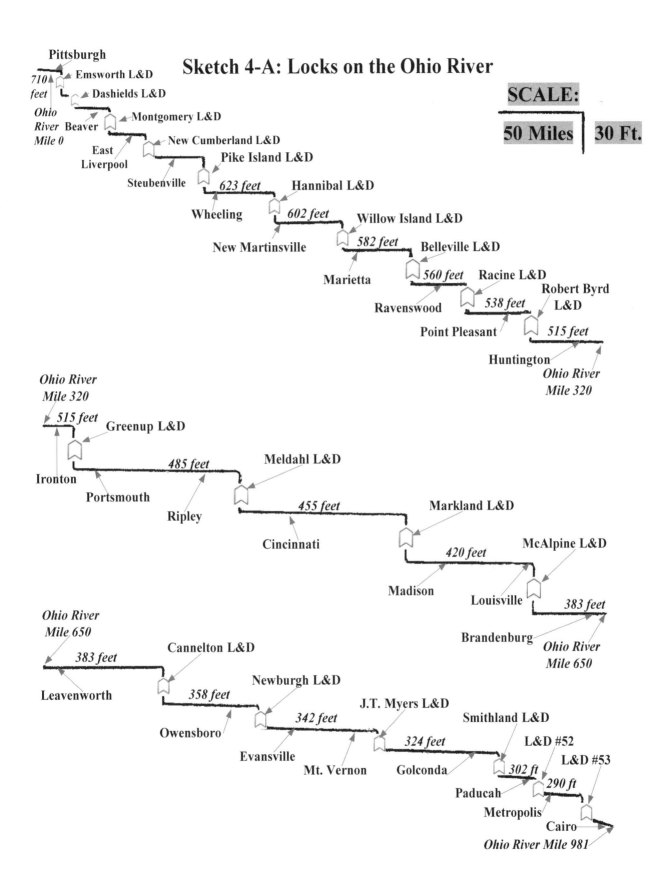

# Sketch 4-A: Locks on the Ohio River

Pittsburgh

Emsworth L&D

710 feet

Dashields L&D

Ohio River Beaver Mile 0

Montgomery L&D

East Liverpool

New Cumberland L&D

Pike Island L&D

Steubenville

623 feet

Hannibal L&D

Wheeling

602 feet

Willow Island L&D

New Martinsville

582 feet

Belleville L&D

Marietta

560 feet

Racine L&D

Ravenswood

538 feet

Robert Byrd L&D

Point Pleasant

515 feet

Huntington

Ohio River Mile 320

**SCALE:**

**50 Miles | 30 Ft.**

Ohio River Mile 320

515 feet

Greenup L&D

Ironton

Portsmouth

485 feet

Meldahl L&D

Ripley

455 feet

Markland L&D

Cincinnati

420 feet

McAlpine L&D

Madison

Louisville

383 feet

Brandenburg

Ohio River Mile 650

Ohio River Mile 650

383 feet

Cannelton L&D

Leavenworth

358 feet

Newburgh L&D

Owensboro

342 feet

J.T. Myers L&D

Evansville

324 feet

Smithland L&D

Mt. Vernon

Golconda

L&D #52

302 ft

L&D #53

Paducah

290 ft

Metropolis

Cairo

Ohio River Mile 981

49

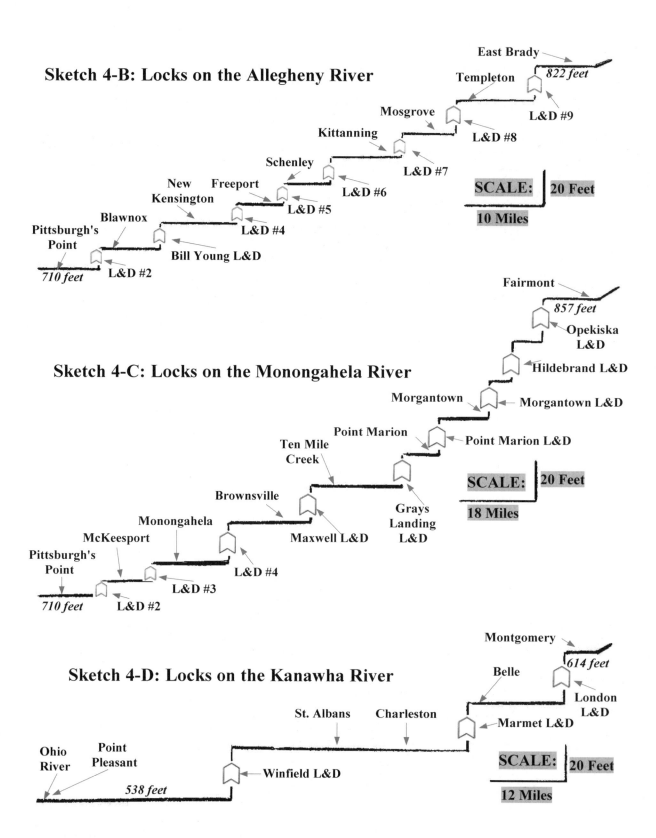

**Sketch 4-B: Locks on the Allegheny River**

East Brady
*822 feet*
Templeton
L&D #9
Mosgrove
L&D #8
Kittanning
L&D #7
Schenley
L&D #6
New Kensington
Freeport
L&D #5
Blawnox
L&D #4
Pittsburgh's Point
Bill Young L&D
*710 feet*
L&D #2

SCALE: 20 Feet
10 Miles

**Sketch 4-C: Locks on the Monongahela River**

Fairmont
*857 feet*
Opekiska L&D
Hildebrand L&D
Morgantown
Morgantown L&D
Point Marion
Point Marion L&D
Ten Mile Creek
Brownsville
Maxwell L&D
Grays Landing L&D
Monongahela
McKeesport
L&D #3
L&D #4
Pittsburgh's Point
*710 feet*
L&D #2

SCALE: 20 Feet
18 Miles

**Sketch 4-D: Locks on the Kanawha River**

Montgomery
*614 feet*
Belle
London L&D
St. Albans
Charleston
Marmet L&D
Ohio River
Point Pleasant
Winfield L&D
*538 feet*

SCALE: 20 Feet
12 Miles

50

# CHAPTER 5
## The Evolution, Growth, and Decline of River Industries

In the late 18th Century, the cities and towns along the Ohio River were settled by an adventurous and optimistic breed of pioneer. Even the names of many towns evoked optimism –Cairo, Rome, Metropolis, America, Enterprise, Point Pleasant, Ironton, and even Cincinnati. Cincinnati was named for the 'Society of Cincinnati.' This was a group of ex-Revolutionary War soldiers who formed their society based on the ideals of an altruistic fifth century Roman Emperor, Lucius Cincinnatus –who inspired high ideals.

Some river towns were situated on a wide bend in the river (e.g., Evansville and Mount Vernon in Indiana; Owensboro in Kentucky; and East Liverpool in Ohio). Some towns were located at important river confluences (e.g., Pittsburgh, Beaver and McKeesport in Pennsylvania; Marietta and Portsmouth in Ohio; Parkersburg and Point Pleasant in West Virginia; and Paducah and Carrollton in Kentucky). A preponderance of smaller Ohio River towns –too many to count, are located off smaller tributaries and even small creeks flowing into the Ohio River. Most cities and towns hopefully were located on high enough ground to avoid flooding. Smaller river towns are often much longer (i.e., along the same axis as the river), than wide. This is true even with a few of the larger cities –Huntington and Charleston in West Virginia, and Evansville Indiana.

Nearly all of the industries that developed along the Ohio River region were of an extractive nature. Minerals were typically extracted from the ground. As these industries became more profitable, they became larger, more competitive, and corporately run with a profit eye more on the 'bottom line.' A century or so later, that 'bottom line,' meant closing down now-enormous facilities in order to find a better 'bottom line' in a similar extractive industry overseas. In the more global economy of the late 20th Century, foreign imports doomed most Ohio River industries –and some of which had thrived for two centuries.

Salt, one of the first industries in the area, became less important with the advent of refrigeration –near the beginning of the 20th Century. Following salt, natural gas and oil production peaked in the early 20th Century. Early natural gas, oil, and coal production developed as a result of technological advancements stemming from the salt industry. In the 1810s, the region's first mined coal came from the high slopes in the Monongahela River Valley south of Pittsburgh. Soon this soft bituminous coal was being converted into a more efficient fuel –coke. Coke, in turn, spurred other industries, including iron and steel. In the 1820s, local deposits of iron ore and limestone, along with plenty of timber, stimulated the pig iron industry. That pig iron industry lasted only until much larger deposits of iron ore were found in Minnesota, less than a half-century later. As the 20th Century dawned, the steel industry arrived. The steel industry was encouraged by iron ore, coke, and a late 19th Century development –the Bessemer process. During the first half of the 20th Century, nobody could economically rival Pittsburgh when it came to steel production.

World War I spurred the development and growth of the huge chemical industry in the Kanawha River Valley of West Virginia. Smaller river industries, like glass, ceramics, and fluorspar also extracted local raw materials. Some of these smaller industries were around for two centuries (e.g., glass) while others did not last nearly as long. By 1965, the Ohio River Basin claimed twenty percent of the nation's Gross National Product (GNP). But starting in the 1960s, foreign imports started making serious inroads into the market share held by many Ohio River Valley industries. Ohio

River ceramic and fluorspar industries were near totally wiped-out on account of imports. One surviving local Ohio River glass company is about all that remains of a once thriving glass industry. The Kanawha Valley chemical industry is under serious economic pressure. The once mighty US steel industry is a thin shadow of its former self –again the result of imported steel and globalization.

A few other Ohio River towns and small businesses fell victim to catastrophic floods (e.g., in Shawneetown Illinois), bad timing and poor management (e.g., in Cairo Illinois), or just bad luck. There's little doubt the extractive industries that developed along the Ohio River, created 'boom' cycles, and then they were followed by that inevitable 'bust.' Oftentimes, in extractive industries, the 'busts' are permanent. Traveling along the rivers, and seeing the once-thriving hulks of steel mills and other once-vibrant factories, evokes a deep melancholy for an Ohio River time since passed –but that time was not long ago. How can one not find that sad?

### Salt

One of the earliest industries commercially developed in the Ohio River region was salt. Salt's value as a preservative for food goes back to at least the 20th Century BC. Salt has been a factor in the development of many economies as well as many wars. Salt has a great ability to preserve meats and butter, as well as to help tan hides. This was especially necessary in those days before refrigeration –before the dawn of the 20th Century. Nonetheless, salt was difficult to obtain, and it became highly valued throughout history. In our Ohio River Valley research, we came across no less than four areas noted for salt production: 1) the Kanawha River Valley of West Virginia, 2) the Kiskiminetas-Conemaugh River Valley off the Allegheny River in Pennsylvania, 3) The saline mines in Gallatin County, Illinois, and 4) salt springs found near Big Bone Lick, Kentucky.

In the Kanawha River Valley, in order to acquire salt, Native Americans would boil water from salt springs. By 1806, colonists were drilling deep wells into the mountains trying to better tap into this briny water. The early 1800s was a prosperous time for Kanawha River Valley salt makers. There were about four dozen salt furnaces commercially producing salt, and the valley was touted as the 'top salt producer in the world.' By the 1830s and 1840s, salt production remained strong, with about 40 salt furnaces operating in the Kanawha Valley. Local salt production peaked in 1846. The Civil War of the 1860s and a weakened economy in the 1870s curtailed salt production, and the Kanawha Valley never regained its former prominence.

Also in the early 1800s, similar salt production success was being experience further north in Pennsylvania's Kiskiminetas-Conemaugh Valley. Wells were being drilled, and by 1819 'The Great Conemaugh Salt Works' had about a dozen producers. By 1833, four million pounds of salt were shipped out of that Allegheny River Valley.

Farther west, there was also salt production. In 1755, when Mary Ingles and Frau Stumf escaped from their Shawnee Indian captors, they were in the custody of two Frenchmen on a 'salt expedition' from southern Ohio to Big Bone Lick Kentucky. In southeastern Illinois, near the Ohio River, Native Americans had been procuring salt from an area known as 'the Great Salt Springs.' In the early 1800s, the federal government took this land from the Indians. The government leased the land back, but required that the lease holder produce no less than a certain amount of salt, or else pays a fine each year. This in turn, encouraged slave labor. By 1820, there were about 300 slaves working the saline mines of Gallatin County Illinois, while the federal government conveniently 'looked the other way.'

In Appalachia, salt production was the engine that led to the development of other industries. Pennsylvania salt wells were being contaminated by oil, thus exciting possibilities for petroleum production. Local coal was soon being mined as fuel for the furnaces and the steam engines that worked the pumps for the salt wells. The salt industry facilitated the development of the Kanawha Valley's chemical industry. Furthermore, salt-related accoutrements such as deep-well boring tools, and casings and tubing, spurred the growth of tapping into that region's natural gas and oil reserves.

## Natural Gas and Oil

Early natural gas vents and oil deposits were considered an annoying interruption for salt producers. Oil that found its way into the Kanawha, Little Kanawha, and Big Sandy Rivers was often nicknamed 'old greasy' by local flatboat men. In 1815, while drilling for salt in present-day Charleston West Virginia, a natural gas vent was struck. It took a few years to understand its value. By 1819, commercial petroleum wells were being sunk off the Little Kanawha River near Parkersburg West Virginia. By 1826, oil-burning lamps were being used in factories and workshops. The equipment developed for salt drilling twenty years prior, now had new applications. Around 1860, on the Little Kanawha River, one operator was producing 200 barrels of oil per day. As the Civil War approached, newly rich oil barons were using their wealth and influence to further the statehood agenda of West Virginia.

By 1876, there were nearly 300 wells in the area, producing a total of 900 barrels daily. On the Ohio River, Parkersburg West Virginia was the transfer point to many other markets. By the 1890s, the shallow 100-foot deep wells had been pretty much tapped-out. Deeper wells needed to be dug. With the deeper wells, the oil and gas industry rebounded, and production peaked at 1,600 million barrels in 1900. Thereafter, oil production declined, although natural gas production continued to grow. Between 1906 and 1917, West Virginia was the leading state in natural gas production. But soon afterward, West Virginia's natural gas production started to steadily decline. To learn more about the local oil and gas industry, visit the 'Oil and Gas Museum' at 119 Third Street in Parkersburg, West Virginia (☎ 304-485-5446 or 304-428-8015).

## Coal and Coke

In 17th and 18th Century North America, there was an abundant wood supply, precluding a need for coal. Nonetheless, coal, as a fuel, had been around for centuries, especially in England. But by the 19th Century, a gradual scarcity of North American timber started encouraging coal production. Typically salt works had continuous fires, and needed to consume large amounts of fuel. By the 1810s, coal was discovered and was being gradually substituted for wood. Some of this early coal came from the Monongahela River Valley near Pittsburgh.

In the mid 1800s, a skilled miner along with a few laborers using pickaxes and shovels could produce several tons of coal per day. Typically, a team would work a vein or surface seam on an exposed riverbank. There were many such exposed veins along the high slopes of the Monongahela River Valley. Furthermore, barges on the nearby Monongahela River facilitated the commercial transportation of coal out of the area. Pickaxe and shovel extraction of surface seams was followed by dynamiting. By about 1890, cutting machinery had largely replaced dynamiting. As the surface mines became depleted, better coal was found in deeper mines. With the advent of more advanced machinery, mining for deeper coal was possible. In those earlier days, miners were typically paid on a per ton rate.

There are a handful of broad classifications of coal, with the two most common classifications being bituminous and anthracite. Bituminous coal has a duller appearance, is softer, gives off more smoke, has lower carbon content, contains more impurities, and burns at a lower temperature than anthracite coal. Most of the coal in the Ohio River region is bituminous, however some anthracite is found in northern West Virginia. Western Pennsylvania and eastern Ohio had many bituminous fields close to the surface. Anthracite, because of its fewer impurities, and higher heat output was the initially preferred coal for smelting pig iron. Later, technology improved to a point where bituminous coal could be converted into coke. Coke is produced when bituminous coal is baked, in the absence of oxygen, and the impurities are burned off. When coke is burned as fuel, its higher heat and lack of impurities facilitate the smelting of iron ore. In the late 19th Century, it became economically profitable to convert southwestern Pennsylvania bituminous coal into coke. By the early 20th Century, in southwestern Pennsylvania, there were over 4,000 coke ovens producing nearly 20 million tons of coke, annually.

In 1805, Pennsylvania began coal production producing about 100,000 tons of bituminous; by 1860, that state was producing 4.7 million tons of bituminous. Ohio production reached 100,000 tons in 1840, and 5.3 million tons by 1872. The 5.0 million ton annual production level was then reached by Illinois in 1876, by West Virginia in 1888, by Kentucky in 1893, and by Indiana in 1899. A century later, in 1995, the region's annual coal production was dominated by West Virginia and Kentucky with 163 million tons and 154 million tons, respectively. In 1995, Pennsylvania produced 57 million tons (bituminous only), Illinois production was at 48 million tons, and Ohio and Indiana each produced 26 million tons.

Coal dominated river freight in southwestern Pennsylvania for 200 years. Around Pittsburgh, coal represents about three-quarters of all the cargo passing through that port, annually. As early as the 1780s, coal found its way onto barges heading down the Monongahela. By the 1830s, Pittsburgh area coal was being shipped to New Orleans. By 1900, one Pittsburgh coal enterprise controlled 80 towboats, 4,000 barges and nearly two-thirds of the coal freight on these rivers.

In the early 20th Century, close to one-half of the electricity supplied in the United States is provided by coal-fired power plants. When you travel down or along the Ohio River or its larger tributaries, you can't help but notice many of these coal-fired power plants. The *Ohio River Way* has counted 49 power generating plants along the

Ohio River itself, and it's estimated that collectively these plants produce more than six percent of total US electrical generating capacity. Coal accounts for more than one-half of all the barge tonnage on the entire Ohio River system and its value is more than $4 billion annually.

By the 1850s, railroads were beginning to stretch into the bituminous coal fields of Ohio and Illinois. After the Civil War, railroads often integrated with coal companies, and purchased huge tracts of land, along with all the mineral rights. Before long, besides their mineral wealth, the railroads were making fortunes transporting large amounts of Appalachian coal. Throughout American history, newly-built railroads, encourage by extractive industries, have typically doomed certain segments of river transportation. In the eastern half of the United States alone, there are dozens of examples of newly-built canals being eclipsed by newer railroad lines, and only a few years after a canal opened for commerce. This 'railroad factor' has often been an adverse factor for many of the smaller river and canal towns. In the Ohio River region, railroads were more efficient moving commodities along a north-south orientation than river transport.

The coal industry, like many other extractive industries found in Appalachia was, and is, not without many downsides. Coal miners lived in coal company towns, were often paid in script, and could only spend their overvalued script at the [coal] 'company store' in order to purchase the bare essentials needed for existence. Since the late 19th Century, there have been many management-labor disputes, often marred by violence. The coal companies had a history of taking extraordinary measures to keep their miners from unionizing. Coal companies hired guards and heavy-handed security forces. These forces often exchanged gunfire with striking miners. Many lives were taken on both sides. It was not until President Franklin Roosevelt's New Deal, that coal company guards were removed, and miners could fully unionize. During World War II, the coal mining industry prospered. However, soon after the war, the industry was near collapse. Throughout its history, Appalachian coal has been an industry of 'feast or famine.'

There has been a grim history of coal mining accidents. Since 1900, there are well over 1,500 documented fatalities in Appalachia coal mines. In 1907, the largest single US mining disaster, claiming the lives of 362 men and boys, occurred in a coal mine near Fairmont West Virginia. A century later, in 2006, there were 47 coal mining fatalities –mostly in West Virginia and Kentucky coal fields. If not injured in a disaster, 19th and 20th Century deep miners often developed 'black lung,' from the daily inhalation of coal dust, leading to a prematurely shortened life.

In the 1950s, less dangerous strip mining started to take hold working those coal seams that were located fairly close to the surface. In strip mines, heavy construction equipment operating on the surface replaced the need for mine shafts and tunnels. However, strip mines also have many downsides. After it rains, acid runoff from strip mined areas pollute streams and rivers. Coal company impoundment dams were often poorly constructed. In 1972, a poorly constructed coal impoundment dam in a tributary of the Guyandotte River burst after normal winter rains. In Logan County West Virginia, 126 lost their lives and more than 4,000 quickly became homeless, as this 15-to-20 foot wave of cold black water obliterated everything in the hollow.

In the last thirty years, great progress in mechanization has made coal mining even more efficient. Entire 'mountaintop removal' followed strip mining. Giant machines, operated by a relatively few men, lopped off entire mountaintops scraping and digging for coal. Mountaintop removal and strip mines can leave huge ugly scars on once pristine mountain landscape. Furthermore, mountainside erosion is typically hastened. Throughout history, Appalachian coal has been both a blessing and a curse.

US Steel Works Coke Plant on the Monongahela River, Clairton, Pennsylvania

## Iron and Steel

Before steel is made into many of the familiar finished products that we know today, many things need to take place. One of those pre-steel processes is that iron needs to be extracted from iron ore. This raw or crude iron, after being extracted from the ore, is called pig iron. Early steel-making needed to be preceded by pig iron blast furnaces. In the early 1800s, iron ore was beginning to be discovered in the Ohio River valley, in about a 100-mide long swath running northward from Greenup County Kentucky into southeastern Ohio. This area became the first large-scale pig iron industry in North America. Besides the iron ore, pig iron furnaces needed limestone plus a fuel supply. The fuel supply was typically charcoal. Charcoal was produced from the abundant supply of local hardwood timber. Similar to producing coke, wood baked in the absence of oxygen becomes charcoal –and a much better fuel source for pig iron furnaces than plain wood. Limestone, another required raw material, was used as a flux. Without adding limestone, the familiar metallic properties of iron couldn't be achieved.

In 1825, the first pig iron blast furnace was built in northeastern Kentucky. A year later, several more furnaces were constructed across the river in Ohio. Heavy iron ore, sometimes found in a seam a foot thick, and limestone were hauled to nearby iron furnaces. In the 1850s, the railroads came to help transport this Ohio and Kentucky pig iron to far-reaching markets. In the late 1800s, pig iron from Ironton Ohio found its way into warships of the foremost European naval powers –England, France, and Russia. However, in 1845, much larger iron ore deposits were discovered around the western edge of Lake Superior in Minnesota's Mesabi Range. This find doomed the industry in the Ohio Valley. Nonetheless, today, near Ironton and Hanging Rock Ohio, you can still find many of these old historic iron furnaces. The Ohio River's 'Hanging Rock Iron Region,' is where America's iron industry got its footing.

Besides the Hanging Rock Iron Region of Ohio, iron ore and coal (for making coke) was fairly abundant around Pittsburgh. Pittsburgh was on its way to becoming the heart of the US Steel industry. Pig iron, molten iron, or scrap iron are some of the basic inputs used in making steel. Under tremendous heat, with varying heating and cooling cycles, iron impurities are removed, and alloys such as manganese, nickel, chromium and vanadium are added to produce a particular grade of steel. Globally, commercial steel production didn't get started until Englishman Henry Bessemer perfected a process that was able to remove impurities such as silicon, oxides and manganese from iron. In 1855, the Bessemer process was developed. Before long, steel was economically replacing wrought iron.

In 1901, Andrew Carnegie, JP Morgan, Elbert H. Gary, and Charles Schwab launched US Steel Corporation. Within a year after being launched, US Steel was making two-thirds of all steel products in the United States. By 1911, the city of Pittsburgh alone was producing between one-third and one-half of our nation's steel. At one time, US Steel was the largest steel producer, as well as largest corporation in the world. In 1904, Bethlehem Steel was remade by the former young president of US Steel, Charles Schwab. Domestic competitors, like Bethlehem Steel were more innovative, while US Steel heavily relied on its massive size. By 1911, US Steel's market share slipped to 50 percent –but it was still very healthy. The city of Pittsburgh's population swelled as European immigrants found work in its local steel mills. In 1943, at the height of World War II, US Steel employed more than 340,000. By 1953, U.S. Steel's production volume peaked at more than 35 million tons.

US Steel's founder, Andrew Carnegie didn't object to high wages for his steel workers, but vowed to limit union activity. Steel mills were, and still are, very dangerous and dirty places to work. In 1959, a union-led strike had the effect of shutting down 90 percent of total US steel production. That strike opened the door for imported steel. Prior to 1959, imported steel was a negligible factor; but thereafter, the US steel industry started its slow painful decline. In the 1970s and 80s, US steel companies were filing dumping complaints with the federal government against cheaper imported steel. Relief did not come. By the end of the 20th Century, tens of thousands of union steelworkers, of whom the vast number, were in the Pittsburgh-Ohio Valley Region, had permanently lost their jobs. Today US Steel produces less than ten percent of all the steel products found in the United States

Boating down the Monongahela and Ohio Rivers today, several rusty hulks of old steel mills can still be seen. Encountering these massive ghostly structures along the side of the river is eerie. To think that less than a half-century ago, that gargantuan facility was a bustling energetic enterprise – the pride of many Americans –employing thousands while supporting a huge local economy…but now sadly, the hulk stands silent …just rusting away. But Pittsburghers have somewhat adapted to the collapse of their once proud steel industry. Several quality universities, high-tech, health care, and service industries have somewhat filled the void left behind by Big Steel.

There is one facility on the Monongahela River, near Pittsburgh that is probably at least a shadow of its former self. At Monongahela River mile 20, the US Steel Clairton Works still produces coke. This is the largest coke manufacturing facility in the country. When you get off your boat anywhere in western Pennsylvania (or even in eastern Ohio, or northern West Virginia), the local talk is nearly always about sports; and as long as I can remember it's primarily been about one beloved team –their five-time world champion, Pittsburgh Steelers. Today, steel may be gone, but Pittsburghers have always had the heart of champions, like their Steelers.

## Chemicals

Today, the navigable Kanawha River has no less than three distinct personalities. The lowermost forty miles is rather bland; the uppermost twenty miles is a spectacular Appalachian Mountain gorge; and the middle thirty miles –downriver and upriver from Charleston –is 'chemical plant alley' –or valley, with a few niceties thrown in – downtown Charleston, many parked old paddlewheelers, and a handful of boating facilities.

The chemical industry started in the 1910s. In 1914, during World War I, US chlorine imports from Germany ceased. A Charleston plant was soon tasked to produce chlorine and caustic acid from Kanawha Valley salt brine for the national market. Soon explosives, compounds, and other chemicals were being produced to aid the war effort. Small Kanawha River towns like Nitro, Institute, and Belle became chemical company towns. In the 1920s and 30s, economic growth in the 'chemical valley' continued as large corporation began moving into the Kanawha Valley. Then World War II spurred growth even more.

The chemical industry, with all its pros and cons, has been an economic mainstay in the area. The Kanawha River provides a means for bulk transportation and a source for mixing and cooling chemicals. Market access is reasonably good. The Kanawha Valley, linked by highways, railways and rivers, has good access to the Great Lake and Mid-Atlantic states. Twenty of our nation's largest 100 metropolitan areas are within 500 miles of the Kanawha River Valley.

Chemical Companies like Union Carbide, DuPont, Monsanto, Dow, Diamond Shamrock, Olin, Bayer, Clearon, Elko Chemical, and FMC, now or at least at one time, have had a presence in the Kanawha Valley. Union Carbide's Research and Development Headquarters is in South Charleston. Only a few of us can probably appreciate some of the valley's products – caustic sodas, phenols, dyes (at least 100 different types), many acids (sulfuric, nitric, benzoic, and others), toluene, naphthalene, ammonia, urea fertilizers, and more. But we probably could recognize the many plastics and other familiar products facilitating our lives today, that have started-out in this valley. DuPont's plant a Belle West Virginia has produced nearly 175 products used in everyday industry, not to mention that they developed nylon.

There is a trade-off in the Chemical Valley though –the specter of a major accident with toxic air pollution. In 1984, a Union Carbide plant in Bhopal India (population 800,000) producing methyl isocyanate had a horrible accident resulting in an initial death toll of around 4,000.

In 1980, Kanawha Valley chemical corporations employed about 12,500. In 2003, in a more global economy, as production has shifted offshore, this same local chemical industry was employing only 3,600. There is a fear that the remainder of the chemical company jobs will go the same way as steel.

## Glass, Ceramics, and Fluorspar

In the late 19th and for much of the 20th Centuries, certain parts of the Ohio and Monongahela River valleys, had thriving glass-making businesses. Local silica sand, limestone, and soda ash were the primary raw materials. Coal fired the ovens. Knowledgeable immigrants provided much of the expertise. The local rivers provided the routes for the raw materials as well as avenues to the marketplace. West Virginia, alone had become home to more than 500 glass companies. Morgantown West Virginia, on the Monongahela River, with such industry leaders as Seneca Glass and Morgantown Glass, was one of the preeminent glass-making centers. In 1971, Morgantown Glass shut it doors, followed in 1983, by Seneca Glass. Cheaper overseas labor rates coupled with a change in the market taste –satisfaction with less exquisite glass, doomed these and most of the other local glass-making companies.

To date, one sizeable Ohio River glass-making company is still hanging on. Fenton Art Glass in Williamstown West Virginia (across the Ohio River from Marietta) has survived by successfully carving-out and maintaining a hand-made, high-end, artisan product line niche. Fenton Glass offers factory tours, and has its own outstanding museum and a gift shop. A visit to Fenton Glass is well worth it. Its local factory tour has been rated among the country's 'top 10' by *USA Today*. Besides a great tour at Fenton Glass (at 420 Caroline Ave, Williamstown, WV 26187 ☎ 304-375-7772 or 1-800-319-7793), there are a few other small museums on the Ohio River which preserve this glass-making heritage. In Wheeling, visit the Carriage House Glass Museum (☎ 304-243-4058 or 1-800-624-6988). In Moundsville, visit the Fostoria Glass Museum (☎ 304-845-9188); and in Huntington, visit the Huntington Museum of Art (☎ 304-529-2701)

Like the glass industry, the ceramic industry once thrived in the Ohio Valley. Thousands of years ago, retreating glaciers in the Ohio River Valley, left behind clays and fine silts that were perfect for ceramic-making. In the late 1830s, a few local entrepreneurs realized that these natural resources could be turned into something profitable. Local coal was used in the ovens, and once again, the rivers provided the highway for moving raw materials and the finished ceramics. From about 1840 to 1930, East Liverpool Ohio was becoming the center of this burgeoning ceramic-making industry. During that time, East Liverpool produced more than half of all the ceramics made in America, including a wide assortment of dinner plates sold in most of the country. East Liverpool's population grew from 2,000 in 1870, to 20,000 by 1910, primarily because of the influx of new immigrants working in the ceramics industry. In 1900, more than 90 percent of East Liverpool's factory workers were directly employed in ceramics. East Liverpool was known as 'America's Crockery City,' and also as 'The Pottery Capitol of the Nation.'

Once again imports –imported ceramics, and competing products –started dooming East Liverpool. By the time of the Great Depression of the 1930s, East Liverpool's ceramic industry was barely a shadow of its former self. Nonetheless, much of this rich past history has been preserved in East Liverpool's 'Museum of Ceramics' located in East Liverpool's large old Post Office Building at 400 East Fifth St. (☎ 1-800-600-7180).

Rosiclare Illinois was another one-industry town, but significantly smaller than East Liverpool Ohio. Large mineral deposits of fluorite were found in southeastern Illinois and western Kentucky. Rosiclare, on the Ohio River about 100 miles upstream from the Mississippi River, soon became the mining center of a local fluorite industry. Fluorite (the mineral) or fluorspar (the commercial name) is used as a flux in steel, aluminum, enamel, and glass manufacturing, and as a glazing and etching material, as well as a few other industrial and non-industrial applications. The derived hydrofluoric acid has many uses. Fluorspar is also used in high-octane aviation fuel and certain plastics. Once again, imports –from China, South Africa, and Mexico –doomed the economy of Rosiclare and neighboring communities.

**The Lower Ohio**

The towns on the lower Ohio River never developed the mammoth extractive industries like those found on the upper Ohio River Region (e.g., steel, coal, chemicals, and natural gas). The four largest river towns on the lower Ohio –Evansville Indiana, Owensboro, Henderson and Paducah, Kentucky seemed to have held their own over the past century and a half. After the War of 1812, and the advent of steamboats, urban growth on the lower Ohio started to accelerate. By the 1850s these four cities were connected to national telegraph lines. These four also allowed fairly high tax rates, which proved far-sighted for the necessary municipal improvements. In the late 19th Century, Henderson thrived as a center for tobacco, agriculture, and river commerce. Likewise, Owensboro's growth came from tobacco, whiskey and river commerce.

Paducah Kentucky, at the mouth of the navigable 650-mile long Tennessee River, has been most positively affected by its river location. During the winter, Paducah is touted as the northernmost ice-free inland port. Several barge line companies have operations in Paducah –from business offices to major dry-dock repair facilities. In the late 19th Century, Paducah also got a shot in the arm when the Illinois Central Railroad located a major north-south trunk line through the city, spurring many other railroad related industries (railroad shops, locomotive re-manufacturing, etc.). But the railroads too have since declined.

Evansville Indiana, the largest city on the lower Ohio, has always seemed to have had a progressive business attitude. Evansville was the first city in the area to have street lighting and paved streets. Construction of the short-lived Wabash and Erie Canal (i.e., only in operation during the 1850s) which connected the Great Lakes to the Ohio River near Evansville, greatly accelerated that city's growth. By 1850, Evansville had its first railroad. In 1885, the first bridge over the Ohio River between Louisville and Cairo (i.e., a 370-mile length of river) was the Louisville and Nashville Railroad Bridge connecting Evansville with Henderson Kentucky. In 1890, Evansville was ranked as the 56th largest city in America. During World War II, Evansville was the largest inland manufacturer of LST's (Tank Landing Ships).

Nonetheless, the economies of many smaller lower Ohio River towns have been turbulently shaken over the past 150 years. Two small lower river towns are stark examples –Shawneetown and Cairo, both in Illinois. In the early 19th Century, Cairo was a mooring area for boats located at the confluence of two great rivers –the Ohio and the Mississippi. Cairo was so named because its relationship with the Ohio and Mississippi Rivers reminded people of the geographical relationship Cairo Egypt had with the Nile River. In the 1830s, a terminus for the Illinois Central Railroad, a main rail line connecting Chicago to the Gulf of Mexico, was planned for Cairo. Expectations for Cairo –and most of these expectations were fueled by absentee investors –were quite high. The city was supposed to surpass Louisville, Cincinnati, and St. Louis as an urban center. Cairo even had its own Customs House. By the 1840s, Cairo had its needed levees in place, and the city was home to about 1,000 people. But the 1830s saw the completion of the Louisville and Portland Canal, along with the rapid growth in Shawneetown, 123 miles upstream on the Ohio River. Louisville and Shawneetown were grabbing larger roles in river commerce. Much commercial traffic passed by Cairo's doorstep, without making a stop. The population of Cairo has been steadily declining since the 1920s. By the late 1960s, racial tensions were high, and race riots further gutted Cairo. It's been stated that throughout much of its history, that Cairo has been plagued by poor municipal leadership.

In 19th Century Kentucky, many of the smaller river towns were dominated by elitists with plantation mentalities. With the wealth being concentrated in just a few hands, growth in these small Kentucky towns was often stymied.

Across the river in Illinois, the story was different. After the American Revolution, Shawneetown was a major administrative center for the Northwest Territories. Shawneetown shares a distinction with Washington DC as being one of only two cities ever chartered by the United States government. Around 1800, Shawneetown, not far from the Wabash River and the Illinois-Indiana state line, started really prospering. Shawneetown had the first bank in Illinois, and the town was touted as the financial center of the state. By the mid-19th Century, Shawneetown was the leading port between Louisville and St. Louis, and had about 1,200 inhabitants.

In the 1830s, investors approached the Shawneetown Bank, to interest it in floating some bonds for a new Illinois city. This Shawneetown Bank refused to finance the bonds, stating something like, 'that city will never work, because it's not on a major river.' Well, that city happened to be Chicago. Shawneetown started declining by the late 19th Century, due to vigorous state growth to the north, and the periodic Ohio River flooding that often ravaged the city. Today, 'Old Shawneetown' is nothing more than a saloon with a few old buildings, including that historic bank.

## Floods

During the 20th Century, floods were the number-one natural disaster in the United States in term of lives lost and property damaged. Periodic horrific floods have taken a toll on many Ohio River towns. The Ohio River locks and dams were primarily designed to facilitate river navigation. These dams offer next-to-no protection during an especially severe flood. In the last 250 years, there have been no less than 105 major floods on the Ohio River. During those past 250 years, more than a score of years have experienced multiple major floods. Many times, the flood stages have exceeded 60 feet in height. In 20th Century Cincinnati alone, floodwaters have crested at least to that 60-foot mark twenty-one times. In total, thousands of lives have been lost to Ohio River floods, and property damage has been immeasurable. Within just the past 100 years, there have been no less than five horrendous floods on the Ohio River system that have claimed no less than 1,100 lives. Visitors new to the area, have often asked, "How often does the river flood?" The best answer that I've heard came from Higginsport Ohio, "Whenever it wants to."

In late March 1913, one of those floods cost over 730 lives, and left more than 40,000 homeless in Ohio and Indiana. In a short period, rainfall amounted from six to eleven inches. Fourteen square miles of downtown Dayton were flooded by the Great Miami River. West of Cincinnati, the Great Miami River crested ten to eighteen feet deep and into residential areas. The Scioto River submerged Columbus, Chillicothe and Portsmouth, and drowned 100 people in Columbus. The Ohio River levees in Portsmouth were topped. In Cincinnati, the Ohio River rose twenty-one feet in 24 hours with the loss of 100 lives. In Zanesville, parts of downtown, on the Muskingum River, were twenty feet underwater.

In January and early February 1937, another major flood along the Ohio River in Kentucky, Ohio, Indiana, and Illinois claimed about 400 lives. Sixty-five communities were evacuated, and more than three hundred bridges were wrecked, with some estimates having up to one million people homeless. Parts of Cincinnati were underwater for nineteen days, and the flood level reached 79 feet. Shawneetown and Cairo were completely underwater. This was the final death knell for Shawneetown. In Evansville Indiana, with flood waters more than 48 feet above flood stage, 400 city blocks were inundated. Rosiclare and the nearby Illinois River towns Elizabethtown and Golconda were completely isolated. In Louisville, the river crested at 57 feet, and 70 percent of that city was underwater. The entire population of Paducah had to evacuate, as the river crested at nearly 61 feet above flood stage. The 1937 flood was caused by rain, sleet, and hail occurring for eighteen straight days in January. Unseasonably warm weather also melted the snow off the mountains in the Ohio River watershed. Soon river levels were rising by two feet per day. In many places besides Cincinnati, the Ohio River crested over sixty feet above normal flood stage. Heroic efforts by the Red Cross and others saved thousands of lives.

There have been many other deadly floods in the Ohio River Valley, but we thought we'd limit ourselves to a particular one more sixty year later. In early March 1997, a major flood slammed into the Ohio River Region following three days of heavy rain. Like many of the wet weather systems in late winter or early spring, a large rotating counter-clockwise low pressure was drawing in huge amounts of moisture from the Gulf of Mexico. Up to thirteen inches of rain fell in some parts of northern Kentucky, southern Ohio and Indiana, and much of West Virginia. Moveable sections of floodwalls were placed in the gaps of many river levee systems. The firm floodwalls and levees stood, and were able to protect many river cities, like Paducah, Louisville, Cincinnati, as well as the river cities across from Cincinnati in Kentucky. Evacuation systems were better than before. Nonetheless, even with the latest technological advancements, in a multi-state area, there were still 67 fatalities, 50,000 homes damaged, and about one billion dollars in property damage.

Seven years later, in mid-September of 2004, Category IV *Hurricane Ivan*

slammed into Pensacola Florida and the Gulf Coast. The remnants of *Ivan* proceeded north-northeast up the Ohio River Valley. Everything in the path was soaked. Some parts of Pennsylvania received up to eight inches of rain. Around Pittsburgh and Allegheny County, hundreds of boats and scores of marinas were damaged by flooding on the Ohio, Allegheny and Beaver Rivers. Several boats broke loose and actually washed over a dam. Boats were lost when they got caught up in the hydraulic (just downstream from the dam) and after going over the dam. There were a few vessels that were able to 'spit out' of the hydraulic fairly quickly and not be total losses.

Nineteen years prior to the remnants of *Ivan*, in early November 1985, the remnants of a minor hurricane took nearly the same path. Category I *Hurricane Juan* also made landfall on the US Gulf Coast. The leftovers of *Juan* proceeded up the Ohio River Valley toward the Great Lakes. When this depression reached sodden West Virginia, the remnants of *Juan* dropped as much as nine inches of rain on certain parts of that state. Among other rivers, the Tygart Valley and Cheat Rivers were cresting 30 feet and 21 feet over their banks. These two overflowing rivers spilled into the Monongahela River. In the Monongahela, scores of boats and marinas were heavily damaged, as well as the many river towns. In West Virginia alone, 48 were either dead or missing, and property damage amounted to around $500 million in this 1985 flood.

In the spring and summer of 1993, there was another horrific river flooding event. This flood encompassed about 150 rivers and nine Midwestern states, and was roughly centered near the upper Mississippi River region. *The Food of 93* was triggered by as much as four feet of rainfall falling over a four-month period –and longer than that in some particular areas. The nature of that rainfall was nearly continuous. Hundreds of levees failed; property damage was around $15 billion; and there were fifty fatalities.

Besides floods, the Ohio River has also experienced serious bank erosion.

Unlike the Mississippi River, which has had its banks basically rip-rapped (i.e., stabilized by small stones), the Ohio River has not done this. As a result, the shoreline is constantly eroding back, and the river is becoming wider and shallower. Large trees along the shoreline eventually fall into the river. Large floating trees, besides creating serious navigation problems for recreational vessels, can also play havoc with large commercial towboats. There has been more than one instance where a large tree trunk has become caught in the huge propeller of a towboat, immobilizing hundreds of tons of waterborne freight, and creating another serious navigational hazard.

Cooling towers of power plant near Willow Island, West Virginia

Dozens of Coal Barges on the Ohio River near Catlettsburg, Kentucky

# SECTION II
# RIVER REGIONS AND HIGHLIGHTS

## A NOTE ABOUT READING THE 23 SKETCHES

Twenty-two of the 23 river sketches accompany this section. The first sketch – and the overall rivers sketch –was found in Chapter 1. The second, third and fourth sketches are found in Chapter 6. All 23 sketches are portrait-oriented (i.e., not landscape-oriented), so that you don't have to turn this book sideways to read them. These sketches are also proportioned and scaled to varying degrees in order to maximize the amount of useful information depicted on each page. North is seldom at the top of every page, but positioned in the top half of each page. On all the river sketches, two river mileage 'pins' are typically located near where that river's mileage (i.e., typically the Ohio River) enters and exits the sketch.

The larger or 'more navigable' rivers are drawn with a heavier line than the 'less navigable' rivers. Occasionally, the same line depicting one river on the same sketch may change from a heavily drawn line to a lightly drawn line (e.g., the Kanawha River). This change would be near the 'head of navigation.' The 'mile scale bar' on each sketch is in statute miles, but it could not be ascertained with precision. Hence, it's only a rough estimate and most useful when comparing the scales on different sketches within this book. Likewise, the position of the north arrow may be off by possibly five degrees. In no way should these 23 sketches be used for actual river navigation. One or more of the appropriate seven Corps of Engineer chartbooks should be used for river navigation. Nonetheless, we hope these sketches will give you a better concept and appreciation, whether traveling along the rivers by boat or by car, of the numerous spatial and river relationships in the Ohio River Region.

We've also depicted most of the 200 river locales (and much more) on these sketches. Besides, the smallest scale sketch of the entire region (found in Chapter 1), we subdivide our sketches into three encompassing regions containing multiple chapters: the Upper Ohio, the Middle Ohio, and the Lower Ohio River Regions. The Lower Ohio River sketch primarily contains most of Chapters 14 (minus the Kentucky River and uppermost area of that chapter), Chapters 15, and 16. The Middle Ohio River sketch contains the Kentucky River area of Chapter 14, the last part of Chapter 9, and Chapters 11, 12 and 13. The Upper Ohio River sketch encompasses Chapters 6, 7, 8, and 10, as well as the first part of Chapter 9. The second sketch in this book –the small-scale sketch of the Upper Ohio River Region –is found on the next page. The first large-scale sketch –the Lower Allegheny River –is found on the page 69. Each of our eleven regional chapters contains one, two, or three large-scale sketches.

We do not have a legend on our sketches, but we have added a few easy-to-understand symbols on the sketches. Asides from labeling rivers and the locations of cities, towns, and even some boating and shoreside facilities, we have depicted the approximate river locations of highway and railroad bridges, and locks and dams. Railroad bridges are represented by one line with cross hashes. Highway bridges are depicted by two close and parallel lines. A 'lock and dam' (i.e., 'L&D') is depicted by a bar going across the river with a chevron-like appendage near one end of that bar. That chevron-like appendage represents the lock. Lock gates open on the upriver side, and that's how we've tried to depict these chevrons. We've also portrayed our locks (i.e., the chevrons) on the side of the river that they are actually situated on.

## Sketch 6-A: The Upper Ohio River Region –from Western PA to the Muskingum River

East Brady

Mahoning Creek

French Creek

Kittanning

Kiskiminetas River

Allegheny River

Freeport

New Kensington

McKeesport

Youghiogheny River

**PA.**

**PA.**

**WV.**

Beaver River

**Pittsburgh**

OHIO RIVER

Brownsville

Cheat River

**OH.**

Beaver

Monongahela River

**Morgantown**

East Liverpool

Ten Mile Creek

Fairmont

Tygart Valley River

**PA.**

N

E

S

W

Steubenville

**Scale: 20 Miles**

**Wheeling**

**WV.**

**OH.**

West Fork River

OHIO RIVER

New Martinsville

Middle Island Creek

Tuscarawas River

St. Marys

Marietta

Waldonding Creek

McConnelsville

Parkersburg

Little Kanawha River

Zanesville

Licking River

Muskingum River

OHIO RIVER

Hocking River

**OH.**

**WV.**

# CHAPTER 6
## The Allegheny River …from Pittsburgh to East Brady, PA

The Allegheny River, about 325 miles long, starts in north-central Pennsylvania and first flows northwestward into southwestern New York.  From southwestern New York, the Allegheny bends southwestward towards Pittsburgh.  The Allegheny watershed drains most of the western portion of Pennsylvania and a small part of southwestern New York.  The pre-colonial inhabitants of the Allegheny watershed went back and forth between the Iroquois and Delaware Indians.  The Iroquois named the local river "Oyo" –meaning beautiful river.  When that name was slightly altered to "most beautiful steam"' and translated back to the Delaware tongue (an Algonquin language), it came out as "Welhikheny."  "Welhikheny" was then later anglicized to "Allegheny."

Early French explorers, going to and coming from the Pittsburgh area, diverted from the Allegheny River at French Creek in Venango County.  French Creek generally went northward for about another 70 miles, to within only about 15 miles of Lake Erie.  In 1753, the French, under the command of the Marquis Duquesne were busy building a series of forts to connect their trade route from Lake Erie to the Ohio Region.  The northernmost fort, Fort Presque Isle was on Lake Erie, near present-day Erie Pennsylvania.  The second and third forts were on French Creek.  Fort Le Boeuf was far up French Creek about 15 miles from Lake Erie, near present-day Waterford Pennsylvania.  The third fort, Fort Machault, was at the junction of the Allegheny River and French Creek near present-day Franklin Pennsylvania.  The southernmost and last fort constructed, Fort Duquesne, was at the Forks of the Ohio –where the Allegheny meets the Monongahela River.

Fish found in the upper Allegheny River include muskellunge, walleye, pike, chain pickerel, rainbow trout, and smallmouth bass.  East of Warren Pennsylvania, the Kinzua Dam (no lock) creates the Allegheny Reservoir.  This large reservoir straddles both Pennsylvania and New York.  For a canoeist, it's about a 125-mile trip from the Kinzua Dam to East Brady in mostly Class I whitewater.  The lowest 70 mile section of the Allegheny River –from 'The Point' in Pittsburgh to East Brady, is maintained by the Corps of Engineers.  Despite being set in relatively steep topography, there are many enchanting low-lying islands in the Allegheny River, including several in the lower navigable portion of the river.  Some of these make favorite picnic spots for summertime boaters.  The present-day Allegheny River locks and dams are old and were constructed from 1920 to 1938.  The first lock, Lock #1 in Pittsburgh, was even older and constructed in 1903.  Lock #1 was removed in 1938 after reconstruction of the Emsworth Lock and Dam, six miles downstream on the Ohio River.

The following table summarizes the locks and pools on the Allegheny River:

**Table 6-A: Locks and Pools on the Allegheny River**

| Lock and Pool Name | Mile | Lock Side | Telephone Number ☎ | Opens Rec. Vessels | Lift (in ft) | Pool Length (miles) |
|---|---|---|---|---|---|---|
| Emsworth (down on the Ohio Riv.) | -(6.2) | RDB | 412-766-6213 | 24/7 | 18 | 12.9 |
| Lock and Dam # 2 (Pittsburgh) | 6.7 | LDB | 412-661-2217 | 24/7 | 11 | 7.8 |
| CW Bill Young L/D (Lock and Dam # 3) (N. Kensington, PA) | 14.5 | LDB | 412-828-3550 | 24/7 | 14 | 9.7 |
| Lock & D # 4 (Natrona Hgths PA) | 24.2 | RDB | 724-224-2666 | 24/7 | 10 | 6.2 |
| Lock and Dam  # 5 (Freeport, PA) | 30.4 | RDB | 724-295-2261 | limited | 12 | 5.9 |
| Lock and Dam  # 6 (Clinton, PA) | 36.3 | RDB | 724-295-3775 | limited | 12 | 9.4 |
| Lock & D # 7 (W. Kittanning PA) | 45.7 | RDB | 724-543-2551 | limited | 13 | 6.9 |
| Lock and D # 8 (Templeton, PA) | 52.6 | LDB | 724-548-5119 | limited | 18 | 9.6 |
| Lock and Dam # 9 (Cosmus, PA) | 62.2 | LDB | 724-868-2486 | closed | 22 | ≈8.0 |

Allegheny River, seen from the mountains near Bradys Bend

Riverfront Park, Kittanning, Pennsylvania

**NOTE:** Next to a city or town name, we indicate on what side of the river the city is situated –either the RDB or the LDB (and in a few instances, like Pittsburgh, it's both sides of the river). The RDB or the LDB mean either **R**ight or **L**eft Descending Bank. Oftentimes, the word 'descending' is omitted, and it's just 'Right Bank' of 'Left Bank.' A stream or a river *flows* or *drains* toward a larger body of water, and these ever larger water bodies eventually empty into a sea. When one orients him/herself to the normal direction of that river's flow, one side of the river is the left descending bank while the opposite side is the right descending bank. The Left Descending Bank is abbreviated 'LDB,' while the Right Descending Bank is abbreviated 'RDB.' With its typical curves and horseshoe bends, a river flowing towards a sea could easily travel north, south, east, and west, and sometimes within the span of only a few miles. On the Ohio River, there are a few five-mile sections that do this. Hence, orienting one side of a river to one of the four cardinal directions can be ambiguous at best. However orienting a river using the Left or Right Descending Bank terminology eliminates this ambiguity.

After LDB or RDB, another important river location variable is the mileage marker. The Corps of Engineer maintained inland rivers have mile markers. The Ohio River is 981 miles long. Mile number zero is off 'the Point' at Pittsburgh, while mile number 981 is near Cairo Illinois. The first eight miles of the Allegheny River (i.e., miles 0 through 8 –seen below) are situated in Pittsburgh. Hence, knowing the river mile and what side of the river is what (i.e., the RDB or LDB), one can pinpoint, and exchange information about any point along the river.

## PITTSBURGH, PA (Miles 0 through 8, RDB and LDB. See **Note Above)

Eighteenth century travel over the Allegheny Mountains was difficult and goods imported into southwestern Pennsylvania were hard to come by. Early settlers to the Pittsburgh area had to become self-reliant. The local topography, with rivers and many hills also added to the challenges of living here. Nonetheless, by the mid-19th Century, Pittsburgh captured the title of "Gateway to the West." Pittsburgh beat out longer established Brownsville Pennsylvania on the Monongahela River as well as Wheeling West Virginia –further down the Ohio River (and in a deeper, more navigable, part of the Ohio), as well as being a terminus of the National Road (i.e., present-day US Route 40). In 1852, when the Pennsylvania Railroad reached it, Pittsburgh was well on its way. The railroad cut a trip from Philadelphia to Pittsburgh from four days to 13 hours. From about the mid-nineteenth century, and lasting for about 100 years, Pittsburgh and the surrounding area, led our United States in the production of coal, iron, steel, and glass.

The hilly topography challenged road and bridge engineers. Today, Pittsburgh is also known as a city of bridges. Around the heart of the city, about 40 bridges cross the three main rivers. There may be well over 2,000 bridges in all of Allegheny County and close to another 500 bridges in Beaver County (i.e., downriver on the Ohio). There are also some very impressive tunnels through the mountains around Pittsburgh. The Fort Pitt and Mount Washington Tunnels carry traffic through tunnels before crossing the Monongahela River. As a non-native driving around Pittsburgh, I found the 'road layout' (and associated bridges and tunnels) to be somewhere between an engineering marvel and sheer madness. To continue in the same direction, it's easy to have to first turn left, then right, then right, then left, and left just to keep going in the same general direction!

Enduring the demise of Pittsburgh's heavy industries during the latter part of the twentieth century, the city's prominence as a world class inland port survived. Pittsburgh sits near the northeastern corner of our nation's 9,000-mile inland waterway system. Waterborne cargo originating in the Port of Pittsburgh can reach 24 other states. From Pittsburgh, there is easy waterborne access to locales as far away as St. Paul Minnesota, Sioux City Iowa, Tulsa Oklahoma, New Orleans, the Gulf of Mexico, Chicago and all the Great Lakes.

Based on 2002 data from the US Army Corps of Engineers, Pittsburgh is the second busiest inland port in the country, as well as the 13th busiest port, of any kind, in the entire nation. Pittsburgh ships more tonnage than Baltimore, Philadelphia, and St. Louis. Pittsburgh, with more than 200 river terminals, is the origin for more tons of raw materials than any other port in the world. The Pittsburgh Port District encompasses eleven counties and 200 miles of commercially navigable waterways located in southwestern Pennsylvania. Pittsburgh waterway industries directly generate around 34,000 jobs. On an annual basis, $8 billion of goods travel through the Pittsburgh Port District. More than 50 million tons of cargo –mostly coal, sand, petroleum, chemicals, and metals pass through Pittsburgh each year. The jet fuel used by planes at Pittsburgh Airport, much of the gasoline found at the local pumps, the salt used to clear the roads of winter ice, the concrete for major projects (e.g., PNC baseball park), as well as the mulch for local gardens arrive in Pittsburgh by barge. With about 2.4 million folks in the metropolitan area, Pittsburgh is the second largest city in Pennsylvania –behind only Philadelphia.

**SPRINGDALE, PA** (mile 16, RDB –Right Descending Bank):
Springdale is home to early environmentalist Rachel Carson. In 1962, Carson forewarned us about the dangers associated with unbridled pesticide (esp. DDT) usage.

**NEW KENSINGTON, PA** (mile 19, LDB –Left Descending Bank):
New Kensington was founded in 1891. The town, situated on level riverfront land, attracted the Pittsburgh Reduction Company –later ALCOA. In 1941, the Mount St. Peter Catholic Church was constructed from the remnants of the torn-down Beatty Mellon Mansion. One-time porch banisters became communion rails; a chandelier became a baptismal font.

**TARENTUM, PA** (mile 22, RDB):
The Tour-Ed Mine and Museum (☎ 724-224-4720) is off Bull Creek Road. It's open during the summer and offers educational tours during these summer months.

**BRACKENRIDGE, PA** (mile 23, RDB):
Like New Kensington, Brackenridge's location also attracted large industries –steel mills and glass factories. Many of those industries are now gone. But Allegheny Ludlum has survived. Allegheny Ludlum is in the business of making specialty steel, including stainless steels, silicon electrical steels, tool steels, titanium and various advanced alloys. Besides the plant in Brackenridge, Allegheny Ludlum has nearby plants in Natrona (also on the Allegheny River) and Bagdad and Vandergrift (both on the Kiskiminetas River).

**FREEPORT, PA** (mile 29, RDB):
Freeport was incorporated in 1833. The town is located at the confluence of Buffalo Creek and the Allegheny River. The water dispersing from Buffalo Creek forms a small eddy in the Allegheny River. This made a good location (i.e., in that slight counter-current) to tie-up Allegheny River boats. Early town leaders took that mantra and declared that no dockage fees would be charged in 'our free port.'

**KISKIMINETAS RIVER, PA** (mile 30, LDB):
There seems to be no definitive interpretation of the origin of the name. It's Native American with interpretations such as, "river of the big fish," "clear, clean stream of many bends," or "plenty of walnuts." Colloquially the Kiskiminetas River is just known as the "Kiski." The Kiski River forms at Saltsburg, 27 miles from the Allegheny, at the confluence of Loyalhanna Creek and the Conemaugh River. In 1889, our nation suffered what would be its fourth deadliest natural disaster about 50 milers up the Conemaugh River when an earthen dam on Stoney Creek broke, and more than 2,000 lives were lost in the Great Johnstown Flood. In the late 19ᵗʰ Century, Johnstown and the surrounding Kiski-Conemaugh valley was a bustling section

# Sketch 6-B: The Lower Allegheny River –from Pittsburgh to Natrona, Pennsylvania

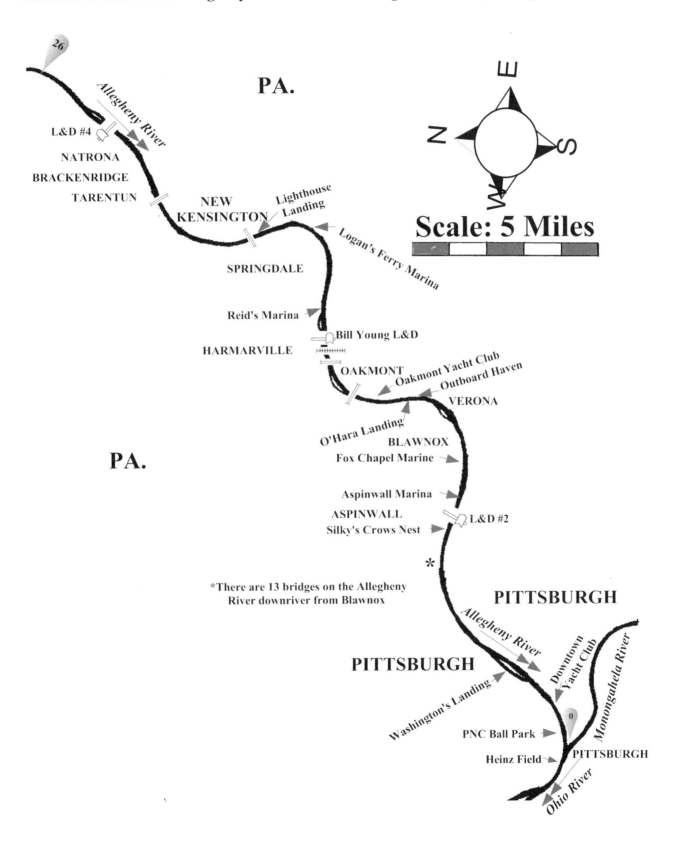

PA.

Scale: 5 Miles

26

L&D #4

Allegheny River

NATRONA
BRACKENRIDGE
TARENTUN

NEW
KENSINGTON

Lighthouse
Landing

Logan's Ferry Marina

SPRINGDALE

Reid's Marina

Bill Young L&D

HARMARVILLE

OAKMONT

Oakmont Yacht Club
Outboard Haven

VERONA

O'Hara Landing

BLAWNOX

Fox Chapel Marine

PA.

Aspinwall Marina

ASPINWALL
Silky's Crows Nest

L&D #2

*

*There are 13 bridges on the Allegheny
River downriver from Blawnox

PITTSBURGH

PITTSBURGH

Allegheny River

Downtown Yacht Club

Monongahela River

Washington's Landing

0

PNC Ball Park

Heinz Field

PITTSBURGH

Ohio River

of the country with steel-making, railroad and coal enterprises, as well as being a magnet for hard-working immigrants.

## LEECHBURG, PA (Kiskiminetas River, mile 5, RDB):

Leechburg is located in a bend five miles up the Kiski River on the right bank (i.e., north side). The town started to prosper around the 1820s, with the construction of the first canal hoping to connect Atlantic flowing rivers to the Mississippi River system. The 'Old Pennsylvania Canal' was constructed near the left bank of the Kiski River and headed upstream toward Johnstown. But by the 1840s, the 'Old Pennsylvania Canal' was made obsolete by a paralleling line of the Pennsylvania Railroad. By the early twentieth century, coal mines, foundries, cement plants, and steel sheet works fueled Leechburg's economy.

## SCHENLEY, PA (mile 31, LDB):

Schenley was the home to the Schenley Distillery which produced a popular brand of whiskey from the late 19th to mid/late 20th Century. A local told me that small fish would feed on the discarded distillery mash. Larger fish, such as walleyes and muskellunges, would in turn feed on these smaller fish. After being caught and fillet, these larger fish tasted and smelled like whiskey. Today the site is an abandoned industrial park along the river. The Schenley Yacht Club is located in the upriver end of this industrial park.

## FORD CITY, PA (mile 42, LDB):

Fort Armstrong, a site north of Ford City, was founded in 1779. It was an outpost to protect against Indians, and named after Major General John Armstrong. Ford City was founded in 1887 as a site for the Pittsburgh Plate Glass Company's (PPG) factory along the Allegheny River. During its heyday, in the 1950s, PPG employed over 3,500 and was the largest and most productive plate glass plant in the world. But by 1993, that PPG plant had closed for good, and all the jobs were lost. Many toilets used in the United States were also once manufactured in Ford City. But by 2005, Eljer brand toilets (and similar fixtures) also had succumbed to imports –mostly from China.

## KITTANNING, PA (mile 45, LDB):

In the 1700s, Kittanning was the largest Delaware Indian town west of the Alleghenies. Kittanning sat on the western terminus of 'the Kittanning Path.' In the 18th Century, this trail was a major overland east-west route over the Allegheny Mountains for the Delaware and Shawnee Indians, as well as colonial settlers. The eastern terminus of this path was in central Pennsylvania on the Juniata River. In the 1750s, as Native American lands were being taken over by colonists, the Indians reacted. The Indians took retribution on the white settlers by taking many hostages. In response, Lieutenant Colonel John Armstrong was sent to dispatch the Indians and retrieve the hostages. In 1756, Armstrong reached Kittanning, liberated about 300 white prisoners, and then destroyed their Delaware village. He was soon christened "the Hero of Kittanning."

By the early twentieth century, Kittanning had coal mines, large iron and steel works, glassworks, flour and lumber mills. Kittanning also had factories producing china, pottery, mirrors, and typewriters. Lime plants and breweries also called the city home. Kittanning's population peaked in the mid-twentieth century. Like so many other western Pennsylvania river towns, Kittanning started its decline in the latter part of the 20th Century. Kittanning is the seat of Armstrong County.

# Sketch 6-C: The Upper Allegheny River –from Freeport to East Brady, PA

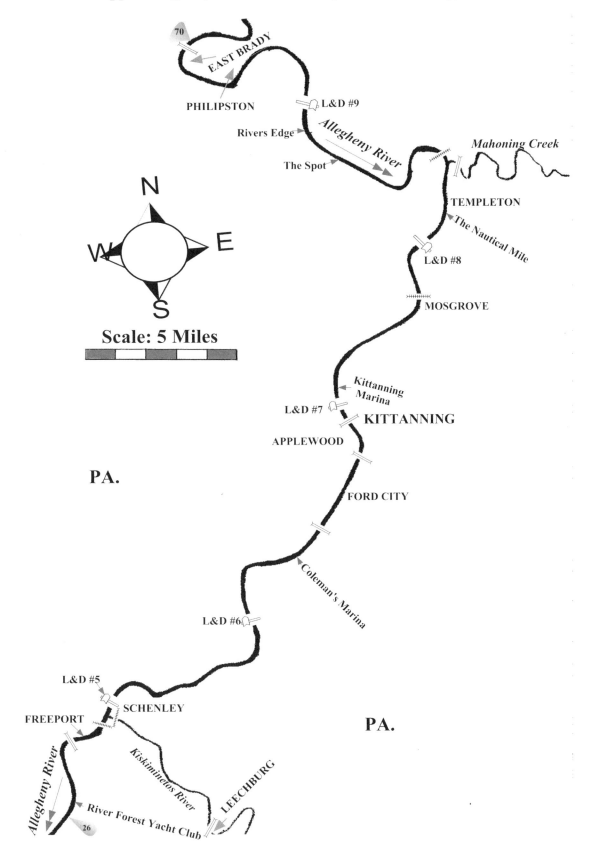

70

EAST BRADY

PHILIPSTON

L&D #9

Rivers Edge

Allegheny River

The Spot

Mahoning Creek

TEMPLETON

The Nautical Mile

N

W        E

S

L&D #8

MOSGROVE

Scale: 5 Miles

Kittanning Marina

L&D #7

KITTANNING

APPLEWOOD

PA.

FORD CITY

Coleman's Marina

L&D #6

L&D #5

SCHENLEY

FREEPORT

PA.

Allegheny River

Kiskiminetos River

LEECHBURG

River Forest Yacht Club

26

Marina near Ford City, Pennsylvania

**MAHONING CREEK, PA** (mile 55.5, LDB):

The town of Punxsutawney lies slightly more than 30 miles up Mahoning Creek. Punxsutawney is the home of that infamous 'late winter' groundhog named 'Phil.'

**EAST BRADY, PA** (mile 69, LDB):

The Allegheny River, in about a six mile length of gorge-like setting, makes a deep 'reverse S-bend.' Nearby Brady's Bend, in the Allegheny River, was named for Captain Samuel Brady, a legendary frontier scout of the late 18th Century. In mid-1800s, the Brady's Bend Iron Company was the first west of the Allegheny Mountains to make iron rails for the railroad companies.

Today, East Brady is the hometown of pro football Hall-of-Fame quarterback, Jim Kelly. In the late 1970s, Kelly, wanted to play college football at home for Penn State, and coach Joe Paterno. But coach Paterno told Kelly, he'd be converted to a linebacker. In 1979, the freshman quarterback at the University of Miami came back to his home state to beat Penn State. After the University of Miami, Jim Kelly had a fruitful professional career as an NFL quarterback with the Buffalo Bills. In late 2006, a new bridge across the Allegheny was under construction in East Brady. East Brady has a few restaurants, a grocer, a motel, a gas station, and a hotel.

# CHAPTER 7
## The Monongahela River ...from Pittsburgh to Fairmont, WV

"Monongahela" is an Indian word meaning "the river of caving banks." Colloquially, the Monongahela is often just called "the Mon." After early immigrants crossed the Allegheny (i.e., the Appalachians) Mountains of Pennsylvania, their next big goal was the Monongahela River. After that grueling ground trek over the Alleghenies, early settlers very much welcomed the westward flowing rivers, like the Ohio and its tributaries. Despite the rigors from the rivers, travel on them was far better than traveling over mountains and through numerous ravines. The Mon actually flows north to the Ohio, and is one of the few major north-flowing rivers in North America. Early flatboats were being built on the Mon at Red Stone Old Fort (i.e., present-day Brownsville), Monongahela, Elizabeth, and McKeesport Pennsylvania.

About 129 miles south of Pittsburgh, the Monongahela forms when the Tygart Valley River meets the West Fork River. Both the West Fork and Tygart Valley Rivers are navigable for small craft for a few miles beyond their confluence with the Mon. The Tygart Valley River is the slightly more navigable fork. The Tygart Valley River, forking from the east also flows generally northward for about 160 miles, before reaching the Mon. Two state parks along the Tygart Valley River are fairly close to the confluence. Valley Falls State Park is downstream from Grafton, while Tygart Lake State Park (☎ 304-265-6184) is upstream from Grafton. The Tygart Valley River is dammed to form a lake at Tygart Lake State Park.

The West Fork River enters from the southwest and flows northward for about 80 miles, rising out from a plateau in north-central West Virginia. Near Weston, on the West Fork River, the Corps of Engineers constructed a dam and created Stonewall Jackson Lake. Daring and unexcitable Confederate General Stonewall Jackson, whose battle credo was 'strength and mobility,' was born near Clarksburg West Virginia. Jackson's parents and all but one sibling died when he was young. Jackson was a determined, persistent and religious man. He started near the bottom of his class at West Point, but preserved. Like Confederate General Robert E. Lee, Jackson's first allegiance was to his state –then Virginia. Like Union General Ulysses S. Grant, Jackson was unpretentious and rumpled. During the early years of the Civil War, Jackson was able to defeat three Union armies, about twice the size of his own army, by jabbing at them with his smaller force and keeping his enemy off balance.

By the mid 1810s, commercial coal was being shipped down the Mon on large flatboats measuring 80 feet long by 18 feet wide. In the late 1830s, a private company, spurred by coal interests, started building locks and dams on the Monongahela, and charged tolls for passage. By 1844, four locks and dams were completed on the river. By 1904, five more locks and dams were extended into West Virginia. This made the Monongahela the nation's first completely slack-water (i.e., pooled) river. In the 1920s, the Monongahela River claimed the second highest volume of freight per ton/mile in the world –behind only the Rhine River in Germany. By the 1940s, another round of lock and dam modernizations had begun. Today, the Mon transports about 70 percent of the cargo flowing through the Port of Pittsburgh.

With the possible exceptions of certain short segments of the Ohio River, the Monongahela may be the most industrialized river in this entire book. This river industry, consisting of mostly now-closed down Pennsylvania steel mills had contributed to a rather polluted situation during the 1960s and early 1970s. However, things have greatly improved. These days, during the warm summer months, folks can be seen swimming in the Mon. If you drive a car alongside the river, and then take boat down the middle of the river, you will likely have two contrasting impressions. Looking down on the river from the winding gritty roads, the river seems unappealing. However, taking a boat down that same stretch of river, and looking back up at the riverbanks, roads, and towns, the river has a much more appealing feel. The riverbanks are lined with sycamore, willow, catalpa and other hardwoods, and are often lush and green.  Much of the once heavy industry is at least partially hidden by the vegetation along the banks.

The following table summaries the locks and pools on the Monongahela River:

**Table 7-A:  Locks and Pools on the Monongahela River**

| Lock and Pool Name | Mile | Lock Side | Telephone Number ☎ | Opens for Rec. Vessels | Lift (in ft) | Pool Length (miles) |
|---|---|---|---|---|---|---|
| Emsworth (down the Ohio Riv.) | -(6.2) | RDB | 412-766-6213 | 24/7 | 18 | 17.4 |
| Lock & Dam #2 (Braddock, PA) | 11.2 | RDB | 412-271-1272 | 24/7 | 9 | 12.6 |
| Lock & Dam #3 (Elizabeth, PA) | 23.8 | RDB | 412-384-4532 | 24/7 | 8 | 17.7 |
| Lock & D #4 (Belle Vernon PA) | 41.5 | RDB | 724-684-8442 | 24/7 | 17 | 19.7 |
| Maxwell L&D (E.Millsboro, PA) | 61.2 | RDB | 724-785-5027 | 24/7 | 20 | 20.8 |
| Grays Lndng L&D (Masontown) | 82.0 | RDB | 724-583-8304 | 24/7 | 15 | 8.8 |
| Pt. Marion L&D (Dilliner, PA) | 90.8 | LDB | 724-725-5289 | 24/7 | 19 | 11.2 |
| Morgantown L&D (M'townWV) | 102.0 | LDB | 304-292-1885 | Daylight | 17 | 6.0 |
| Hildebrand L&D | 108.0 | LDB | 304-983-2300 | Weekend | 21 | 7.4 |
| Opekiska L&D | 115.4 | RDB | 304-336-4224 | Weekend | 22 | ≈16.0 |

**STATION SQUARE/BESSEMER FURNACE, PA** (Mile 0.7, LDB –Left Descending Bank):

The Station Square/Bessemer Court area is where Pittsburgh's iron and steel industry was launched.  In 1859, the first pig iron blast furnace, the Clinton Furnace, started here.  From this humble beginning, Pittsburgh's steel industry would dominant the world for the next century.  Today, the trendy Station Square/Bessemer Furnace area houses several upscale restaurants, offices, and hotels.  The Gateway Clipper Steamboat Fleet parks less than one-quarter mile downriver from Station Square/Bessemer Furnace.  Here locals and tourists can catch a ride on one of several 'old-time' riverboats navigating through the heart of Pittsburgh.

**HOMESTEAD, PA** (miles 6-8, LDB):

Homestead was settled in 1871.  In a few short years, Homestead had a bustling US Steel Mill which was owned by Andrew Carnegie.  In 1892, after the steel workers' union refused to sign a new contract, Carnegie locked-out the union workforce, and used hundreds of Pinkerton Guards to protect his mill from disgruntled workers.  Nobody knows for sure, who fired first, but the result was eleven deaths and dozens of injuries.  The governor of Pennsylvania had to call out the National Guard to restore order.  In the aftermath of 'The Battle of Homestead,' Carnegie effectively eliminated union resistance in Homestead and elsewhere in his steel mills.  After the Homestead mill reopened, output remained strong for another fifty years, up to Word War II.  During its World War II heyday, this 'flagship' plant employed more than 20,000, and covered 300 acres on the left bank of the Monongahela River.  But by the 1970s, imported steel made this and many other steel mills unprofitable.  Before long, the mill was permanently closed…and then dismantled.

Today, the site of that once vibrant steel mill houses the upscale 'Homestead Waterfront' and the 'Sandcastle Water Park.'  The 'Homestead Waterfront' contains many restaurants, movie theaters, hotels, condos, and a variety of stores, including a Lowe's Hardware Store.  For you baseball fans, there's another historical vignette to Homestead.  That Negro League powerhouse team, the 'Homestead Grays,' once played here.  The 'Grays' won 12 national titles, including nine in a row.  The 'Grays' produced such legends as Josh Gibson, Buck Leonard, Smokey Joe Williams, and Cumberland Posey.  Many of these tough Negro League baseball players were also Homestead steel mill workers.

## Sketch 7-A: The Lower Monongahela River –from Pittsburgh to Fredericktown, PA

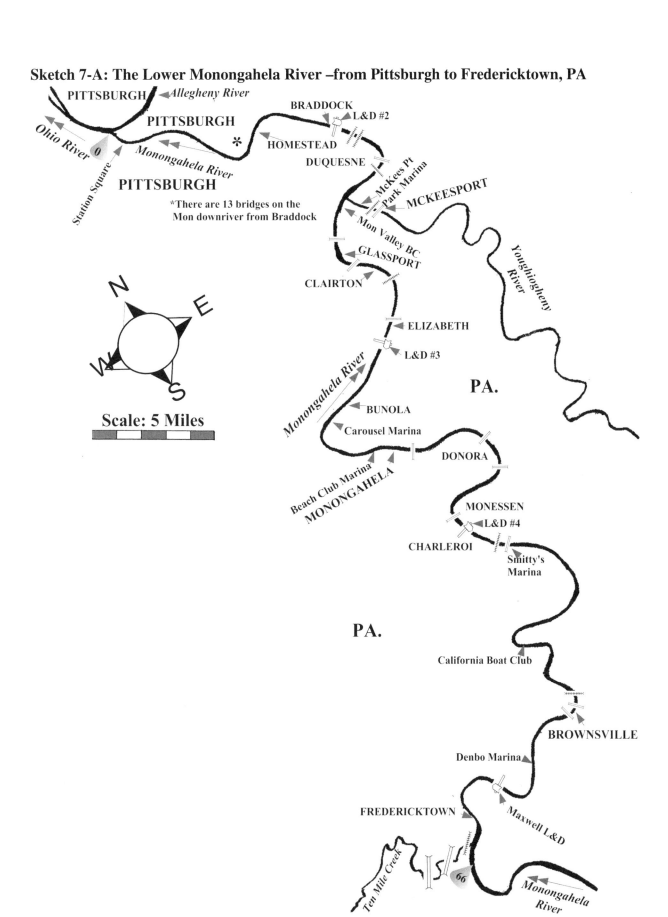

PITTSBURGH

Allegheny River

PITTSBURGH

Ohio River

0

Station Square

Monongahela River

PITTSBURGH

BRADDOCK

L&D #2

HOMESTEAD

*

DUQUESNE

McKees Pt Park Marina

MCKEESPORT

Mon Valley BC

GLASSPORT

CLAIRTON

Youghiogheny River

*There are 13 bridges on the Mon downriver from Braddock

N

E

W

S

Scale: 5 Miles

ELIZABETH

L&D #3

Monongahela River

PA.

BUNOLA

Carousel Marina

Beach Club Marina

MONONGAHELA

DONORA

MONESSEN

L&D #4

CHARLEROI

Smitty's Marina

PA.

California Boat Club

BROWNSVILLE

Denbo Marina

FREDERICKTOWN

Maxwell L&D

Ten Mile Creek

66

Monongahela River

75

# Pittsburgh's Three Rivers

Near Station Square on the Monongahela River

**BRADDOCK, PA** (miles 10-11, RDB –Right Descending Bank):

Braddock is named after General Edward Braddock, and is near the location of his ill-fated second river crossing in 1755. The town of Braddock was started about forty years later. In 1873, the town started booming after Andrew Carnegie had founded another steel mill here. Like just about all US steel mills, this one succumbed to imports during the 1980s. 'Kennywood,' Pittsburgh's longstanding amusement park, is located on the Left Descending Bank (LDB) and across the Monongahela River from Braddock.

**McKEESPORT, PA** (miles 15-16, RDB):

McKeesport was settled in 1795 by John McKee. McKee was soon running ferry services on the Monongahela and Youghiogheny Rivers. Nearby, large bituminous coal deposits were found. By the 1830s coal mining began in earnest. Besides the coal related industries, another major employer was an iron pipe company that employed as many as 10,000. When steel-making started to decline, so did McKeesport. The first GC Murphy 'five and dime' store was located in McKeesport.

The Youghiogheny River empties into the Monongahela at McKeesport. The 'Yough' originates in northern West Virginia, then flows north-northeast into Maryland, before turning northwestward to meet the Mon in Pennsylvania. In 1754, on George Washington's first westward trip to the 'Forks of the Ohio,' he followed the 'Yough' for a ways. In Maryland, a section of the 'Yough' has been set aside as 'The Youghiogheny Scenic and Wild River.' The 'Yough' is noted for exciting whitewater rafting.

**CLAIRTON, PA** (miles 19-21, LDB):

Clairton began when the United States Steel Company acquired this level river-bottom thousand-acre site soon after the turn of the 20th Century. It was to be the location of a huge integrated steel mill complex. During the first several decades of the 20th Century, Clairton and its steel mill thrived. Today, the still-standing Clairton Works, no longer produces steel; but it is the nation's largest coke-producing facility. Annually, about 6.6 million tons of coal is converted into 4.7 million tons of coke at this Clairton facility. Clairton was the setting for the 1978 movie 'Deer Hunter.'

**ELIZABETH, PA** (mile 23, RDB):

Many historians believe that Meriwether Lewis' keelboat was constructed at the Walker Boatyard in Elizabeth. This boat was 55 feet long, 8 feet wide, and supported a 32-foot mast. Glass-making and ship-building were among some of the earlier industries in Elizabeth. Today, the small downtown section has a few boat-accessible diners as well as a few other stores.

**BUNOLA, PA** (miles 26-28, RDB):

Between miles 26 and 27, on the Right Descending Bank, there are about four boating facilities. There are several sets of recreation docks in this area –in various stages of business operation (e.g., open? closed? or somewhere in between?). The Carousel Marina and Restaurant is the one most consistently opened, and is the largest facility in the area.

**MONONGAHELA-NEW EAGLE, PA** (miles 30-32, LDB):

The city of Monongahela was a river starting point for thousands of early pioneers who were continuing westward on their journey from the East. It's also one of the oldest settlements in the Mon Valley, having been settled in the late 18th Century. In 1794, Monongahela was the site of the famed Whiskey Rebellion. President George Washington summoned about 13,000 federal troops to western Pennsylvania, after federal tax collectors had been harassed and occasionally attacked trying to collect the badly-needed federal dollars which were levied on distilled spirits. This was one of the first 'test cases' of federal authority. A federal force was able to apprehend about twenty tax-evading lawbreakers. Two were sentenced, and later hanged. But the successful federal suppression of the Whiskey Rebellion had the unintended consequence of driving small local illicit whiskey distillers deeper into the frontier –becoming the forerunners of Kentucky, West Virginia, and Tennessee moonshiners.

## DONORA, PA (mile 37, LDB):

Donora is the site of one of the worst air-pollution incidents in the country. In the fall of 1948, effluent gases emitted by a local steel and wire plant, and a zinc works trapped polluted air, in an air inversion. Some have speculated that fluoride emissions contributed to the severity of the incident. Eighteen folks died during this air inversion, and another fifty succumbed soon after the inversion was over. There's no telling how many folks were adversely affected with permanently damaged lungs. Donora is the birthplace of several baseball stars –Stan Musial, Ken Griffey, Sr., and Ken Griffey, Jr.

## CHARLEROI, PA (miles 41-42, LDB):

Charleroi received its name from its sister city –Charleroi in Belgium. That name came from the French King, 'Charles II.'

## BROWNSVILLE, PA (mile 56, RDB):

About 200 years ago there was a saying in Brownsville, "Pittsburgh might amount to something if it wasn't so close to Brownsville." In 1750, before the French and Indian War, historic Brownsville had been established as Redstone Old Fort by the British as a trading vanguard into the Ohio Territory. Redstone Old Fort benefited from being located near Indian trails and on the Monongahela River. One of Brownsville early frontier residents, Christopher Gist, saved young officer George Washington's life on no less than two occasions. Many great westward expeditions had started-out in Brownsville. During the American Revolution, George Rogers Clark started his successful military conquest of the West from Redstone Old Fort. In 1814, the Steamboat *Enterprise* was constructed at Brownsville.

## FREDERICKTOWN-MILLSBORO-TEN MILE CREEK, PA (miles 64-66, LDB):

Fredericktown is a fair sized town with restaurants, a grocer, motel, gas stations, hardware store, laundromat, and a library. Millsboro, just upstream from Fredericktown, has an historic old hotel on the riverfront. There are a few docks still remaining in Millsboro, but the better amenities for travelers will be found in Fredericktown. Furthermore, the first mile and a half of navigable Ten Mile Creek is loaded with boating facilities. There are more concentrated boating facilities in Ten Mile Creek than anywhere else on the entire Monongahela River.

## RICE'S LANDING, PA (mile 68, LDB):

One hundred years ago, Rice's Landing was an important river and transportation hub, moving clay, sand, coal and lumber through this portion of southwestern Pennsylvania.

## NEMACOLIN, PA (mile 76, LDB):

The small town of Nemacolin was named after a Delaware Indian Chief. In the 1740s, Nemacolin blazed a trail through the mountains and laurel thickets from Wills Creek on the Potomac River (i.e., what would become Cumberland Maryland –and draining into the Chesapeake Bay and the Atlantic Ocean) to what would become Brownsville (on the Monongahela River –draining toward the center of the continent). During the next two centuries, Nemacolin's Trail would be involved in much continental history. In 1755, ill-fated General Edward Braddock marched up, with what-would-be-ineffective heavy artillery along Nemacolin's Trail into French territory. About a hundred years later, The US Congress established the first National Highway using the old trail. This was our young nation's first east west non-river route until the railroads. Today, a good part of Nemacolin's Trail is known as US Route 40 or 'The National Road.'

**FRIENDSHIP HILL, PA** (miles 86-87, RDB):

Friendship Hill National Historic Site was the 1780s home of early American Statesman, Albert Gallatin. Gallatin served as Congressman, Secretary of Treasury, and ambassador. In 1804, when Lewis and Clark arrived at the headwaters of the Missouri River, they named the three rivers found there after the three most prominent politicians of their day, Jefferson, Madison, and Gallatin. From 1801 to 1814, Gallatin served as the US Secretary of the Treasury. He was able to successfully juggle financing westward expansion on a very limited federal budget. Gallatin left behind a great legacy of responsible fiscal federal management. Our new nation owed a great debt to Albert Gallatin for getting us on firm financial footing, coupled with the foresight to wisely program a sound system for future federal expenditures. Gallatin was often personally attacked by other American politicians because he was not native born. He was Swiss-born, but he did take an oath of allegiance to Virginia before the Revolutionary War.

**POINT MARION, PA** (mile 90, RDB):

Point Marion is the last town in Pennsylvania (or possibly the first town if you're coming from the south). There are a few restaurants and stores in Pt. Marion, but there is no boat dock – only a boat ramp. Near this concrete boat ramp, there's adequate boat trailer parking, an athletic field, and a playground. On the nearby non-navigable Cheat River, there is a dam (with no lock) three and half miles upstream.

The Monongahela River, near Brownsville, Pennsylvania

# Sketch 7-C: The Upper Monongahela River –from Ten Mile Creek to Fairmont WV

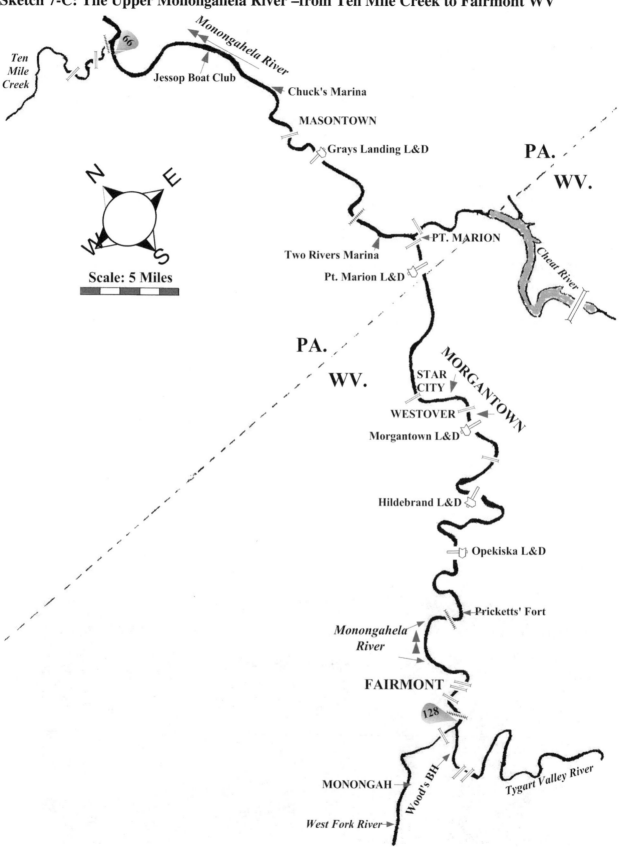

Ten Mile Creek

66

Monongahela River

Jessop Boat Club

Chuck's Marina

MASONTOWN

Grays Landing L&D

N E W S

Scale: 5 Miles

PA.

WV.

Cheat River

Two Rivers Marina

PT. MARION

Pt. Marion L&D

PA.

WV.

STAR CITY

MORGANTOWN

WESTOVER

Morgantown L&D

Hildebrand L&D

Opekiska L&D

Pricketts' Fort

Monongahela River

FAIRMONT

128

MONONGAH

Wood's BH

Tygart Valley River

West Fork River

**MORGANTOWN-STAR CITY-WESTOVER, WV** (miles 98-102, R & LDB):

In 1772, Morgantown was settled by Zaquill Morgan. Today, Morgantown, the seat of Monongalia County, is the fifth largest city in West Virginia. In the 1860s, Morgantown became home to West Virginia University, the largest school in the state –and my alma mater. During the 1970s, the US Department of Transportation began building an experimental personal rapid transit system (PRT) to connect the two separated college campuses. The city –and the campuses, was chosen because of Morgantown's many abrupt elevation changes, as well as its significantly diverse seasonal climates. On the RDB of the Monongahela River, from about mile 97 (i.e., north of Star City) to about mile 121 (i.e., Prickett's Fort), the level old railroad bed, paralleling the river, has been turned into a beautiful hiking-biking trail –the 'Mon River Trail.'

**PRICKETT'S FORT, WV** (mile 120.7, RDB)

In 1774 during Lord Dunmore's War, Prickett's Fort had been built to provide protection for about 80 white families during a time of increased Indian hostilities. In areas near Hildebrand and Opekiska Locks and Dams (i.e., downriver from Prickett's Fort), the Indian name for the river, 'Banks Caving In,' does seem most appropriate.

**RIVESVILLE, WV** (mile 1226, LDB):

In 1694, Rivesville was the location of the first temporary white settlement on the Monongahela River.

**FAIRMONT, WV** (miles 126-128, mostly on the LDB):

Fairmont is the seat of Marion County. Marion County was so-named after South Carolina's famous Revolutionary War hero, Francis Marion –'the Swamp Fox.' The 'Father of West Virginia," Francis Pierpont was also from Fairmont. In 1861, Pierpont served as provisional governor of West Virginia, and later as the governor of a Union-backed 'Restored Virginia' during the latter stages of the Civil War, as well as for a time shortly thereafter.

In 1863, during the Civil War, Confederate cavalry troops, under the command of General W.E. Jones, after having attacked Morgantown, successfully sacked and raided Fairmont and destroyed the railroad bridges. Today, a busy railroad hugs the steep banks of the Monongahela, starting out on the RDB of the Tygart Valley River, and then crossing the Mon several times. Fairmont, the seventh largest city in West Virginia and the seat of Marion County, hosts its annual 'Three Rivers Festival" around Memorial Day weekend.

**MONONGAH, WV** (mile 129, LDB –four miles up the West Fork River):

The town of Monongah lies barely four miles up the RDB of the West Fork River. Here in December 1907, the worst mining disaster in US history occurred. Three hundred and sixty-two men lost their lives when two connected deep mines of the Fairmont Coal Company exploded. Most of these workers were Italian immigrants, and many were young boys working for as little as a $1 per week. The explosions and subsequent fires were presumed to have ignited when flammable coal dust caught fire after having been ignited by a smaller methane explosion. In 1968 –barely sixty years later, and less than five miles away, another very similar explosion occurred at Consolidated Coal Company's Farmington deep mine when another 78 West Virginia miners lost their lives.

Heinz Field, Carnegie Science Center, and Submarine Requin, Pittsburgh

Beaver River, Pennsylvania

# CHAPTER 8
# The Wheeling Area …on the Ohio River, from Pittsburgh to New Martinsville WV, including the Beaver River

The Ohio River starts at 'the Point' in Pittsburgh where the Allegheny and Monongahela Rivers merge. The Iroquois Indians name, "Oyo" (or "Ohio") translates to beautiful river. The Iroquois likely bestowed that name somewhere on the present-day Allegheny River –which they considered to be the 'upper Ohio.' With its many twists and turns the river generally flows west-southwest for nearly a thousand miles before meeting the mighty Mississippi River near Cairo Illinois. The Ohio, Allegheny and Monongahela Rivers originate in the rugged terrain of central Appalachia. By the time the Ohio reaches western Kentucky and Illinois, the terrain has become quite different –gently rolling low hills.

The Ohio River has always been a major transportation artery since the earliest Native Americans discovered it. The Ohio, with its eastern tributaries, was the main east-west traveling artery west of the Appalachian Mountains (called the Allegheny Mountains in an earlier era). Indians traveling east or west, and Colonial settlers expanding primarily westward found this river route to be an invaluable early highway. Slightly more than two centuries ago, when westward migrating settlers reached the banks of the Ohio (or Monongahela) they must have felt that they were well on their way to their destined promised land –wherever that was in the West. Several times during the late 19th and early 20th Centuries, three of our nation's 12 largest cities were situated on the Ohio River –Cincinnati (reaching the 6th largest in the 1840s and 1850s), Pittsburgh (the 8th largest in the 1910s), and Louisville (the 12th largest in the 1860s). There's little doubt, that their strategic location on the Ohio River, was the primary reason for the success of these cities. Today, the uppermost Ohio River region is heavily industrialized. There are steel mills (most now are closed-down), coal, sand, gravel, petroleum, and chemical terminals, as well as many coal-fired power plants along this part of the river. In certain stretches on this river (e.g., far western Pennsylvania), the barge staging areas and towboat traffic can be intense.

In 2005, the Bassmaster Classic Fishing Tournament was hosted off the Point on the Ohio River, in downtown Pittsburgh. Plenty of bass were caught. This is indicative of the great improvement in water quality, because bass cannot tolerate polluted waters. In the 1970s catfish and carp were about the only fish that could survive in these polluted rivers. Today the river quality has much improved!

In 1885, the first lock and dam on the upper Ohio River was completed at Davis Island, about five miles below the Point in Pittsburgh. In 1921, the Emsworth Lock and Dam, about six miles below the Point was completed. Emsworth replaced the Davis Island Lock and Dam. By 1929, the first round of lock and dam construction along the entire 981-mile Ohio River length had been finally completed. In 1938, the Emsworth Lock and Dam was reconstructed, raising the uppermost Ohio River pool level by seven feet. That Emsworth Pool also extended well into the Allegheny and Monongahela Rivers. Hence, the lowest locks and dams on both the Allegheny and Monongahela Rivers (i.e., both called Lock and Dam #1) were no longer needed, and thus removed. The Pittsburgh area (i.e., the Emsworth Pool) now had water frontage of nearly 50 miles in one navigational pool. The uppermost, and oldest, three locks (i.e., Emsworth, Dashields, and Montgomery) on the Ohio River do not have floating bollards in their smaller recreational vessel chambers. However, at river mile 54.3, the New Cumberland Lock, built in 1961, and all the locks further down river, except for the very last two locks (i.e., Locks #52 and #53) do have floating bollards, making the locking-though process for a recreational vessel easier.

The following table summarizes the locks and pools on this uppermost portion of the Ohio River:

**Table 8-A: Locks and Pools on the Uppermost Ohio River**

| Lock and Pool Name | Mile | Lock Side | Telephone Number ☎ | Opens for R. Vessels | Lift (in ft) | Pool Length (miles) |
|---|---|---|---|---|---|---|
| Emsworth Lock & Dam (Pgh, PA) | 6.2 | RDB | 412-766-6213 | 24/7 | 18 | 6.2 |
| Dashields L&D (Glenwillard, PA) | 13.3 | LDB | 724-457-8430 | 24/7 | 10 | 7.1 |
| Montg'ry L&D(Shippingsport,PA) | 31.7 | LDB | 724-643-8400 | 24/7 | 18 | 18.4 |
| N.Cumberland L&D (Stratton,OH) | 54.3 | RDB | 740-537-2571 | 24/7 | 21 | 22.6 |
| Pike Island L&D (Warwood, WV) | 84.2 | LDB | 304-277-2240 | 24/7 | 21 | 29.9 |
| Hannibal L&D (Hannibal OH) | 126.4 | RDB | 740-483-2305 | 24/7 | 21 | 42.2 |

**CHARTIERS CREEK, PA** (mile 2.5, LDB –Left Descending Bank)

Chartiers Creek drains into the Ohio behind Brunot Island. In 1743, half-breed French-Indian, Pierre Chartiers, established a trading post on this creek. In 1749, when Celoron de Bienville visited the area, he declared the creek, "as the most beautiful he has ever seen on the Ohio River." In 1752, George Washington and Christopher Gist later visited the area. By the mid 19th Century, Chartiers Creek was used as an important railroad bed between Pittsburgh and points south.

**McKEES ROCKS, PA** (miles 3-4, LDB)

In 1764, Alexander McKee was granted this tract of land which stretched from a rocky projection to the Ohio River. In 1803, Meriwether Lewis had great difficulty getting through this section. All hands were needed to carry Lewis' keelboat through a 30-yard section of extremely low water.

**DAVIS ISLAND, PA** (mile 4.7, LDB)

In 1885, the upper Ohio River's first lock and dam was completed at Davis Island. When it was constructed, it was the world's largest moveable (i.e., wicket) dam and had the widest locking chamber. In 1921, the Davis Island Lock and Dam was replaced by the Emsworth Lock and Dam, one and half miles downriver.

**NEVILLE ISLAND, PA** (miles 5-10, LDB)

Neville Island has often been a prominent ship building site. During World War II, two large shipbuilding plants contributed hundreds of steel ships towards the successful war effort. Today, there are a few residences on the downriver, and northwestern, end of still mostly industrial Neville Island.

**BEAVER, PA** (mile 26, RDB –Right Descending Bank):

During the American Revolution, near the confluence of the Beaver and Ohio Rivers, Fort McIntosh was constructed. This was the first fort built north of the Ohio River by the newly-formed United States. After the war, Fort McIntosh was the home of the First American Regiment, which was the oldest active Army unit. In 1785, this fort was the site of the one-sided Treaty of Fort McIntosh between Native Americans and the government. The Indians were forced to cede to the U.S. their 'Ohio lands' east of the Muskingum and Cuyahoga Rivers as well as much land in Michigan. In 1788, the fort was abandoned because the frontier had moved farther west, and there was no more need for a permanent garrison in this area. In 1792, the town of Beaver was laid out. The town is also the seat of Beaver County.

# Sketch 8-A: The Ohio River –from Pittsburgh, PA to Brilliant, Ohio

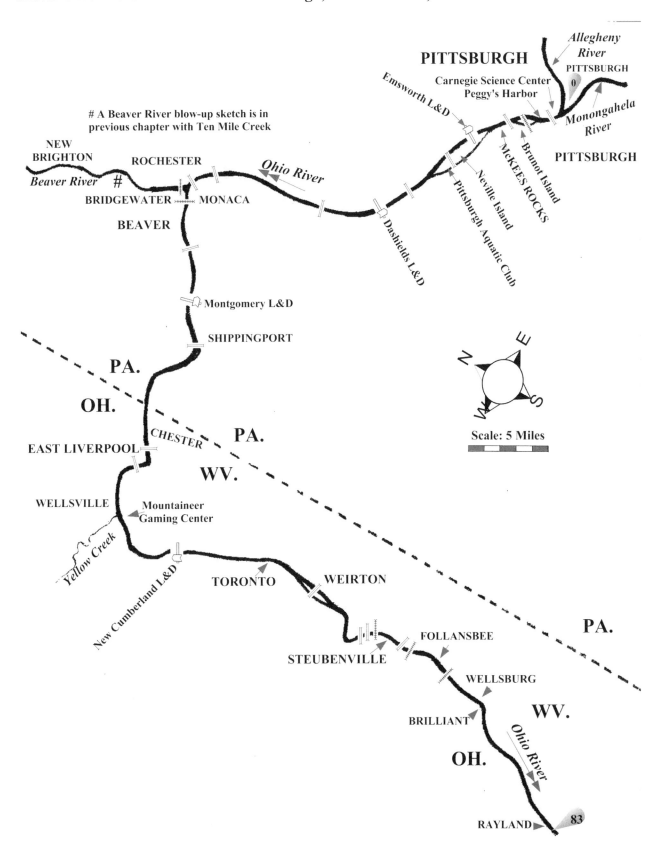

PITTSBURGH

*Allegheny River*

PITTSBURGH

Carnegie Science Center
Peggy's Harbor

Emsworth L&D

*Monongahela River*

PITTSBURGH

Brunot Island

McKEES ROCKS

Neville Island

Pittsburgh Aquatic Club

# A Beaver River blow-up sketch is in previous chapter with Ten Mile Creek

NEW BRIGHTON

ROCHESTER

*Ohio River*

*Beaver River* #

BRIDGEWATER    MONACA

BEAVER

Dashields L&D

Montgomery L&D

SHIPPINGPORT

PA.

OH.

N E S W

Scale: 5 Miles

CHESTER

PA.

EAST LIVERPOOL

WV.

WELLSVILLE

Mountaineer Gaming Center

*Yellow Creek*

New Cumberland L&D

TORONTO

WEIRTON

PA.

FOLLANSBEE

STEUBENVILLE

WELLSBURG

BRILLIANT

WV.

OH.

*Ohio River*

RAYLAND

83

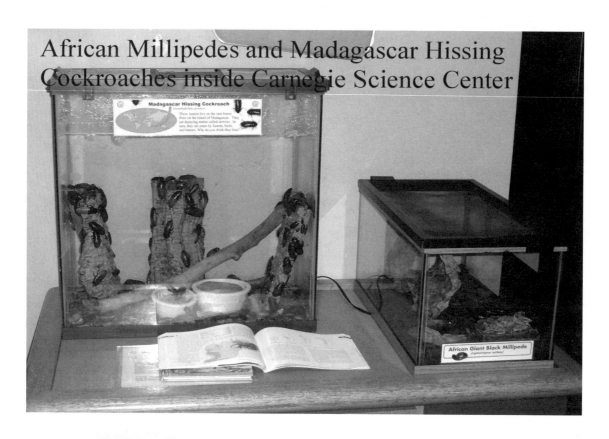

African Millipedes and Madagascar Hissing Cockroaches inside Carnegie Science Center

St. Peters Catholic Church, Steubenville, Ohio

**MONTGOMERY LOCK AND DAM, PA** (mile 31.7, LDB):

There was a horrible accident here on the night of January 9, 2005. The towboat *MV Elizabeth M.* was pushing six coal laden barges upstream against extremely heavy current. After clearing the lockwall, two of the six barges ripped loose from the tow in the 12 MPH current. The towboat pilot then tried to snag his barges to keep them from going back over the dam. He wasn't able to do so. The towboat and three of the barges went over the dam. Four lives were lost, but four people were luckily rescued. A condition called an 'outdraft' helped push the entire rig toward the center of the river soon after it had cleared the upstream end of the lockwall. The 2,200 HP diesel engine of the *Elizabeth M* was no match for the 12 MPH current and the exacerbated outdraft created by the extreme river conditions on that awful day.

**SHIPPINGPORT, PA** (mile 34.8, LDB):

In 1957, the Beaver Valley Nuclear Generating Station became the first commercial nuclear power plant operating in the United States. Note the five cooling towers.

**CHESTER, WV** (mile 43, LDB)

Chester is the northernmost city in the northernmost, and smallest, county of West Virginia. Hancock County West Virginia was named after the first signer of the Declaration of Independence, John Hancock. Iron furnaces in Chester made the cannonballs used by Commandant Oliver Hazard Perry during the pivotal Battle of Lake Erie in 1813. US Route 30 crosses the Ohio River between Chester and East Liverpool. US Route 30 was part of what would become the Lincoln Highway. The Lincoln Highway was the first highway route to cross the entire continent, and was constructed as a hard surface with the automobile in mind. This 3,400-mile road was started in 1915, and completed in 1934. The route extended from New York to San Francisco, by way of Philadelphia, Pittsburgh, Chicago, Omaha, Cheyenne and Reno.

**EAST LIVERPOOL, OH** (miles 43-45, RDB):

When one approaches East Liverpool, along the Ohio River traveling either east or west, the 126-foot tall East Liverpool High School Alumni Clock Tower will be seen dominating the skyline. East Liverpool was earlier named Fawcettstown and St. Clair –after Arthur St. Clair, the governor of the Northwest Territory. But in 1834, the town became East Liverpool because its pottery industry reminded English settlers of that same industry in Liverpool, England. With abundant clay deposits, ready river transportation, and hard-working immigrants, East Liverpool dominated the domestic ceramic industry for close to a century, producing more than one-half of America's annual ceramic output. This industry started taking off around 1841. Before long, East Liverpool had become known as 'Crockery City,' and 'The Pottery Capital of America.' At one time, East Liverpool hosted 200 pottery factories. Once again, in the second half of the 20th Century, imported pottery coupled with the rapid growth of plastics doomed this industry. To learn more about this rich history, please visit the East Liverpool Museum of Ceramics (☎ 330-386-6001 www.themuseumofceramics.org).

The Land Ordinance of 1785 required that public lands be surveyed before any distribution or sale. The 'Point of Beginning' is a surveyor's mark just east of East Liverpool, on the Ohio-Pennsylvania border. This point marks the beginning location for surveying public lands to the west needed for opening the Northwest Territory. The 'Point of Beginning' is the starting point, as well as the prototype for future surveys of all other public lands west, eventually reaching all of the way to the Pacific Ocean. This government system of recta-linear Surveys included Base Lines (east-west lines), Principal Meridians (north-south lines), Ranges (north-south strips enclosed by Range Lines), and Townships (east-west strips enclosed by Base Lines). One thirty-sixth of a township was called a Section. A 640-acre Section was the smallest unit of land offered for sale by the federal government. The first westward Base Line was created here near the north shore of the Ohio River.  This site, on the Ohio River, was chosen because Pennsylvania's boundary had been recently established.

**WELLSVILLE, OH** (mile 48, RDB):

Wellsville was settled in the late 18th Century by William Wells.  By 1815, steamboats were regularly stopping in Wellsville.  The town also became a stop for the Cleveland-Ohio River stagecoach line.  In 1852, the Cleveland & Pittsburgh Railroad reached Wellsville, making the town its southern terminus.  Much of Wellsville's early history is preserved by the Wellsville Historical Society in The Wellsville River Museum.  There is also a Pennsylvania Railroad caboose car located outside the museum.

**YELLOW CREEK, OH** (mile 50.5, RDB):

In 1774, two miles downstream from Wellsville, the Yellow Creek Massacre occurred.  A group of whites ambushed and murdered the relatives of Mingo Indian Chief Logan, as they exited a local tavern after celebrating a successful hunting expedition.  Chief Logan retaliated.  That retaliation pleased Colonial Virginia Governor, Lord Dunmore, because now he had the excuse to initiate his war.  Some knowledgeable accounts maintain that Lord Dunmore had used the Native Americans as pawns for other devious purposes.  For more details, please read the Point Pleasant Section –215 miles downriver on the Ohio.

**TORONTO, OH** (miles 58-60, RDB):

Newburg's Landing was first settled in the 19th Century.  In 1881, when the railroad arrived, the name was changed to Sloan Station.  Later, after a vote, the name was changed again to Toronto, hoping to emulate that clean large city in Ontario Canada.  By the 20th Century, Toronto became a center of heavy industry with several large factories around the town. Toronto is also known as the 'Gem City.'  In the late 20th Century, as many other towns in the region had done, Toronto's heavy manufacturing plummeted as industries went overseas.  Today, only Titanium Metals Corporation remains.

Late movie-actor Robert Urich is from Toronto.  A local who graduated high school with Urich, told me that Urich was a real good guy –a clean liver, a non drinker, etc, and was unlike so many others who grew-up here –thus reinforcing the adage that 'only the good die young.'

**WEIRTON, WV** (miles 62-65, LDB):

In the late 1700s, Holliday's Cove was founded.  In 1909, Ernest Weir built a steel mill, the Weirton Steel Company, north of town.  By 1940, the area of 'Weirton,' located near that steel mill, was said to be the largest unincorporated city in the country.  In 1947, unincorporated Weirton, Holliday's Cove and two unincorporated towns merged to form an incorporated Weirton.  ISG Weirton Inc. –formerly the Weirton Steel Company, is the nation's second largest tin maker, and the fourth largest private employer in West Virginia.  There is no 'Weirton Waterfront.'  The main part of Weirton is more than a couple of miles away from the Ohio River.

**STEUBENVILLE, OH** (miles 67-69, RDB)

In 1787, Fort Steuben was named after Baron Frederich Steuben, a Revolutionary War veteran.  Fort Steuben was a log fort, constructed to protect government land surveyors laying out the first seven Ranges (i.e., six-mile wide vertical strips of land) in the Northwest Territory.  The town of Steubenville, and the seat of Jefferson County, followed.  The government surveyed land was then sold or offered to soldiers as payment for their services during the Revolutionary War.

In 1803, when Meriwether Lewis passed Steubenville, he described it as "a small well built thriving place with several respectable families."  One can still visit a tastefully done reconstructed Fort Steuben (☎ 740-283-1787 or www.oldfortsteuben.com) off Third Street near the Ohio River –at its original location.  Also in Steubenville, one can find many large river floodwall murals, the Jefferson County Historical Museum, and the Creegan Animation Factory. The Creegan Company (☎ 740-283-3708 or www.creegans.com) is the nation's largest manufacturer of animated and costume characters. Entertainer Dean Martin is Steubenville's favorite son.

**FOLLANSBEE, WV** (miles 70-71, LDB):
The large plant on the river is a coke plant. It was originally owned by the Wheeling-Pittsburgh Steel Company, but now operates as Mountain State Carbon. Successful college and professional football coach Lou Holtz was born in Follansbee.

**WELLSBURG, WV** (mile 74, LDB)
Wellsburg was founded in 1789. Soon, Wellsburg was a busy port sending flatboats with their down-bound cargo south and west. Wellsburg became the seat of Brooke County. Patrick Gass, one of the Corps of Discovery's members, resided in Wellsburg. Gass joined the Corps of Discovery as a private, but was soon voted on to be one of its sergeants. He was an adept carpenter and one of the Corps most reliable members. Gass published a journal of the Lewis and Clark expedition, more focusing on the human aspects of the Corps of Discovery. Gass out-lived his Corps comrades, living to the age of 98 years old in 1870. When Gass was nearly 90 years old, he tried to volunteer in the Union Army at the onset of the Civil War. The house that Gass built still stands on the corner of 10th and Main Streets in Wellsburg.

**BRILLIANT, OH** (mile 75, RDB):
The town of Brilliant was named after a glass factory that was once located here.

**MARTINS FERRY, OH** (miles 88-89, RDB):
As early as 1779, settlers began arriving in the Martins Ferry area, but a town was not permanently settled until much later. In 1865, Martins Ferry officially became a city. By the turn of the 19th Century, Martins Ferry had become an important river port, rail hub, and industrial center. During the latter part of the 20th Century, local industries moved overseas, and the population was reduced to a fraction of what it once was.

**WHEELING, WV** (miles 89-93, LDB):
'Wheeling' is a Native American name, perhaps meaning the 'place of the skull.' One legend has it that an Indian chief placed the decapitated head of a prisoner on a pole near the mouth of the nearby creek as a message to warn off intruders. In 1769, Ebenezer, Jonathan, Andrew, and Silas Zane arrived, and started Virginia's first permanent settlement on the Ohio River. In the late 18th Century, this site was chosen because it was then situated at the head of the 'very navigable' portion of the Ohio River, and was perceived to be a great potential transportation hub. In 1774, Fort Fincastle was built on the order of colonial governor Lord Dunmore. Fort Fincastle was to be an outpost during forthcoming Lord Dunmore's War. In 1776, the fort was renamed Fort Henry in honor of Virginia first post-colonial governor, Patrick Henry. In 1781 and 1782, during the American Revolution, Fort Henry had either been under siege or attacked by forces of British and Indians. In 1782, one of the last battles of the American Revolution was fought at Fort Henry. Folklore was made, when teenager Betty Zane volunteered to risk her young life by making a 60-yard dash outside the barricaded fort in order to retrieve some badly needed gunpowder. She successfully returned with several pounds of gunpowder stuffed into a tablecloth. The surprised potential attackers outside the fort were either bewildered or unwilling to fire upon the young heroine. Thus, during the closing days of the American Revolution, an attack on Fort Henry was thwarted. In Martins Ferry, across the river, where Betty eventually settled, she is honored every year with the Betty Zane Frontier Days celebration.

**Sketch 8-C: The Ohio River –from Rayland, OH to New Martinsville, WV**

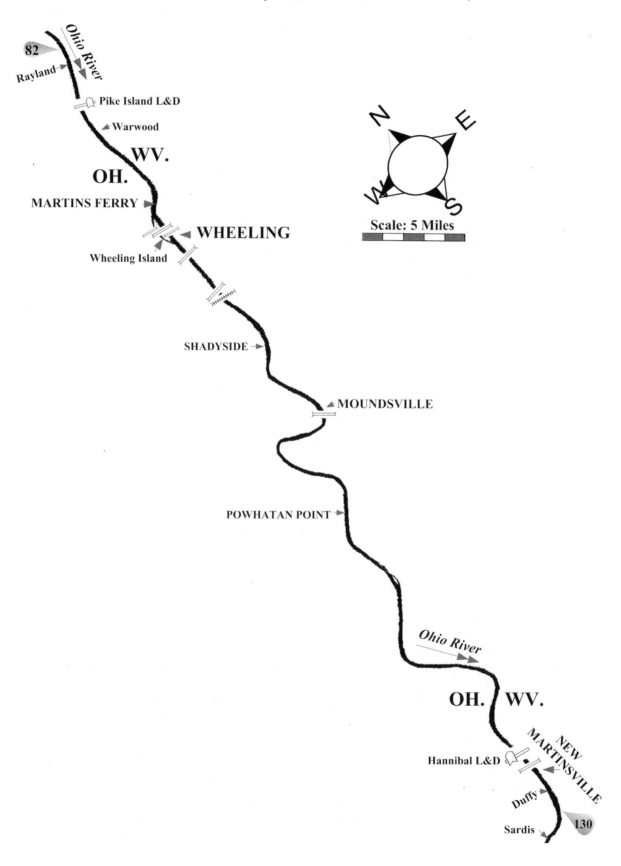

82

Ohio River

Rayland

Pike Island L&D

Warwood

WV.

OH.

MARTINS FERRY

WHEELING

Wheeling Island

SHADYSIDE

MOUNDSVILLE

POWHATAN POINT

Ohio River

OH. WV.

Hannibal L&D

NEW MARTINSVILLE

Duffy

Sardis

130

N E W S

Scale: 5 Miles

In the early 19<sup>th</sup> Century Wheeling was vying with Pittsburgh for the gateway to the west. Spearheaded by Albert Gallatin and Henry Clay of the Jefferson Administration, Congress passed legislation in 1806 approving a 'national road.' In 1811, the National Road was started at Cumberland Maryland and was initially called the Cumberland Road. By 1818, the National Road, also known as 'Main Street of America,' had reached Wheeling. Later it became US Route 40. When the National Road ended in Wheeling, the Ohio River was just the natural westward extension. The National Road expanded already existing towns, created new ones, and became a vital artery carrying folks to the rapidly growing area on the western side of the Allegheny Mountains, and on the north side of the Ohio River. By the 1830s the National Road was 750 miles long, passed through six states, and had reached Vandalia Illinois. Besides the important river cities of Wheeling and Brownsville, the National Road also passed through the river cities of Zanesville (on the Muskingum River) and Terre Haute (on the Wabash River). By the 1840s the National Road (www.HistoricNationalRoad.org) was likely the busiest route in the entire country. In 1849, the 1,010-foot long suspension bridge to Wheeling Island was the world's longest.

Nevertheless, by 1852, Pittsburgh beat out Wheeling in local importance when the Pennsylvania Railroad arrived there. Wheeling retained importance as a river, rail, and road hub establishing successful industries in glass, cut nails, cigars, tobacco, and beer. The LaBelle Nail plant, constructed in 1852 in South Wheeling, was once the largest cut nail plant in the world. The Bloch Brothers Tobacco Company, famous for its huge 'Chew Mail Pouch Tobacco' signs appearing on thousands of barns in a six state area, was located in Wheeling. Many of these barns became historical landmarks because of this classic advertising scheme.

During the late 19<sup>th</sup> Century, Wheeling had become the third city in the nation to have electric streetcars as well as the fourth city to install electric street lights. In 1907, an Ohio River flood crested at 50 feet and drowned many folks in Wheeling. Wheeling Island, a large island two miles long, is home to many unique old Victorian homes as well as to the Wheeling Island Racetrack and Gaming Center. The Wheeling Custom House, built in 1859, is now known as West Virginia's Independence Hall Museum (☎ 304-238-1300) and is considered the birthplace of West Virginia in 1863. This first capitol building of West Virginia is located at the corner of 16<sup>th</sup> and Market Streets. Wheeling, the fourth largest city in West Virginia, is the seat of Ohio County. The Kruger Street Toy and Train Museum (☎ 304-242-8133, www.toyandtrain.com) is located in a restored Victorian era schoolhouse.

**SHADYSIDE, OH** (miles 97-98, RDB):
In June 1990, 26 people lost their lives, 80 homes were completely destroyed, and another 250 homes were damaged. Localized weather maps that morning gave only a slight foreboding of the flash floods that would unfold later that day. A slow-moving front was draped across the Midwest. Over the state of Ohio, rain was heavy, but not excessive. But slow-moving thunderstorms were drenching the hills of southeastern Ohio with 3-to-4 inches of rain. Also it had been a wet spring. The ground was saturated, and it couldn't absorb any more water. Before long, a 15-to-20 foot wall of water was racing towards the Ohio River along three small creeks near Shadyside. Buildings, cars, and bridges were swept into the Ohio River. Two bodies were found as far away as the Hannibal Lock and Dam, 30 miles downstream on the Ohio River. Flash flooding had never been experienced in these streams before, although these streams did have similar characteristics to other flash flood-prone streams common in the eastern Ohio River Valley.

# Old Victorian House on Wheeling Island, West Virginia

Municipal Wharf and Heritage Port, Wheeling, West Virginia

**MOUNDSVILLE, WV** (mile 102, LDB):

The Moundsville area had been settled by Native Americans before the Greek and Roman Empires of Europe. The city derives its name from Indian mounds built by the Adena Culture. The largest mound, the Grave Creek Mound [and State Park], is located near the center of town about six blocks from the Ohio River. This mound is 69 feet high, 295 feet in diameter, and consists of 60,000 tons of displaced earth. In the 1830s, a vault dug into the mound revealed skeletal remains, ivory beads, seashells, cooper bracelets, and an un-deciphered inscription in stone. The nearby museum (☎ 800-843-4128) is well done and worth a visit.

In 1752, Christopher Gist, an Ohio River exploring companion of George Washington, was known to have visited the area. In the early 1770s, a stockade known as Fort Tomlinson was constructed on the flats near Grave Creek. Moundsville was on its way. The old Moundsville High School was built atop Fort Tomlinson. In 1852, in nearby Rosby's Rock, the first continuous railroad line from the Atlantic Ocean to the Ohio region was established when the B&O Railroad joined the Baltimore & Wheeling Railroad. This feat was accomplished after constructing 11 tunnels and 113 bridges.

The former West Virginia Penitentiary is located two blocks southeast of the Grave Creek Mound. This Gothic-style prison was the second public building constructed in the newly formed state of West Virginia. In 1995, the prison closed it doors, in part because the five foot by seven foot cells were deemed to be cruel and unusual punishment. Today, the prison is open for tours. The Stand Theatre, the Marx Toy Museum, and the Fostoria Glass Museum are also located in Moundville. Moundsville, the seat of Marshall County, hosts its annual 'Riverfront Festival' in mid-September.

**POWHATAN POINT, OH** (mile 109, RDB):

Powhatan Point, founded in 1849, was named after the powerful Indian chief who lived in tidewater Virginia at the time of the early colonists. Powhatan ruled over 30 tribes, and fathered the legendary daughter, Pocahontas. Before succumbing to smallpox in her very young life, Pocahontas is alleged to have done some remarkable things to improve relations between Native Americans and early colonists.

**NEW MARTINSVILLE, WV** (miles 127-128, LDB):

New Martinsville was named after early settler Presley Martin. About 1846, the name was changed from Martinsville to New Martinsville. This friendly town is the county seat of Wetzel County. Wetzel County is the first West Virginia County south of the northern panhandle and the Mason-Dixon Line. The four West Virginia counties north of New Martinsville all border on two states –Pennsylvania and Ohio. In the central part of town, there's a general store, grocer, post office, and a nice restaurant. A couple of miles north of town, there's a large shopping center along with several restaurants, auto parts stores, a few motels, and a Walmart. New Martinsville hosts its annual 'River Heritage Days' in late June.

The Ohio River's Long Reach, near Sistersville, West Virginia

Pomeroy, Ohio Riverfront

# CHAPTER 9
# The Parkersburg Area ...on the Ohio River from Sardis to Gallipolis OH, including the Hocking and Little Kanawha Rivers

This section of the upper Ohio River is slightly over 150 miles long. It contains the better part of four pools –the Willow Island, Belleville, Racine, and Robert Byrd Pools. The longest straight section of the entire Ohio River, the Long Reach, is included in this chapter. The Long Reach extends about 16 miles downriver from Paden City West Virginia. About 70 miles beyond the downriver end of the Long Reach, and for about another 30 miles our river twists, turns, and flows in just about every conceivable direction, including northeast and southeast (i.e., far from that west-southwesterly trend). In this chapter, the terrain softens a bit. A few modest-sized cities (i.e., Marietta Ohio and Parkersburg West Virginia) and many small and modest-sized towns (Paden City, Sistersville, St. Marys, Williamstown, Vienna, Ravenswood and Point Pleasant –in West Virginia, and Belpre, Pomeroy, Middleport, and Gallipolis –in Ohio), in large part owe their existence to the Ohio River. Along the river, there are still pockets of heavy industry, but this industry is not as dense as in the previous upriver chapter. While heavy industry exists, there are many sections of the Ohio River that seem remote, and look like they were 200 years ago –except for the river being pooled (i.e., affording higher water with less current).

Two major tributaries flow into the Ohio River in this section –the Muskingum flowing southward from the heart of Ohio, and the Kanawha flowing northwestward from southeastern West Virginia. These two rivers are addressed in the next two chapters. The Muskingum River and most of Marietta Ohio are addressed in Chapter 10. The Kanawha River and Charleston West Virginia are addressed in Chapter 11. Chapter 12 will address the next downriver section of the Ohio River.

The following table summarizes the locks and pools on this section of Ohio River with some overlap into adjacent river sections:

**Table 9-A, Locks and Pools on the Ohio River, from New Martinsville to Gallipolis:**

| Lock and Pool Name | Mile | Lock Side | Telephone Number ☎ | Opens for R. Vessels | Lift (in ft) | Pool Length (miles) |
|---|---|---|---|---|---|---|
| Hannibal L & D (Hannibal. OH) | 126.4 | RDB | 740-483-2305 | 24/7 | 21 | 42.2 |
| Willow Island L & D (Reno, OH) | 161.7 | RDB | 740-374-8710 | 24/7 | 20 | 35.3 |
| Belleville L & D (Reedsville, OH) | 203.9 | RDB | 304-863-6331 | 24/7 | 22 | 42.2 |
| Racine L&D (Letart, WV) | 237.5 | LDB | 304-882-2118 | 24/7 | 22 | 33.6 |
| R. Byrd L&D (Gallipolis Fry,WV) | 279.2 | LDB | 304-576-2272 | 24/7 | 23 | 41.7 |

**PADEN CITY, WV** (mile 133.4, LDB –Left Descending Bank –I.E. West Virginia)

Paden City is at the upriver end of the Ohio River's Long Reach. The town was settled in 1796 by Revolutionary War Veteran and Pennsylvania Quaker Obediah Paden. In 1877, Paden City was the site of West Virginia's first organized labor union meeting when the Knights of Labor –a predecessor to the Industrial Workers of the World –met. There's a motel, gas station, hardware store, general store, and restaurants in town. A very nice park/campground/ boat ramp is situated on the Ohio River, but it's about a half-mile from the center of town.

**SISTERSVILLE, WV** (mile 137.5, LDB):

In 1770, George Washington camped in this area during a survey trip. Washington was likely one of the first to label this part of the river, 'the Long Reach.' In 1776, Sistersville was settled by Charles Wells. The town was named for the Wells' sisters. In 1815, a ferry service, that still operates today, was started between Sistersville and Fly across the Ohio River. In the late 19th Century, Sistersville became a small oil boomtown. Sistersville hosts its annual 'Oil and Gas Festival' in mid-September.

Sistersville has a hardware store, general store, auto parts store, pharmacy, a few restaurants, and the historic Victorian style Wells Inn. Between Sistersville and St. Marys (i.e., about 17 miles downriver), there are several riverfront campgrounds on both sides of the river, and many of these campgrounds have boat docks.

**WAYNE NATIONAL FOREST, OH** (miles 137-163, RDB –Right Descending Bank)

National Forests are protected areas managed by the US Department of Agriculture, for multiple uses –recreation, limited hunting and limited timber harvesting. The quarter-million acre Wayne National Forest has three separate large tracts of land –all located in southeastern Ohio. Oak and hickory dominate the hardwood tree species in this part of the Wayne National Forest (☎ 740-373-9055).

**ST MARYS, WV** (mile 155, LDB)

St. Marys was chartered in 1815. Its founder, Alexander H. Creel, named the town in honor of the Virgin Mary. According to legend, the Virgin appeared to Creel in a vision one night as his steamboat passed by this location. St. Marys is the seat of Pleasants County. The county was named for James Pleasants –a Virginia governor and senator. In St. Marys, there's a motel, convenience story, grocer, several restaurants and gas stations.

Nearby, Middle Island is a part of the much larger Ohio River Islands National Wildlife Refuge System, administered by the US Fish and Wildlife Service. The Ohio River Wildlife Refuge is scattered on floodplains over 360 miles and in three states. The system consists of over 20 islands, and it is still expanding. The Ohio River Refuge makes a great habitat for hundreds of bird species –many are migratory, more than 50 fish species, many mammals, amphibians, reptiles, with scores of species of endangered freshwater mussels (in many cases threatened by the introduction of non-native zebra mussel). The Middle Island Refuge may be the only Ohio River Wildlife Refuge Island accessible by car. Nearly all the other islands are accessible only by boat. If you do visit any Ohio River Wildlife Refuge Island by boat, please go at a 'no wake' speed. You're not permitted to camp, have wood fires, or to tie-up overnight on these enchanting and enlightening little islands.

**NEWPORT, OH** (mile 156, RDB)

In 1862, Captain Gordon Greene was born in Newport, Ohio. During the 1890s, in Cincinnati, Greene started one of the most successful and long-lived steamboat lines –the Greene Steamboat Line. During his lifetime, Captain Gordon owned 25 packet boats. Also in 1890, Captain Gordon married Mary Becker Greene of the Newport area. Captain Mary Becker Greene was one of the first women to earn her pilots and masters license, all while raising three sons – two of which also became captains. For more than a half century Mary Becker Greene, was one of the more noted figures on the Ohio and Mississippi Rivers. The Greene Steamboat Line evolved into the Delta Queen Steamboat Company. Captain Gordon Greene died in 1927, and is buried in Newport Cemetery. In her latter years, Captain Mary was the hostess aboard the Delta Queen. In 1949, Captain Mary passed away at 79 years old in her cabin aboard the Delta Queen.

**WILLIAMSTOWN, WV** (mile 172, LDB)

In 1787, Isaac Williams settled on the present site. In 1790, as Marietta was starting out, there was a crop failure due to a late planting and an early frost. The helpful settlers on the Williamston side of the river saved the new settlers in Marietta from famine by sharing their bounty. The big narrow island in the Ohio River northeast of Williamston and Marietta has been called Kerr, Duvall's, Meigs, Muskingum, Buckley's, and Marietta Island.

## Sketch 9-A: The Ohio River –from Sardis, OH to Blennerhassett Island, WV

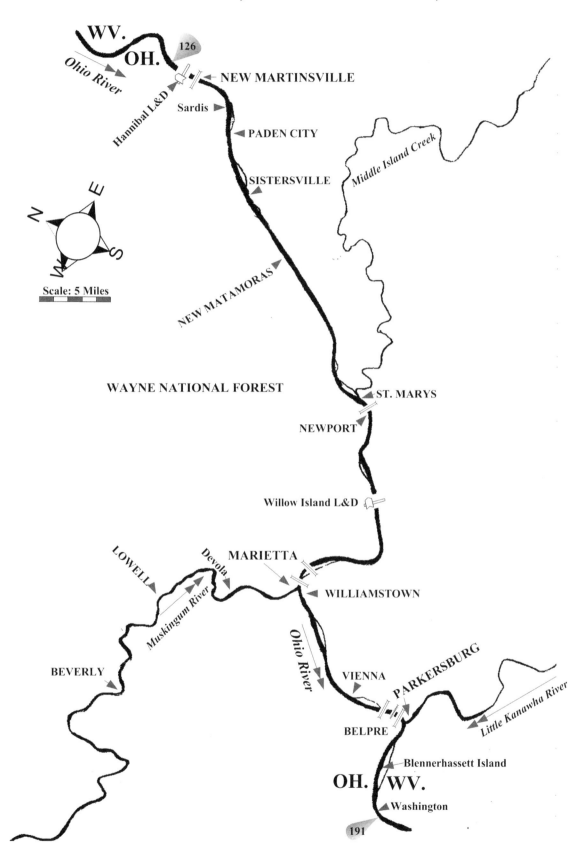

WV.
OH.
Ohio River
126
NEW MARTINSVILLE
Hannibal L&D
Sardis
PADEN CITY
SISTERSVILLE
Middle Island Creek

N
E
S
W
Scale: 5 Miles

NEW MATAMORAS

WAYNE NATIONAL FOREST
ST. MARYS
NEWPORT

Willow Island L&D

LOWELL
Devola
MARIETTA
WILLIAMSTOWN
Muskingum River

BEVERLY
Ohio River
VIENNA
PARKERSBURG
BELPRE
Little Kanawha River

OH. WV.
Blennerhassett Island
Washington
191

Unfortunately the once prodigious 19<sup>th</sup> and 20<sup>th</sup> Century glassmaking of West Virginia has succumbed to mass-produced and cheaper imported products. Nonetheless, today Fenton Art Glass is still the town's largest company with over 450 employees. In 1905, brothers Frank and John Fenton started a glass decorating company in Martins Ferry Ohio. In 1906, their third and fourth brothers joined them as they broke ground for a new glass factory on the present site. Williamston was chosen because of its proximity to a source of natural gas. As imported glass was snatching the marketplace by the mid-20<sup>th</sup> Century, Fenton retained its focus on high-end, meticulously crafted, handmade glass and utilized a wide array of distinctive colors (as many as 30 different colors), and unique crimping patterns, adorned with painstaking hand painting. This strategy worked, and Fenton was able to remain in business, while many other local glass companies folded. Today, Fenton is among the world's foremost producers of handmade glass. Knowledgeable collectors often await new Fenton editions. The free glass-making factory tour, in-house museum, and gift shop are outstanding. If you find yourself anywhere near this area, we highly recommend stopping for a visit at Fenton Art Glass (☎ 304-375-7772 or www.fentonartglass.com) at 420 Caroline Street.

**MARIETTA, OH** (mile 172, RDB)

Marietta, along with the Muskingum River, is addressed in the next chapter, Chapter 10.

**VIENNA, WV** (mile 179-181, LDB)

In 1794, Vienna was founded by a Revolutionary War physician, Dr. Joseph Spencer. For his war time services, Spencer was given a 5,000-acre land grant. He named his new farming community after Vienna New Jersey, where he had participated in a Revolutionary War battle. Not until the 20<sup>th</sup> Century, did this area prosper. When the roads between Parkersburg and Marietta improved, Vienna morphed from farming to a desirable residential community that it still is today.

**BELPRE, OH** (mile 184, RDB)

In 1789, Revolutionary War veterans and New England farmers started settling Belpre after arriving by flatboat. They named the area 'Belle Prairie'. In the early years agricultural goods (e.g., fruits, vegetables, and grain) where shipped from Belpre as far as New Orleans. By the mid 18<sup>th</sup> Century, industry had replaced agriculture, and polymer production (a large group that includes synthetic plastics) began dominating local industry.

**PARKERSBURG, WV** (mile 184, LDB):

Parkersburg, originally named Newport, was first laid out in the 1780s. Revolutionary War Captain Alexander Parker was granted land in this area. In 1809, title conflicts between the Newport city planners and the Parker estate were settled in favor of Parker's heirs. The area was soon renamed Parkersburg. By 1811, steamboats were regularly stopping in Parkersburg. In 1857, a spur of the Baltimore and Ohio Railroad reached Parkersburg, but train cars had to be ferried across the river to Belpre Ohio. In 1860, one of the world's largest oil fields at the time had been discovered 40 miles from Parkersburg, on the Little Kanawha River.

By 1863, Parkersburg had also become a power center shaping the new state. West Virginia's first elected governor, Arthur Boreman, was from Parkersburg, as were three of the state's next ten governors. During the Civil War, Parkersburg served as an important troop transfer point and medical center. By the end of the Civil War, Parkersburg had changed from a sleepy southern town to a bustling northern city. By 1871, the B&O Railroad Bridge across the Ohio River –the longest railroad bridge in the world at that time –was completed, thus further spurring growth. During the 1880s, an oil and natural gas boom positioned the town as a refining and shipping hub. By 1900, oil production had significantly ebbed, but natural gas production remained strong. The city's oil and gas heritage is revived at the Oil and Gas Museum, located

# Sketch 9-B: The Middle Ohio River Region –from Marietta to the Kentucky River

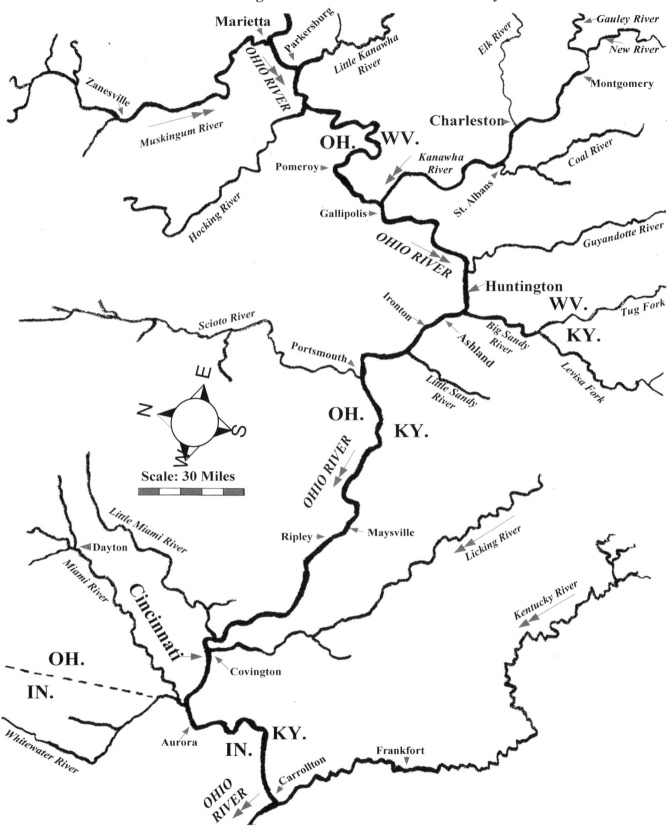

downtown at 119 Third Street (☎ 304-485-5446).  The Blennerhassett Museum of Regional History (☎ 304-422-0611, www.wvparks.com/blennerhassett) is located at 2<sup>nd</sup> and Juliana Streets in the compact downtown.  The red-tiled roof of the Wood County Courthouse, built in 1899, looms over Parkersburg's skyline.  Today, Parkersburg is the third largest city in West Virginia.

Parkersburg sits at the confluence of the Little Kanawha and Ohio Rivers.  Point Park is at the LDB of the Ohio, and the RDB of the Little Kanawha River.  The Point Park boat landing is within walking distance from the museums.  In its early days, Point Park was a public landing for flatboats, as well as the site of a dozen local buildings, including a military blockhouse. Parkersburg has seen its share of flooding.  In 1913, flood water crested at 59 feet.  In 1950, the city completed a floodwall through the Point Park area.  In 1977, when the Ohio River crested at 55 feet, Parkersburg was mostly spared, thanks to that floodwall.

## BLENNERHASSETT ISLAND, WV (miles 186-190, LDB):

At nearly four miles in length, Blennerhassett Island is the fifth largest island in the Ohio River.  In 1796, 31-year old Irish aristocrat Harman Blennerhassett married his niece, Margaret. The couple, ostracized by their families, soon moved to a relatively remote island in the Ohio River.  In 1798, they constructed their mansion on the island.  By 1805, the Blennerhassetts had befriended controversial Revolutionary War colonel, and ex-vice president Aaron Burr.  The Blennerhassetts, intrigued by Burr's plan, provided liberal funds, and offered their island as a location for training troops and storing supplies for Burr's scheme to create a new North American republic.

Aaron Burr, albeit a Revolutionary war hero, was likely a reckless adventurer more than anything else.  Although he served as a US Senator from New York, and vice-president (in Thomas Jefferson's first administration), he showed a casual disregard for public service, and was quoted as saying, "…politics were for fun, honor, and profit."  In 1804, Burr eliminated his political arch enemy, Alexander Hamilton, in a New Jersey pistol duel.

At a critical time for westward expansion in America, Burr was concocting a scheme that was highly incompatible with President Jefferson's grand plan.  Burr wished to carve out an empire from the territory west of the Appalachians as well as from parts of Mexico.  In several ways –with agricultural goods and commerce, this newly concocted southwestern republic could thwart the ambitions of a westward expanding America.  Part of Burr's scheme involved provoking a rebellion in the Spanish-held west.  Learning of Burr's scheme, President Jefferson ordered the arrest of Burr, Blennerhassett, and anyone else contemplating such an overthrow in Spanish Territory.  In the hot seat, Burr surrendered to authorities.  He was charged with treason, for assembling an armed force (on Blennerhassett Island), plotting to take New Orleans, and planning to separate the Atlantic states from potential western states.

In 1807, Chief Justice John Marshall presided at Burr's trial.  Marshall subpoenaed President Jefferson in order to provide solid documentations against Burr.  Jefferson declared, as the president, he should not be required to provide the Court with their requested paperwork due to his executive privilege.  Jefferson further argued that he should not be held subject to the demand of the Judiciary.  Marshall sided with Burr's defense.  This ruling was most significant, because it suggested that like all citizens, the US President was also subject to the law.  Burr's trial brought into question the powers of executive privilege and the independence of the Judicial Branch.  Burr's case also required Marshall to reconsider the definition of treason.  Marshall ruled that because Burr had not committed an act of war, he could not be found guilty of treason. The First Amendment guaranteed Burr the right to voice opposition to the federal government and that 'merely suggesting war, or engaging in a conspiracy, was not enough to require a conviction of treason.'

Despite encountering the full force of the Jefferson Administration, Burr was acquitted. For the next four years, Burr lived in Northern Europe.  Burr returned to America in 1812.

Ironically, in 1835, when Burr lived to see an American-backed Texas Revolution concocted against Mexico, he wryly stated, "What was treason in me thirty years ago is now patriotism."

As the Burr's conspiracy collapsed, Harman Blennerhassett fled down the river, but was caught, and remained a prisoner until well after Burr was released. The ill-fated Blennerhassetts died close to poverty. In 1811, the Blennerhassett mansion accidentally burned to the ground. In 1973, the process of rebuilding the mansion was started. Today, the 500-acre island is now a state park and a popular tourist attraction.

**LITTLE KANAWHA RIVER, WV** (mile 184.7, LDB):

The Little Kanawha River has been a fairly important commercial waterway in the development of West Virginia. The early petroleum and logging industries took advantage of this slow-moving, often muddy Ohio River tributary. Today, the first five miles of the narrow Little Kanawha is peppered with industrial activity, including sand and gravel pits with a fair amount of barge activity. The river, about 160 miles in total length, generally flows northwestward from the center of the state.

**WASHINGTON, WV** (mile 191, LDB)

In 1948, the Dupont Chemical Company opened a factory here. This plant produces a wide variety of polymer products, and is the world's largest producer of Teflon. Little Hocking Ohio is across the river from Washington West Virginia.

**BELLEVILLE DAM, OH** (mile 203.9, RDB):

On January 6, 2005, only days before the fatalities at the Montgomery Lock and Dam, there was another similar towboat accident at the Belleville Lock and Dam. The towboat *MV Jon J. Strong* didn't have enough power to push 12 coal-laden barges far enough away from the Belleville Lock. The *Jon J. Strong* didn't go over the dam like the *Elizabeth M*, and no lives were lost. However, nine of the twelve coal barges broke lose after going through the lock. Three barges crashed into the dam and got caught in the tainter gates. The dam was jammed opened, and the pool level was lost. The 42-mile Belleville Pool was closed for nearly two weeks, until the smashed half-sunken barges could be pulled from the teeth of the dam's gates. In lost revenue alone, this accident was estimated to have cost about $2.5 million per day.

Point Pleasant, West Virginia and Riverfront Park

# Sketch 9-C: The Ohio River –from Little Hocking to Gallipolis, Ohio

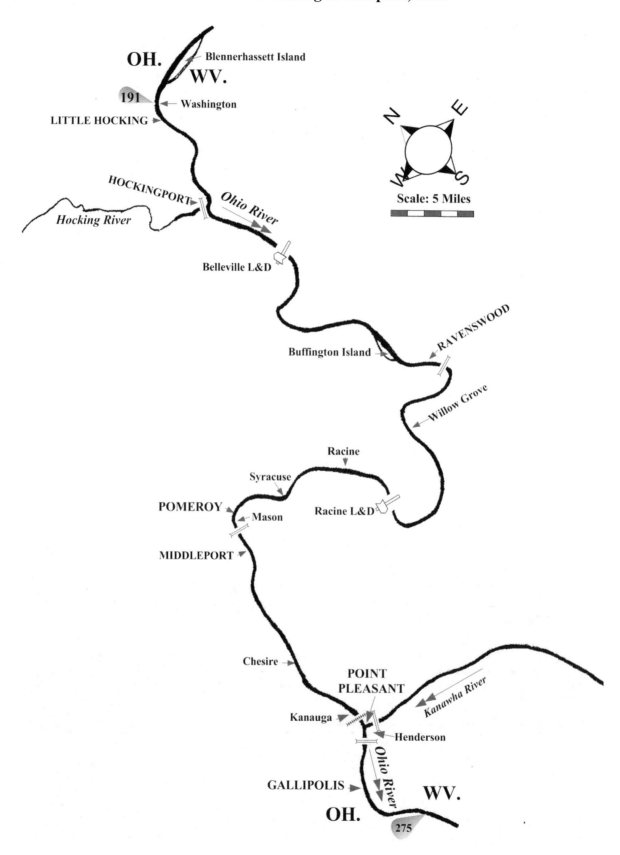

OH.

WV.

Blennerhassett Island

191

LITTLE HOCKING

Washington

HOCKINGPORT

*Ohio River*

*Hocking River*

N
E
W
S

Scale: 5 Miles

Belleville L&D

RAVENSWOOD

Buffington Island

Willow Grove

Racine

Syracuse

POMEROY

Mason

Racine L&D

MIDDLEPORT

Chesire

POINT
PLEASANT

*Kanawha River*

Kanauga

Henderson

*Ohio River*

GALLIPOLIS

WV.

OH.

275

**BUFFINGTON ISLAND, OH** (mile 217, RDB):

Buffington Island was the site of a July 1863 Civil War Battle. After going on a ten day rampage through Indiana and Ohio, Confederate Cavalry General John Hunt Morgan tried to return to the South by crossing the Ohio River at a ford near Buffington Island. But the Union anticipated this too, and sent gunboats and troops to Buffington Island to block Morgan's escape route. About three hundred Confederates soldiers were successfully able to ford the river, before a pitched battle broke out. During the battle close to 1,000 Confederates were either killed or captured. John Hunt Morgan and about 700 soldiers broke off the conflict and continued retreating northward. Most of Morgan's men were captured a week later near Salineville Ohio. During and after the Battle at Buffington Island, the locals from Portland Ohio cared for the dying and wounded Union as well as Confederate soldiers. Three Ohioans who fought for the Union at Buffington Island would later go on to become US presidents –Rutherford B Hayes, James Garfield, and William McKinley. Near the road, there are covered picnic pavilions, outdoor grills, and an Indian mound. We safely anchored overnight out of the main Ohio River channel near the northern tip of Buffington Island.

**RAVENSWOOD, WV** (mile 220, LDB):

In 1770, George Washington acquired about a 2,500 acre parcel of land here. By 1810, the settlement of Ravenswood was firmly established. There are restaurants, gas stations, a grocer, a hardware store, an auto parts store, and a few stores in a shopping center at the north (i.e., upriver) end of town.

**NEAR WILLOW GROVE, WV** (mile 228, LDB):

In the spring of 1910, the 235-foot steamboat *Virginia* ended-up in a cornfield 600 feet away from the Ohio River, as high water receded. The *Virginia* stayed here for six months, until the high water returned and she was able to refloat herself. This incident provided the fodder for the colorful ballad, *"Steamboat in a Cornfield"* by John Hartford.

**HOCKINGPORT AND THE HOCKING RIVER, OH** (mile 199.2, RDB):

In 1774, during Lord Dunmore's War, it's believed that the contingent of Virginia militiamen led by Lord Dunmore departed the Ohio River near the mouth of the Hocking River for an overland march to the Shawnee Village (i.e., near present-day Circleville Ohio). Hockingport sits on the LDB of the Hocking River near its confluence with the Ohio River. "Hocking" or "Hokhochen" is a Native American word meaning something like "gourd shaped" –referring to the river's shape near Logan Ohio. In 1843, the short-lived Hocking Canal once linked Athens with Lancaster Ohio and the Ohio & Erie Canal. Athens Ohio, a little more than 25 miles up the Hocking River from Hockingport, is home to Ohio University. Between Athens and Nelsonville, and paralleling the Hocking River, the Hockhocking-Adena Bikeway serves as a major source of recreation for students from Ohio University.

The depth of the enchanting Hocking River, near Hockingport and its mouth, is ample. However, overhead clearances could be restrictive. The second overhead clearance, a power line, appears lower than the first obstacle –a highway bridge. Even though you have enough overhead clearance for that bridge, you may not have enough clearance for those powerlines? Nonetheless, the low dangling powerlines are not level across the entire width of the Hocking River.

**POMEROY, OH** (mile 250, RDB):

This narrow strip of level land along the river owes it existence to the salt, coal, and the river. In 1805, the first coal mine was opened. By the early 1820s, the first salt wells and furnaces were built. The salt furnaces required much fuel. Coal was that fuel. Around 1819, a village was formed. By about 1825, wood became so scarce, that the villagers had to turn to coal in order to heat their homes. Valentine Horton and Wyllys Pomeroy were two early coal industrialists. In the 1830s, Horton designed coal barges that were able to replace coal flatboats and rafts. By 1835, Horton had developed the first coal-powered (i.e., replacing wood as fuel) steam towboat, the *Condor*. As well as being shipped downstream to Cincinnati, coal was also shipped upstream to Pittsburgh. The Pomeroy area soon developed an iron industry. Showboats and excursion boats frequently visited the Pomeroy's Wharf

The main street through town, Front Street, actually borders the Ohio River on one side of the street. Most of Pomeroy is narrow – only a couple blocks wide, and along the river. The Meigs County Courthouse was built into a hillside, and is uniquely mentioned in 'Ripley's Believe it or Not' as a building that can be entered from the ground level on three separate floors. During the last weekend in September, Pomeroy hosts its Sternwheeler River Festival.

## MIDDLEPORT, OH (mile 252, RDB):

Middleport started being settled in 1797, when a Revolutionary War officer built a log cabin for his family on the banks of the Ohio. Middleport was so named because it's nearly half-way between Pittsburgh and Cincinnati. Steamboats departing those two cities simultaneously would typically pass each other near Middleport. Actually Middleport is slightly closer to Cincinnati, but the journey from Cincinnati was upstream. In 1850, the steamboat *Buckeye State* made the 470-mile upriver run from Cincinnati to Pittsburgh in a record time of 43 hours.

## RELICS OF WORLD WAR II TNT PLANT, WV (mile 261, LDB):

During the early 1940s, the West Virginia Ordinance Works (commonly called the TNT Plant) was a very busy place. Point Pleasant, four miles downriver, was a boom town housing hundreds of chemists, scientists, engineers, and laborers. Today, there's a trail through the relics, including 100 storage magazines, of this old explosives manufacturing site. The present hiking trails are administered by the nearby West Virginia State Farm Museum (☎ 304-675-5737).

## KANAUGA AND THE SILVER BRIDGE, OH (mile 265, RDB):

In December 1967, the Silver Bridge connecting Kanauga Ohio with Point Pleasant West Virginia collapsed into the Ohio River. Thirty one vehicles carrying 67 people plunged into the water. Forty-six people were killed, but 21 others escaped serious injuries. The Silver Bridge was unique because it was the first to be painted with aluminum paint. The vertical suspension members were 'I-bar chains' (versus woven wire cables). This was only the second 'I bar chain' bridge in the entire world and the first one in the United States. According to some legends, a moth-like humanoid was seen by several Point Pleasant residents in the weeks leading up to the bridge disaster. This creature is said to have predicted the collapse. This is the source of the book and movie, *The Mothman Prophecies*. The bridge was constructed in 1928. The NTSB determined that the bridge failed because of a cleavage fracture in one lower limb of an I-bar chain connection point. That failure point, located on the upstream side of the bridge near the Ohio side of the river, had eroded badly over the past 40 years.

## POINT PLEASANT, WV (mile 265, LDB):

For a relatively small town on the Ohio River, Point Pleasant West Virginia may hold more American history than any other town of comparable size. In 1770, George Washington explored the site and named this enchanting spot at the confluence of the Kanawha River, 'Point Pleasant.' A couple of years later, in 1772, a 20-year old George Rogers Clark first visited.

In 1774, Lord Dunmore's War was started under self-serving pretences. Virginia Tory Governor Lord Dunmore devised a two pronged attack against the Indians. One prong, lead by Dunmore himself, would proceed southwestward along the Ohio River after reaching Fort Pitt. The second prong, lead by Colonel Andrew Lewis would proceed northwestward from present-day southwestern Virginia, following the Kanawha River to it's confluence with the Ohio River. The two forces were supposed to hook-up at Camp Union (i.e., present-day Point Pleasant).

Some historians have speculated that the treacherous Lord Dunmore split his force in two, secretly hoping that Lewis' prong of about 1,100 men would be attacked and decimated by the Indians. Then a much weaker Virginia militia would be less able to mount an effective resistance in the next foreseen insurrection –the American Revolution. Should Colonel Lewis have been defeated, the colony of Virginia would have been so occupied in protecting her western frontier that she couldn't have been of much help to the other colonies during the Revolution. About 65 miles upriver from Point Pleasant, and instead of uniting with Lewis's prong at the 'prearranged,' but probably never intended, Camp Union, Dunmore's prong struck westward, departing the Ohio River near the mouth of the Hocking River. At the very least, Dunmore was planning to cut his 'own deal' with the Indians, with no input from Lewis. Some even suggest that Dunmore was colluding with the Indians well before the Battle of Point Pleasant –double crossing Lewis in his forthcoming battle.

Colonel Andrew Lewis was a very capable and experienced leader. Lewis was a Captain in George Washington's regiment that tried to hold Fort Necessity. Later, he was part of the General Forbes Expedition that eventually routed the French from Fort Duquesne. Lewis also spent a year as a French prisoner in Quebec. On October 10, 1774, Lewis' prong, having recently arrived at Camp Union –the pre-arranged meeting place, was attacked by a force of Shawnees, Mingos and other Native Americans lead by Chief Cornstalk. The *Battle of Point Pleasant* ensued. After a five-hour brutal battle, much of it hand-to-hand, Lewis was victorious. But Lewis lost many men including his trusted brother. Cornstalk retreated back across the Ohio River. Within no time Cornstalk was (again?) negotiating with Lord Dunmore who was now in Pickaway Plains Ohio.

After the Battle of Point Pleasant, Lewis pursued the Indians. As they neared Dunmore's Camp, they were told by messengers to retreat and return to Point Pleasant more than once. Incensed, Lewis disobeyed this direct order from Lord Dunmore. This was the first (and far from last) time that a 'Colonial Officer' would defy an order from his superior British military authority. Dunmore eventually went out to meet Lewis to inform him that a treaty, the *Treaty of Camp Charlotte*, was about to be concluded, and Lord Dunmore's War would be over. Many argue that the *Battle of Point Pleasant* was the first battle of the American Revolution because its flames were likely being fanned by the double-crossing British Lord Dunmore.

After the *Treaty of Camp Charlotte*, a frail stockade named Fort Blair was constructed in Point Pleasant to house the wounded men. In 1775, evacuated Fort Blair burned down. By early 1777, a much larger Fort Randolph had been constructed on the site of old Fort Blair. During 1777 and 1778, Fort Randolph was often under Indian attack. In 1777, Cornstalk and his son, on a peace mission, were murdered at Fort Randolph. In his dying words, Cornstalk placed a 200-year curse on the area. And perhaps he did? This area has had it its strange twists of bad luck – barge accidents, the Silver Bridge collapse, etc.

Continental Brigadier General Andrew Lewis may have had the better parting shot at Lord Dunmore. In July 1776, during the heat of the American Revolution, Lord Dunmore continued to attack the Revolutionary forces from his stronghold at Gywnn Island Virginia on the Chesapeake Bay. Lewis had the honor of firing the first gun as Dunmore's fleet was sent packing to the Caribbean.

Many of the men in the Lewis expedition went on to join George Rogers Clark in his successful conquest of our western frontier. In 1778, Clark, himself, while heading down the Ohio, during his momentous campaign to Fort Massac, Kaskaskia, and Vincennes stopped to regroup in Point Pleasant. In 1779, Fort Randolph was evacuated, and burned by the Indians. In 1785, a second Fort Randolph, needed because off continuing Indian skirmishes, was rebuilt on the former site.

During Colonel Lewis' 1774 campaign, Daniel Boone served as an Indian scout. In 1788, after losing all of his Kentucky land holdings due to an administrative technicality over land titles, Daniel Boone settled in Point Pleasant to work as a surveyor. By 1790, Daniel was also operating a trading post in town. But by 1800, Daniel had left Point Pleasant for the less populated Missouri frontier. Daniel Boone's hard luck with land titles didn't end in Missouri. After the Louisiana Purchase of 1803, he again lost all his property titles. In 1814, only six years before his death, the US Congress rightfully restored Daniel Boone's Missouri land claims.

In 1909, the 84 foot granite shaft , the tallest battle monument at that time west of the Alleghenies was dedicated in Tu-Endie-Wei State Park (☎ 304-675-0869, www.tu-endie-weistatepark.com) in Point Pleasant. Tu-Endie-Wei means 'mingling of the waters.' The park is very well-kept and serene, and not far from the city boat landing housing the Mansion House [Museum] –the oldest hewn log house in the Kanawha Valley. There is also an Ohio River Museum in Point Pleasant (☎ 304-674-0144 www.pprivermuseum.com) that focuses on the history, lore and economics of the Ohio and Kanawha Rivers. This museum is across from Tu-Endie-Wei Park. Point Pleasant hosts its annual 'Sternwheel Regatta and River Festival' around the Fourth of July, and its 'Battle Days' in early October. Point Pleasant is also the seat of Mason County.

## KANAWHA RIVER, WV (mile 265.6, LDB)
The Kanawha River, as well as Charleston West Virginia, is addressed in Chapter 11.

## GALLIPOLIS, OH (mile 269.5, RDB):
Gallipolis is known as 'the City of the Gauls (i.e., the French). In the late 1780s, the Scioto Company was enticing Europeans, especially French, to buy land in southern Ohio. The Scioto Company supposedly had 3.5 million acres of land on the Ohio River east of the Scioto River. So in January 1790, about 500 Frenchman arrived in Alexandria Virginia to soon hopefully be heading to their new 'land of milk and honey.' But the Scioto Company had swindled them. The Scioto Company owned no land, and their titles were worthless. The New England-founded Ohio Company of Associates (i.e., not the same as the Virginia-founded Ohio Company) agreed to step-in and prepare a much smaller tract of land that it owned about 80 miles upstream from the Scioto Company's 'alleged land.' Thirty-six craftsmen from Marietta and New England spent about a month building blockhouses and cabins for the French at the location that was soon to become known as Gallipolis.

In October 1790, those 500 Frenchmen arrived via flatboats from Pittsburgh, and moved into the hastily constructed cabins. Most of these Frenchmen were upper-middle class, and were smartly fleeing their own country on the eve of the French Revolution. As noblemen, doctors, manufacturers, tradesmen, etc., they were poorly prepared for early American frontier life. Within two years, one-half of the French inhabitants had left. Nonetheless by 1795, the Frenchmen were able to repay the Ohio Company for the land. But by 1807, only 20 French families remained in Gallipolis. Nonetheless, the remaining hardcore group of Frenchmen did persist and eventually do well.

By the early 19th Century, Virginians, New Englanders, and Welch started arriving in Gallipolis. The Welch, seeking more religious tolerance than they found in Britain, started arriving in 1818. Subsequent waves of Welch immigrants arrived in the 1830s and 1840s and many of the Welch settlers farmed the land west of Gallipolis.

During The Civil War, Gallipolis was an important embarkation point for Union soldiers heading to campaigns further south. An Army hospital administered to wounded Civil War veterans. Riverfront warehouse and steamboat depots also supported the Union effort.

Today, Gallipolis is the seat of Gallia County and the hometown of Bob Evans, founder of Bob Evans Restaurants. The first restaurant is located 12 miles away in Rio Grande, Ohio. There's a Wal-Mart, a Kmart, shopping centers, and several restaurants on the upriver end of Gallipolis, about two miles from the town's center. Gallipolis hosts its annual River Recreation Festival in early July.

# CHAPTER 10
# Marietta and the Muskingum River to Zanesville OH

The Muskingum River, at 112 miles long, is the longest river lying wholly within the state of Ohio.  The Muskingum and its tributary system is the largest entirely within the state, and it drains about one-fifth of the state.  The Muskingum River forms in east-central Ohio where the Tuscarawas River and Walhonding Rivers meet  in Coshocton.  The Walhonding is fed by many small tributaries coming from the north and west of Coshocton.  The Tuscarawas comes from the north-northeast, and forms outside of Akron.

The Native American name "Moos-kin-gung" means "Elk Eye River."  Large herds of elk and bison once roamed the river valley.  Native Americans had long used the river as part of a corridor extending from Lake Erie to the Ohio River.  The Delaware Indians once had small villages in the upper Muskingum River Valley.

In the 1820s, ground was broken for the long-planned Ohio and Erie Canal.  That waterway was to connect Lake Erie to the Ohio River.  The general plan was for a canal to head south from Lake Erie and Cleveland, pass through Akron, then utilize the Tuscarawas River to reach Coshocton, then utilize the Muskingum River water to reach Dresden –15 miles south of Coshocton, then head west in canals to near Columbus, and then head south again utilizing the Scioto River, before finally arriving at the Ohio River near Portsmouth.  By the 1840s, this Ohio and Erie Canal was completed.  But the canal was never an economically profitable venture.  By the 1850s, especially with the oncoming railroads, the western prongs of the Ohio and Erie Canal were all but abandoned.  Nonetheless, the lowest 90 miles of the river maintained some viability, since no nearby railroad traversed north-south, as the Muskingum River did.

In the late 1820s steamboats were plying the lower Muskingum River, but the river was dangerously shallow.  By 1837 work was started to deepen the lowest 91 miles of the river –from north of Zanesville to Marietta.   By 1841, 11 locks, and 10 dams, on the river had been constructed which provided a channel controlling depth of 4½ feet.  At that time, this was the largest capital improvement project in the state of Ohio.  The first dams were timber cribbing, and the locking chambers were designed at 160 foot long by 30 foot wide.  Several side-cut canals, where many of the locks would be situated, were constructed to bypass dams or rapids.  When this canalization was completed, Marietta had access to Cleveland and the Great Lakes, via the Muskingum River and the upper part of the Ohio and Erie Canal.

By the 1880s, the original bulging timber cribbing dams and aging locks on the Muskingum River were in sorry shape.  In 1887, the U.S. Army Corps of Engineers accepted the responsibility for maintaining the river, and began making necessary repairs.  In 1913, a massive flood further damaged the locks and dams, and they remained closed for the next five years.  In 1918, when the Muskingum River finally reopened, trucking had come onto the scene, and this took a bite out of the Muskingum River's commercial viability.  For a brief time around World War II, Muskingum River traffic picked-up when large quantities of Ohio coal were being shipped out of the state.  But by the late 1940s, river traffic was again way down.

By 1948, the Corp of Engineers decided to end its maintenance of the Muskingum River.  In 1958, the state of Ohio took over ownership of Muskingum River maintenance.  In 1968, the Muskingum River Parkway State Park (☎ 740-674-4794) was designated as an Ohio State Park by the Ohio Department of Natural Resources.  Today, it remains the longest continually navigable river within Ohio.  The Muskingum River Parkway features the nation's only remaining hand-operated lock system. The ten locks are manually operated by lock tenders in the same way as they were in 1841. The Muskingum River Parkway provides about 86 miles of recreational river navigation from Lock Number 11 (i.e., in Ellis, and south of Dresden) to Lock #2 (in Devola, three miles north of Marietta). The Muskingum is like no other that we've ever been on –shallower, with hand-cranked locks, very limited navigation aids, limited lock hours of operation, and not maintained to the same degree as your typical Corps of Engineers waterways.

The following table summarizes the locks and pools on the Muskingum River:

| Lock and Pool Name | Mile | Lock Side | Telephone Number ☎ | Opens [1] | Lift (in ft) | Pool Length (miles) |
|---|---|---|---|---|---|---|
| Belleville L&D (Reedsville, OH) | 31.7 mi dn Oh | RDB | 304-863-6631 | 24/7 | 22 | 5.8 |
| Lock and Dam # 2 (Devola, OH) | 5.8 | LDB | 740-674-4794 | [1] | ≈ 12 | 8.4 |
| L & D # 3  (Lowell, OH) | 14.2 | LDB | 740-896-2296 | [1] | ≈ 12 | 10.9 |
| L & D # 4 (Beverly, OH) | 25.1 | LDB | 740-984-4195 | [1] | ≈ 12 | 9.0 |
| L & D # 5 (Luke Chute, OH) | 34.1 | RDB | 740-984-2282 | [1] | ≈ 12 | 6.1 |
| L & D # 6 (Stockport, OH) | 40.2 | LDB | 740-559-2371 | [1] | ≈ 12 | 9.2 |
| L & D # 7 (McConnelsville, OH) | 49.5 | LDB | 740-962-2724 | [1] | ≈ 12 | 8 |
| L & D # 8 (Rokeby, OH) | 57.6 | LDB | 740-962-4223 | [1] | ≈ 12 | 10.9 |
| L & D # 9 (Philo, OH) | 68.6 | RDB | 740-674-6191 | [1] | ≈ 12 | 8.3 |
| L & D # 10 (Zanesville,  OH) | 76.6 | LDB | 740-452-4137 | [1] | ≈ 12 | 9.3 |
| L & D # 11 (Ellis, OH) | 85.9 | LDB | 740-453-0033 | [1] | ≈ 12 | Unk. |

[1] Muskingum River locks are only open around weekends during the summer and early fall months.

Lock Tender Hand Cranking
Muskingum River Lock Gate

# Old B&O Railroad Bridge to Harmar Village over the Muskingum River

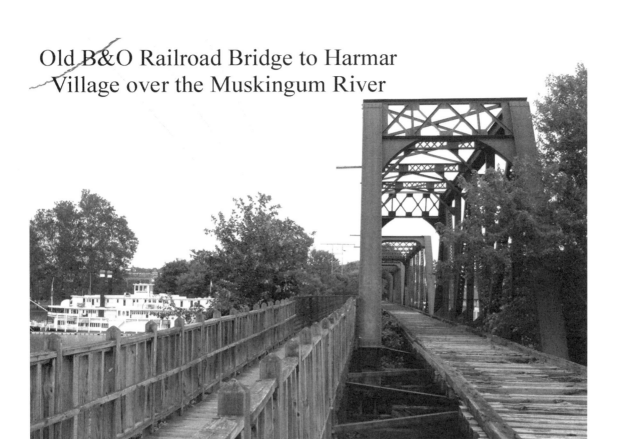

Sternwheeler *Valley Gem* near Marietta, Ohio

**MARIETTA, OH** (Ohio River miles 171-172, RDB; Muskingum River miles 0-3, LBD)

Marietta Ohio is the Northwest Territory's first town. But well before the white settlers arrived, from about 800 BC to 100 AD, the Adena Native American Culture lived here. These were the same people that built the great mound in Moundsville West Virginia, 70 miles upstream on the Ohio River. In the 1760s a few white missionaries reached the Muskingum River trying to convert the local Native Americans.

In the winter of 1785-86, before the permanent settlement of Marietta, Fort Harmar was constructed on RDB (i.e., southwest bank) of the Muskingum River at its confluence with the Ohio River. Fort Harmar was a stockade constructed by, and named for, Revolutionary War General, Josiah Harmar. The initial purpose of this fort was to dissuade squatters from settling on Native American lands. But after it was constructed, the fort had the opposite effect. Settlers [correctly] figured they could flee to the protection of the new stockade during Indian attacks. Today, Harmar Village is a part of West Marietta. The old B&O Railroad Bridge, over the Muskingum River, has been converted into a footbridge connecting Harmar Village with downtown Marietta. In today's Harmar Village, one will find the 'Children's Toy and Doll Museum' (☎ 740-373-5900) and the Harmar Station Model Railroad Museum (☎ 740-374-9995). The Children's Museum displays items that entertained and educated children in the late 19th and early 20th Centuries.

In 1770, when George Washington was exploring the area, he was most favorably impressed. Washington later shared his impressions with fellow Revolutionary War General Rufus Putnam. In 1788, Putnam spearheaded this first settlement in the Northwest Territory. By the end of 1788, about 140 settlers, dominated by Revolutionary War veterans and their families, were living in Marietta Later that year Arthur St. Clair arrived to assume the governorship of the Northwest Territories. A fortification of Campus Martius was soon constructed to serve as the base for these early settlers. Marietta was first named Adelphia –meaning brethren –by Revolutionary War Soldiers. Soon the name was changed to Marietta in honor of French Queen Marie Antoinette, for her assistance during the American Revolution. During the early 1790s, Marietta was often threatened by the Native Americans.

Shipbuilding was one of the first industries in Marietta, thanks to the shipbuilding skills of many New Englanders and the abundance of local hardwood trees. By the early 1810s, there were eight local shipyards, and 29 ocean-voyaging vessels had been constructed. But by the 1840s, local shipbuilding had all but ended. Brick kilns, sawmills, iron furnaces, and even oil and gas spurred early industrial development in Marietta. In 1824, American Revolutionary War hero and French nobleman Marquis de Lafayette returned to the country he helped liberate. He took a one and a half year tour through our new nation. Lafayette started out on a steamer from New Orleans, and stopped in Marietta in May 1825. When he arrived at Pittsburgh, Lafayette went overland to Boston where he laid the cornerstone of the Bunker Hill monument.

In the earlier part of the 20th Century, presidents Theodore Roosevelt, Howard Taft and Franklin Roosevelt had visited Marietta to speak and to dedicate monuments recognizing Marietta's role as an important 'Start Westward' place in American History. The 'Start Westward' monument in East Muskingum Park was created by the same person who chiseled the four presidents on Mount Rushmore.

The museum of the Northwest Territory, 'Campus Martius,' means 'fields of war' in Latin. Today, the Campus Martius Museum has a gift shop, many early artifacts, exhibits on western expansion (including a Conestoga wagon), other interesting assortments that pertain to the early Northwest Territory, as well as information on later immigrations and demographic patterns going all of the way up to 1979. This museum is located on site of the original Campus Martius stockade. Included, as part of Campus Martius, is the 200+ year old house of Rufus Putnam and the headquarters of the Ohio Company of Associates. This museum is located at 601 Second Street (☎ 740-373-3750 or 800-860-0145, www.ohiohistory.org/places/campus).

**Sketch 10-A: The Muskingum River –from Marietta to Zanesville, Ohio**

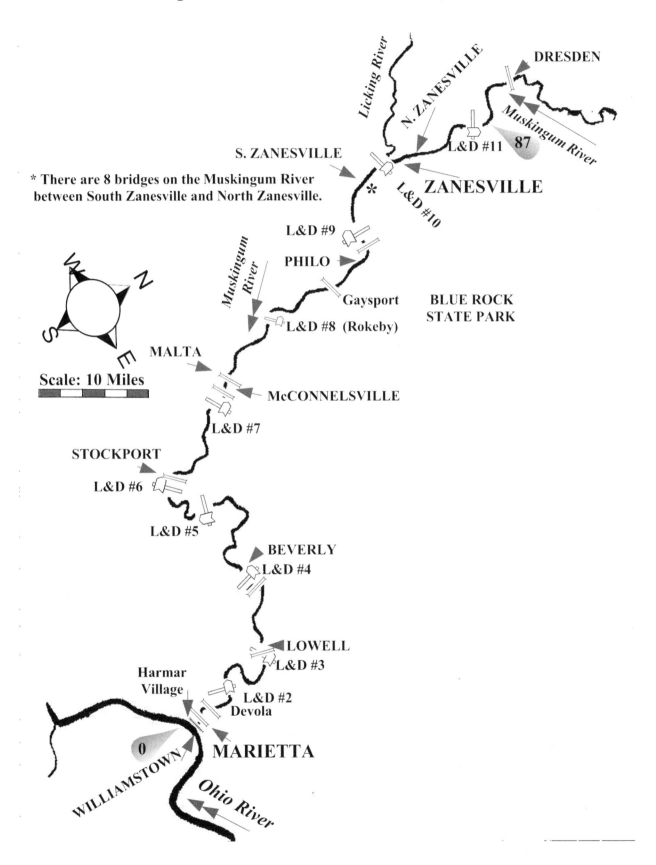

* There are 8 bridges on the Muskingum River between South Zanesville and North Zanesville.

Scale: 10 Miles

The Ohio River Museum (☎ 740-373-3717 or 800-860-0145, www.ohiohistory.org/places/ohriver), founded by Captain Fred Way, is located about two blocks from Campus Martius and on the Muskingum River at 601 Front Street. Inside the Ohio River Museum, one can find about 40 steamboat models (including a 24-footer), paintings, artifacts, early boat-building tools, as well as a 30-minute video on steamboat history. Outside the Ohio River Museum, you'll find a pilothouse section from the steamer *Tell City,* built in 1885. The *WP Snyder Jr.*, floating on the Muskingum River, is also part of this museum. The *WP Snyder Jr.,* built in 1918, is the last intact steam-powered stern-wheeled towboat in the United States. It was donated by the Crucible Steel Company, and arrived here under her own power in 1955. The Ohio River Museum also depicts the high water marks of many of the floods that have ravaged the Marietta during the 20th Century. Both museums have limited hours –usually open around the weekends, and are generally closed from November until spring. Both the museums are operated by the Ohio Historical Society. The 296-passenger rated *Valley Gem* Sternwheeler (☎740-373-7862, www.valleygemsternwheeler.com) parks just downstream from the *WP Snyder Jr.* The *Valley Gem* offers several types of cruises –from 90 minute excursions to three-hour dinner cruises to wedding charters.

Besides the better known Camp Martius and Ohio River Museums, Marietta has another nine museums. Downtown Marietta also has a post office, laundry, many restaurants, the historic Lafayette Hotel, an auto parts store, and many antique shops. A grocer, hardware store, and Marietta College are about a mile east of central downtown. There is a great bicycle trail running through the park area extending on the LDB of the Muskingum River for more than a couple of miles –from Harmar Village to well past the Ohio River Museum. Marietta also hosts its annual Ohio River Sternwheeler Festival every mid-September. For the latest happenings around Marietta, contact the Marietta/Washington County Convention and Visitors Bureau at 316 Third Street (☎ 740-373-5178, www.mariettaohio.org).

**DEVOLA TO LOWELL, OH** (miles 6-20, L /RDB, Left and Right Descending Banks):

There are probably about a dozen small colorful paddlewheelers parked in pool two and in the lower end (i.e., downriver end) of pool three. Many of these unique colorful vessels are between 30 and 50 feet long.

Inside leaky Muskingum River Lock near Lowell, Ohio

**BEVERLY, OH** (mile 24.9, LDB):

In 1852, the worst steamboat disaster on the Muskingum River occurred when the *Buckeye Bell* exploded. The *Buckeye Bell* was en route from Newport on the Ohio River to Zanesville. Twenty-four lives were lost, and a dozen were injured. There were only a few other steamboats disasters on the Muskingum River. In 1879, also near Beverly, the *LC McCormick* exploded and one life was lost. The town of Beverly has a few restaurants and gas stations.

**STOCKPORT, OH** (mile 40.2, RDB):

In 1834, Stockport was founded. The Buckeye Trail crosses the Muskingum River at Stockport. This hiking trail makes a lengthy 1,435-mile loop within the state of Ohio, reaching just about every corner of the state –from a beachhead overlooking Lake Erie near Cleveland to a hilltop overlooking our Ohio River in Cincinnati.

The last remaining grist mill, grinding flour, corn and grain, on the Muskingum River is located in Stockport. The first mill here was built in 1842; the present building was built in 1906. The 1913 flood wiped out most of the mills and bridges on the Muskingum River, but the Stockport grist mill survived. When the mill finally fell silent in 1997, it was renovated, and soon reopened its doors as 'The Stockport Mill Country Inn and Restaurant.' The building is now a 14-room hotel and restaurant (☎ 740-559-2822, www.stockportmill.com). Similarly, in 2002, the old hardware store, was renovated and reopened its doors as 'The Hardware Inn of Stockport' (☎ 740-559-2822, www.hardwareinnofstockport.com). Stockport also has a convenience store and the Stockport RV Park and Campground (☎ 740-559-2239).

**McCONNELSVILLE, OH** (mile 50.2, LDB) and **MALTA, OH** (mile 50.4, RDB):

In 1817, settlers started arriving in McConnelsville and Malta. During the 1820s and 1830s, flatboats were carrying grain, lumber, and livestock down the Muskingum River. After the locks and dams were completed in 1841, both towns grew rapidly because they were now accessible by steamboats. Malta was home to a leading farm implement manufacturer while McConnelsville was home to many flour and grain mills. Today, McConnelsville has several restaurants, a historical museum, an auto parts store, a hardware store, gas stations, a few taverns, an inn, and three grocers. McConnelsville is also the seat of Morgan County. McConnelsville and Malta are known as twin cities.

**ROKEBY, OH** (mile 57.4, LDB):

In 1847, the *Newark* exploded on the Muskingum River near here killing four people. In 1863, during the three-week raid of Confederate General John Hunt Morgan north of the Ohio River, Morgan's men had forded the Muskingum River at Rokeby Lock. Learning of Morgan's approach, the Ohio militia in McConnelsville and Malta converted their local ferryboat into a gunboat, and headed upstream to intercept Morgan. But by the time the ferryboat, with its mounted cannon, arrived in Rokeby, Morgan had already crossed the Muskingum. The Muskingum River Parkway hosts a Lock Festival in Rokeby every June.

**BLUE ROCK STATE PARK, OH** (near mile 63.4, RDB):

Near Philo, Blue Rock State Park (☎ 740-674-4794) has cabins, 95 campsites, several picnic areas, a camp store, a sandy beach on a lake, and three miles of hiking trails.

**ZANESVILLE, OH** (miles 77-78, L/RDB):

In the late 1790s, the area at the Licking River's confluence with the Muskingum was nothing more than a ferry crossing. In 1797, Colonel Ebenezer Zane was commissioned by Congress to blaze a 230-mile road from Wheeling Virginia to Maysville Kentucky through the dense forest and rolling hills of present-day southeastern Ohio. This route would soon be known as 'Zane's Trace.' Several ferry crossings, including the two over the Ohio River (i.e., at

Wheeling and at Mayville) were needed.  Colonel Zane was yet another Revolutionary War veteran.  Zane's brother, Jonathan, and his son-in-law, John McIntire were soon operating a ferry service over the Muskingum River.  They became the area's first settlers.  A town, laid-out by McIntire, was first named Westbourne.  By 1801, the settlement was renamed Zanesville in honor of Ebenezer Zane.

From 1810 to 1812, Zanesville was the second capital of Ohio.  The present-day distinctive Muskingum County Courthouse stands atop the site of this once Ohio State Capital Building.  With the two rivers in Zanesville, early pioneers had a slight logistical problem: "build two bridges, or can we get by with just one bridge?'  The dilemma was solved by building their first 'Y Bridge' in 1814.  The 'Y Bridge' spans both rivers.  The current bridge, in downtown Zanesville, is the fifth version.  'Ripley's Believe It or Not' calls the Zanesville 'Y Bridge,' "the only bridge in the world which you can cross and still be on the same side of the river."  When given directions, visitors are perplexed by the advice, "Drive to the middle of the bridge and then turn right (or left)."

Like East Liverpool, Zanesville was known for its ceramic and pottery industries.  Zanesville has a National Ceramics Museum and Heritage Center (☎ 740-697-7021, www.ceramiccenter.org) and the National Road-Zane Grey Museum (☎ 740-872-3143).  By about 1830, the National Road reached Zanesville.  Novelist Zane Grey was born in Zanesville, and is a descendant of the early Zane family.  Besides ceramic and pottery, 'the Port of Zanesville' was noted for its early glass and steel industries.  Twelve historic churches grace downtown Zanesville.  The city is also the seat of Muskingum County.

Muskingum County Courthouse, Zanesville, Ohio

Muskingum River Marina, North Zanesville, Ohio

Small Stern-wheeler on the Kanawha River

Tu-Endie-Wei State Park from the mouth of the Kanawha River

Sharing Robert C. Byrd Lock with a Coal Tow near Gallipolis, Ohio

116

# CHAPTER 11
# Charleston and the Kanawha River, from Point Pleasant to Alloy, WV

The Native American word 'Kanawha' means 'place of white stone.' The Kanawha River is the largest inland waterway inside the state of West Virginia (the 130-mile long Monongahela River has only about 40 navigable miles inside the state of West Virginia). The 90-mile navigable Kanawha River has at least three, and possibly more, distinct personalities. The lowest 31-mile section –the Robert C. Byrd Pool on the Kanawha River, is rather bland with an unspectacular flood plain on at least one side of the river. The next 40 or so mile section is a real mixed bag. This middle section has portions that are almost recreational lake-like, followed by chemical plants along the banks, followed by the urban environs of Charleston, and then followed by more chemical plants. But the last 20 or so navigable miles is extremely enchanting. In this uppermost navigable portion, there are still a few industrial plants along the river, but the river flows in an almost mountain gorge-like setting. It's worth traveling those lower 70 miles to arrive here.

Beyond the head of navigation, there's about a seven-mile non-navigable section of the river before the Kanawha ends. At Gauley Bridge West Virginia, about 97 miles from the Ohio River, the Gauley River and the New River meet to form the Kanawha. The Gauley River, flowing westward for about 50 miles, originates in the Monongahela National Forest of southeastern West Virginia. The Gauley has become a linchpin in the local economies due to its exhilarating white water rafting. Dozens of river outfitters along the Gauley accommodate this form of outdoor adventure. Over the last 25 or so years, the Gauley River has become one of the most popular advanced white water runs in the entire Eastern United States.

The other Kanawha fork, the New River, originates in the northwest corner of North Carolina and flows northward through three states. Some geologists believe that the New River is one of the oldest rivers in the world (behind only the Nile) as well as being the oldest in North America. The New River flows for about 320 miles, 'against the grain' of the Appalachian Mountains –supporting the geological hypothesis that the New River is even older than the well worn-down Appalachian Mountains. In 1978, about 53 miles of the New River's course through West Virginia was designated as the New River Gorge National River. The New River, steeped in American History (e.g., the Mary Ingles Story), is also designated as an 'American Heritage River' by the US Environmental Protection Agency. Several West Virginia State Parks dot the New River. Like the Gauley River, the New River in West Virginia is also noted for its white water rafting.

In 1977, after a three-year construction project, the New River Gorge Bridge was built – only about 10 miles from the head of the Kanawha River. In 1976, a drive that took close to an hour was reduced to about one minute, thanks to this New River Gorge Bridge. This arch bridge (US Route 19), 876 feet above the New River is the second tallest bridge in the United States (behind only Royal Gorge in Colorado) as well as being world's second longest single arch steel span bridge. The third Saturday of October is 'Bridge Day' and pedestrians are allowed to walk across the bridge.

Since the early 19th Century, the Kanawha River Valley has been a force for growth in the area. The valley contained significant deposits of salt, coal, and natural gas. In the 1840s, boulders and snags started being removed from the river, providing improved navigation. In 1875, the construction of locks and dams began. By 1898, there were 10 locks and wicket dams on the river that provided a six-foot deep navigation channel. In the 1930s, a new round of four higher locks and dams were being constructed, that provided a nine foot channel. Today, there are four pools corresponding to this chapter –the Robert Byrd (starting about 14 miles downriver on the Ohio), the Winfield, the Marmet and the very short London Pool

The following table summarizes the locks and pools on the Kanawha River:

**Table 11-A: Locks and Pools on the Kanawha River:**

| Lock and Pool Name | Mile | Lock Side | Telephone Number ☎ | Opens for R. Vessels | Lift (in ft) | Pool Lgth (mi) |
|---|---|---|---|---|---|---|
| R Byrd L&D, Gallipolis Fry WV | -13.6 Oh. | LDB | 304-576-2272 | 24/7 | 23 | 44.7 |
| Winfield L& D (Redhouse WV) | 31.1 | RDB | 304-586-2501 | 24/7 | 28 | 36.6 |
| Marmet Lock & D (Belle, WV) | 67.7 | RDB | 304-949-1175 | 24/7 | 24 | 15.1 |
| London L & D (London, WV) | 82.8 | RDB | 304-442-8422 | 24/7 | 24 | ≈ 8 |

**NITRO, WV** (mile 42.5, RDB –Right Descending Bank):

During World War I, the federal government was running low on gunpowder. A crash project to build a manufacturing plant for the production of nitroglycerin, as well as the supporting community to house the plant's workers was established here. After the war, the local chemical industry continued to grow.

**COAL RIVER, WV** (mile 45.5 LDB –Left Descending Bank):

Coal deposits along its banks, gave this river its name. In the 19th Century, this was a navigable waterway, transporting coal and timber out of southern West Virginia. A series of locks and dams supported this commercial barge traffic.

**ST. ALBANS, WV** (mile 46, LDB):

The town was laid out in 1816. St. Albans had been previously named Philippi, Coalsmouth, and Kanawha City. In 1871, the name was changed to St. Albans upon the suggestion by a member of the town council from St. Albans Vermont. The 'Port of St. Albans' hosts its annual Riverfest near the Fourth of July weekend.

**INSTITUTE, WV** (mile 49, RDB):

Institute is home to West Virginia State University. In 1865, Samuel Cabell, a wealthy industrialist and land owner left a sizeable fortune to his slave mistress and the couple's 13 children. Before he was murdered, Cabell made sure that his mulatto children all received good educations –something very rare at that time. In 1890, one of Cabell's daughters took her share of land to help start a land-grant institution for African-Americans –The West Virginia Colored Institute. That institution later became West Virginia State University.

**DUNBAR, WV** (mile 52, RDB)

Dunbar was surveyed in 1774. After the American Revolution, the site was granted to George Washington. It's believed that the present city was named for Mary Dunbar –a relative of George Washington.

**CHARLESTON, WV** (miles 56-61, L/RDB):

In 1774, a few settlers started arriving at the confluence of the Elk and Kanawha Rivers. In 1786, the land was sold to Colonel George Clendenin. By 1788, Colonel Clendenin and his company of Virginia Rangers built Fort Lee. Some historians believe that Charleston was named for Colonel Clendenin's father, Charles. By 1794, there were still only 35 folks inhabiting Charleston. From 1786-97, Daniel Boone also lived in the area, and served in the Kanawha County Militia.

# Sketch 11-A: The Kanawha River –from Point Pleasant to Alloy, West Virginia

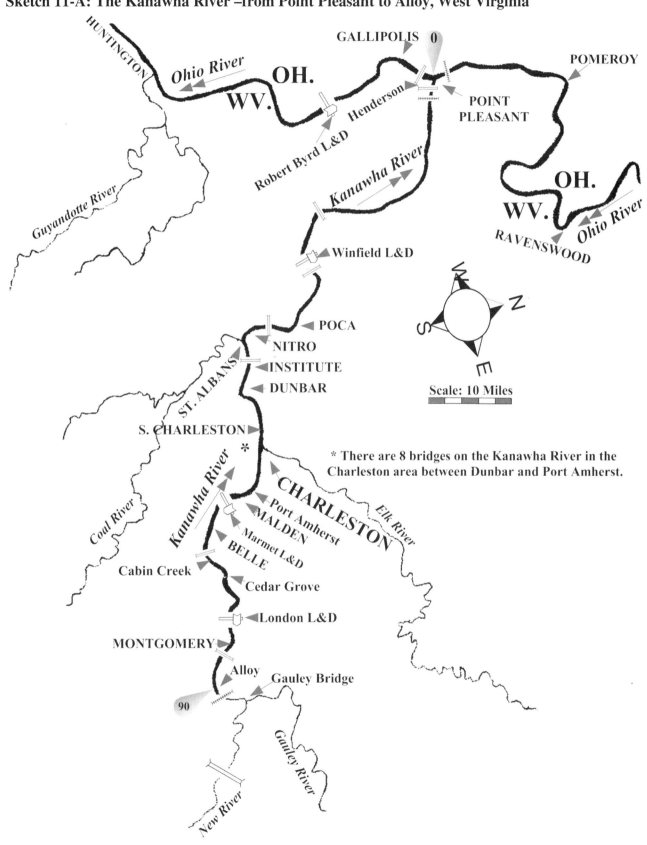

HUNTINGTON

*Ohio River*

OH.

WV.

GALLIPOLIS  0

Henderson

Robert Byrd L&D

POMEROY

POINT PLEASANT

*Kanawha River*

OH.

WV.

*Ohio River*

RAVENSWOOD

*Guyandotte River*

Winfield L&D

POCA

NITRO

INSTITUTE

DUNBAR

ST. ALBANS

S. CHARLESTON

*Kanawha River*

*Coal River*

\* There are 8 bridges on the Kanawha River in the Charleston area between Dunbar and Port Amherst.

Scale: 10 Miles

\*

CHARLESTON

Port Amherst

MALDEN

Marmet L&D

BELLE

*Elk River*

Cabin Creek

Cedar Grove

London L&D

MONTGOMERY

Alloy    Gauley Bridge

90

*Gauley River*

*New River*

119

By the turn of the 19<sup>th</sup> Century, local salt extraction was becoming profitable. In 1806, the first salt well was drilled. Salt would continue driving the local economy from the 1810s to the 1850s. In the 1810s and 1820s, the great-grandson of Mary Ingles, John P. Hale, built a fleet a paddlewheelers to run Kanawha Valley salt from Charleston to Cincinnati. Hale's steamboats lead to other local modernizations which in turn increased the cargo carrying capacities of vessels operating on the Kanawha River.

Charleston continued to grow until the Civil War. When the state of Virginia joined the Confederacy, Charleston's loyalties were divided. In September 1862, a minor encounter –the *Battle of Charleston*, was fought. The Confederates had a short-lived victory, but Union forces returned within weeks, and took control of the city for the remainder of the war. When the Civil War ended, the once flourishing Kanawha Valley salt industry was all but gone.

During the Civil War, in June of 1863, West Virginia became our 35<sup>th</sup> state. In 1870, the state capitol moved from Wheeling to Charleston. In 1875, it moved back to Wheeling. In 1877, state citizens voted on the final location. Charleston won; and by 1885, the capitol was back on the Kanawha River for good. In 1921, the first capitol building was destroyed in a fire. A hastily constructed second capitol building burned down in 1927. In 1931, the present capitol building was completed. In 2005, this capitol's gold dome got a face-lift and a new paint job.

By the early 20<sup>th</sup> Century, besides being the center of state government, Charleston was well positioned to take advantage of the areas natural resources –coal, natural gas, and timber. Railroads expanded into the area. Industries such as chemicals and glass moved into the region.

During World War II, the largest synthetic rubber plant in the country opened outside Charleston. In February 1942, when Singapore fell to the Japanese, the Allies lost 95 percent of their source of rubber. Many experts believed that the loss of this source of rubber was one of the greatest threats facing the Allied cause. The federal government set up an entity –the Rubber Reserve Company. The Rubber Reserve Company was tasked to get four competitors –Uniroyal, Goodrich, Goodyear, and Firestone, along with Standard Oil to share their trade secrets and pool their technology for the war effort. They did. Twenty five plants were soon constructed, with the largest plant just outside Charleston. By the end of 1943, the last of these new plants was at full production. In an unbelievably short period of time, a new synthetic rubber industry was producing enough polymers to keep the war effort on track. Today, synthetic rubber is much more widely utilized than natural rubber.

In the early 1940s, the old Charleston airport, Wertz Field, had to be closed down to make room for that new synthetic rubber plant. The new airport's construction was one of the more remarkable engineering feats of the 1940s. At that time, this airport was the second-largest earth-moving project in history, –behind only the Panama Canal. More than nine million cubic yards of earth was displaced, and 360 acres were cleared. In order to create enough flat surface for two long airport runways, the tops of seven small mountains needed to be lopped-off and the spoil material was used to fill-in the connecting valleys. In 1947, after more than three years of construction, the Kanawha Airport opened. In 1985, this airport was renamed the Yeager Airport, for the West Virginia pilot Chuck Yeager. Brigadier General Yeager had a storied 36-year military career, including piloting the world's first supersonic flight in 1947.

With a population of slightly over 51,000, Charleston is the largest city in West Virginia. Charleston hosts many festivals and events throughout the year. The annual 'Sternwheel Regatta' is held on the Kanawha River near Haddad Riverfront Park, and concludes Labor Day weekend.

## ELK RIVER, WV (mile 57.9, RDB):

The Yeager Airport sits about three miles up the Elk River and less than one-half mile from that river on the LDB side. Today, there are no recreational boating facilities on the Elk River because ice has damaged such facilities in the past. Nonetheless, there are still several industrial docks on the Elk River. The Elk originates in the Monongahela National Forest and flows generally westward for about 170 miles.

The London Lock and Dam on the Kanawha River

The Norfolk and Western Railroad Bridge –
the 'End of the Line' on the Kanawha River

**MALDEN, WV** (mile 64, RDB):
During the salt production heydays of the early 1800s, Malden was one of the largest producing areas. Malden's 'red salt' (rich with iron) was a prized meat-preserving commodity.

After the Civil War, a young Booker T. Washington, moved to, grew-up, worked on a Kanawha River steamboat, and started self-educating himself in Malden. Many consider Booker T. Washington one of the most influential African Americans of the late 19th and early 20th Centuries. Washington realized that many whites would be cynical of the newly-emancipated African Americans. He believed that his race would have to prove itself as being responsible and reliable citizens. Washington realized that the main ingredient for that was education. In 1881, the 25-year old Washington became the first principal of what-would later become Alabama's Tuskegee Institute. During his era, white politicians routinely consulted with Booker T. Washington on important matters of the day.

**BELLE, WV** (miles 68-70, RDB):

The Dupont plant in Belle West Virginia was constructed soon after World War I. By the 1920s, this plant began making synthetic ammonia, eliminating the need to import such. Synthetic ammonia provides the basic inputs for fertilizers, chemicals, and explosives. During World War II, the nylon used in Army parachutes for the war effort came from here. In the 1950s, when production peaked, this Belle plant employed over 5,000. The plant supposedly has one of the best safety records of all Dupont plants.

The dock at the WVU Tech facility
near Montgomery, West Virginia

**CEDAR GROVE, WV** (mile 77.5, RDB):

In 1774, Cedar Grove was the first permanent settlement in the Kanawha Valley. This early settlement had a fort, church, school, and boat yard.

**MONTGOMERY, WV** (mile 85.5, LDB):

After the Revolutionary War, Major Henry Montgomery operated a ferry boat service across the Kanawha River. The town is the largest in this uppermost Kanawha River section, as well as the first town outside of large Kanawha County. Montgomery is home to West Virginia University Institute of Technology.

In 1902, Mother Jones (Mary Harris Jones) helped organize about 7,000 coal miners in the nearby Kanawha Coal Fields. Years earlier, in 1867, Mother Jones had lost her husband and four children to yellow fever. In 1871, she lost all her property in the Great Chicago Fire. Forced to support herself, at a time when next-to-no women did so, she soon became involved in the upstart labor movement. Mother Jones took special interest in child labor and mine worker issues. In 1925, two men, hired by an anti-labor interest attacked her. This indomitable elderly lady fought off the pair of thugs. When she was 83 years old, ex-president Theodore Roosevelt nicknamed her "the most dangerous woman in America." She made enemies in 'high places,' but had some success bringing the issue of child labor to the forefront of public agenda and forced the US Congress to consider and address the horrid conditions in coal mines. She remained a union organizer for the United Mine Workers, and continued to speak-out against labor injustices until her death in 1930. Some suggest Mother Jones is the inspiration for the popular folk song "She'll be Coming 'Round the Mountain, When She Comes." The 'She' was coming to promote the formation of labor unions in the Appalachian coal mining camps, and the 'white horses' were a symbol of the mythological stature of Mother Jones.

**ALLOY, WV** (mile 89.5, RDB):

The large facility on the RDB of the Kanawha River, near the head of navigation is Elkem Metals. Elkem is home to the largest silicon metal smelter in North America. This smelter operates every day, around the clock. This plant produces over 350,000 pounds of high-grade silicon metal each day. This amount represents nearly 30 percent of all the industrial and commercial demand for high-grade silicon metal in the United States, Canada and Mexico. About one-half of all the world's computers contain chips with silicon refined at this plant.

**GAULEY BRIDGE, WV** (mile 97, RDB –ON THE NON-NAVIGABLE KANAWHA RIVER):

In the early 1770s, George Washington, as a young surveyor, was looking for a potential water route, through Virginia, and over the Allegheny Mountains, that would connect Atlantic coastal Virginia to the Mississippi-Ohio River system and the Gulf of Mexico. Washington's preference of river connections was: 1) the James River from the east; and 2) the Kanawha River from the west. The Potomac River, farther to the north, was deemed less desirable, because states other than Virginia could also get a 'piece of the action.' In 1785, the 'James River Company' was formed and the 'James River and Kanawha Canal' was conceived. By 1790, the first canal built in the United States –a short seven-mile section heading west from Richmond Virginia, and paralleling the James River, was constructed. But the company soon went bankrupt.

In 1820, the state of Virginia picked-up the pieces of the old 'James River Company's project, and work on the 'James River and Kanawha Canal' resumed. The project again stalled. In 1835, a new 'James River and Kanawha Canal Company' resumed westward work. By 1840, the canal, reached Lynchburg Virginia. By 1851, the canal extended nearly 200 miles west of Richmond, while still paralleling the James River, to Buchanan Virginia (i.e., near present-day highway Interstate 81). From here, the canal hooked-up with the 'James River and Kanawha Turnpike,' which provided a road passage through the most rugged portions of the mountains before reaching the Kanawha River –which was still more than 150 miles west of Buchanan.

During the Civil War, portions of the Virginia canal were damaged. By 1873, the Chesapeake and Ohio Railroad had reached the Ohio River, and the canal was forever doomed. Today the old canal's towpath, is used by CSX trains to transport coal heading to Norfolk.

Nevertheless, the 'James River and Kanawha Turnpike' soon became a part of the Midland Trail. The Midland Trail crossed some of the most rugged terrain in West Virginia. The earliest trail was believed to have been carved into the mountains by migrating buffalo, and later improved upon by Native Americans. During the Civil War, the Midland Trail had become suitable enough for stage coaches. The trail later evolved into US Route 60. By 1932, US Route 60 spanned the continent from Norfolk Virginia to Los Angeles California, while passing through Gauley Bridge West Virginia.

# The West Virginia State Capitol on the banks of the Kanawha River, Charleston

# CHAPTER 12
# The Huntington Area …on the Ohio River, from Gallipolis Ferry, WV to Manchester, OH

This chapter addresses about a 120-mile section of the Ohio River from the Robert Byrd Lock and Dam, and about 30 miles upriver from Huntington West Virginia, to slightly downriver of Manchester Ohio. Besides Huntington, the cities of Ashland Kentucky, and Portsmouth and Ironton Ohio are passed along the river. Downriver from Huntington, there are a few, but not many, good facilities for recreational boaters. The river takes on a more industrial flavor than it did in the past Ohio River chapter. Coal towboats dominate transport on the river. And the towboats also are getting bigger here! Many of the tows from here and downriver are of the 'three by five' variety (i.e., a towboat pushing a load of three barges wide and five barges long). When we visited, the industrial cities of Ashland and Ironton had next-to-no stopovers for recreational boaters. Portsmouth is only slightly better. Huntington does have a handful of boating facilities nestled along their mostly industrial waterfront. There is only one lock, the busy Greenup Lock, near the middle of this stretch of river. From about Portsmouth downriver, there are many places on the shoreline that are sandier (and less stony). This sandiness feature will continue all of the way to the Mississippi River. Downriver from West Portsmouth, the shore topography becomes less Appalachian Mountain-like and gentler.

The following table summarizes the locks and pools on this section of Ohio River with some overlap into adjacent river sections:

**Table 12-A: Locks and Pools on the Ohio River, from the Robert Byrd Lock and Dam to Manchester, Ohio:**

| Lock and Pool Name | Mile | Lock Side | Telephone Number ☎ | Opens for R. Vessels | Lift (in ft) | Pool Length (miles) |
|---|---|---|---|---|---|---|
| R. Byrd L&D,(Gallipolis Fry, WV) | 279.2 | LDB | 304-576-2272 | 24/7 | 23 | 41.7 |
| Greenup L&D, (Greenup, KY) | 341.0 | LDB | 606-473-7441 | 24/7 | 30 | 61.8 |
| Capt. Meldahl L&D, (Chilo, OH) | 436.2 | RDB | 513-876-2921 | 24/7 | 30 | 95.2 |

**GUYANDOTTE, WV** (mile 305, LDB –Left Descending Bank):
In 1799, the town of Guyandotte, an Indian name, was settled. In 1809, it was designated as the county seat. Guyandotte soon became an important stop on the 'James River and Kanawha Turnpike.' During the Civil War, Guyandotte, unlike much of present-day West Virginia voted to stay with Virginia, and secede with the Confederacy. In 1861, with the assistance of many locals, a small Confederate force attacked a Union recruitment station. The Union Army retook the town, and set a good portion of it ablaze to punish the citizenry for aiding the Confederates. The 'Wheeling Intelligencer' newspaper declared "Guyandotte …the worst secession nest in that whole country. It ought to have been burned two years ago."
In the late 1860s, when Collis P. Huntington visited the area, he had initially hoped to place his railroad terminus in Guyandotte. After he hitched his horse to the post in front of the local hotel, he was fined by the mayor, because his horse had inadvertently backed itself onto the sidewalk. A fuming Mr. Huntington then decided to place the terminus of his railroad elsewhere –about four miles west of Guyandotte –in what was to become Huntington. Decades later, Guyandotte would merge into an expanding Huntington. Today, in this part of eastern Huntington, one can still find homes dating back to the 1820s and the early Guyandotte days.

# Sketch 12-A: The Ohio River –from the Robert Byrd L&D to Manchester, OH

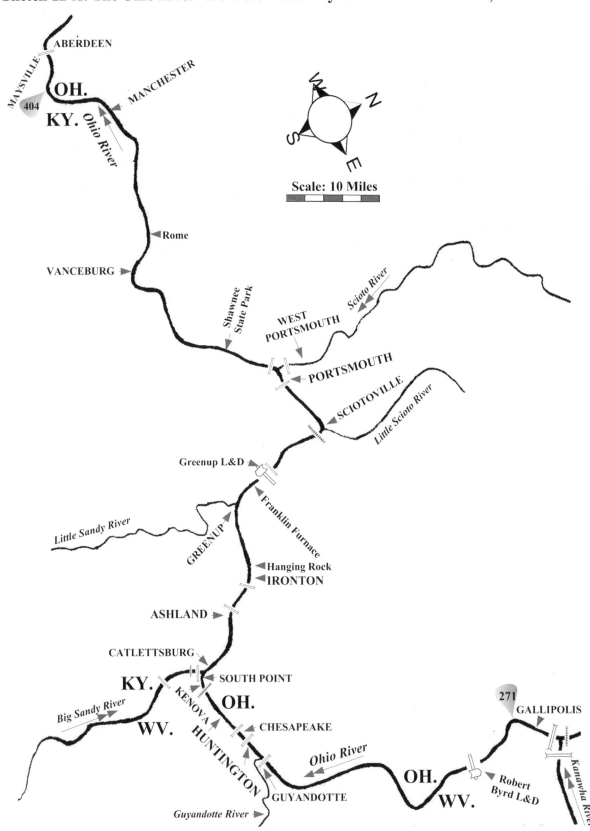

ABERDEEN

MAYSVILLE

OH.

404

KY.

MANCHESTER

Ohio River

Rome

VANCEBURG

Shawnee State Park

WEST PORTSMOUTH

Scioto River

PORTSMOUTH

SCIOTOVILLE

Little Scioto River

Greenup L&D

Franklin Furnace

Little Sandy River

GREENUP

Hanging Rock

IRONTON

ASHLAND

CATLETTSBURG

SOUTH POINT

KY.

KENOVA

OH.

271

GALLIPOLIS

Big Sandy River

WV.

HUNTINGTON

CHESAPEAKE

Ohio River

OH.

GUYANDOTTE

WV.

Robert Byrd L&D

Kanawha River

Guyandotte River

Scale: 10 Miles

**GUYANDOTTE RIVER, WV** (mile 305.2, LDB):

The Guyandotte River flows north-northwestward for over 150 miles, originating in southwestern West Virginia. The town of Barboursville is situated seven miles upstream on the Guyandotte, and at the confluence of the Mud River. Barboursville was an early Shawnee Indian crossroad.

In February 1972, a tributary of the Guyandotte River, Buffalo Creek, suffered a major catastrophe. A shoddily-constructed coal slurry impoundment dam on Buffalo Creek burst after a period of typical winter rains, and with some anticipated warning. One hundred and twenty-six folks lost their lives, another 1,121 were injured, more than 4,000 were left homeless, sixteen coal mining communities were heavily damages, and one poor coal-mining community, Saunders, was completely wiped-out.

**HUNTINGTON, WV** (miles 306-311, LDB):

James Holderby was one of the first settlers in the area. In the early 1820s, Holderby purchased land situated on the high, somewhat narrow, Ohio River floodplain. Soon an Ohio River landing, in an area called Brownsville, was up and running. In 1869, Holderby's Landing was visited, and chosen to be the site for the western terminus of the Chesapeake and Ohio Railroad by Collis Huntington. In 1871, when the area incorporated, it was renamed Huntington. By 1873, trains from as far east as Richmond were arriving in Huntington. By the 1950s, Huntington had established a firm industrial base owing to coal, steel, chemicals, glass, and train assemblies.

Downtown Huntington is also home to Marshall University, the second largest university in West Virginia. Marshall Academy was founded in 1837. It later became Marshall College in 1857 and Marshall University in 1961. The school was named for three-decade serving Supreme Court Chief Justice, John Marshall. Marshall affirmed that the federal high court had the power to exercise judicial review as well as to strike down state laws that violated the US Constitution. For the better, Marshall strengthened the role of our third branch of government –the judiciary.

In November 1970, a chartered plane carrying the Marshall University football team and supporters (75 folks) slammed into a mountainside while approaching the Tri-State Airport, killing everyone aboard. The pilot misjudged his altitude during a rainy and foggy night approach returning from a game with East Carolina University. A touching 2007 movie, *We Are Marshall*, has been made about the aftermath of this incident.

In 1953, the 'Port of Huntington' surpassed Pittsburgh as the busiest port on the Ohio River. Prior to 2000, the 'Port of Huntington' was defined as a fourteen mile stretch on the Ohio River fronting the Huntington waterfront. In 2000, the Corps of Engineers approved a redefinition for the 'Port of Huntington-Tri-State.' The port expanded from those 14 Ohio River miles to 100 Ohio River miles (i.e., from Cheshire to Portsmouth Ohio), plus the 90 navigable miles of the Kanawha River, plus another nine miles into the Big Sandy River. In terms of both total tonnage and ton-miles, the 'Port of Huntington-Tri State,' is the largest inland port in the entire United States, and typically handles over 80 million tons per year of cargo. In terms of 'total tonnage,' the 'Port of Huntington' has no equal. Second place St. Louis handles less than half Huntington's tonnage. But in terms of 'ton-miles,' St. Louis and Pittsburgh are not that far behind still first-place Huntington. 'Ton-miles' factors in the distance a cargo travels on the inland rivers between its loading and unloading points. Two of the biggest contributors towards the 'Port of Huntington-Tri State' high river tonnage are railroad cars offloading coal, and petroleum coming from the Marathon refinery in Catlettsburg Kentucky.

With a population close to 50,000, Huntington is the second largest city in West Virginia. The western end of downtown Huntington, the old central city, is home to the Cabell County Courthouse. The courthouse, built in 1901, is the gold domed building. There are also three small museums on this western end of Huntington –the Antique Railroad Museum (☎ 304-736-7349), the Museum of Radio and Technology (304-525-8890, www.mrtwv.org), and well out of town, the Heritage Farm Museum (☎ 304-552-1244, www.heritagefarmmuseum.com). The Antique Railroad Museum displays one of the last working steam locomotives, #1308, and built in 1949. Huntington has its annual Ribfest Festival at Harris Riverfront Park (☎ 304-696-5990) during the third weekend in August.

**KENOVA, WV** (miles 316, LDB):
        In 1817, Ceredo-Kenova was founded as an abolitionist settlement against slavery in the western part of Virginia. 'Kenova' was named for the meeting place of three states –Kentucky, Ohio, and Virginia.

**SOUTH POINT, OH** (mile 316, RDB –Right Descending Bank)
        The town of South Point is the most southerly point in the state of Ohio. From this point downriver, the Ohio generally flows north of due west, and will not again reach this low latitude for another 275 miles downriver, or about 10 miles upriver from Louisville.

**BIG SANDY RIVER, WV-KY** (mile 317.1, LDB):
        The Big Sandy River forms the boundary between West Virginia (near Kenova) and Kentucky (near Catlettsburg). A section of the Ohio River, for many miles both upstream and downstream of the Big Sandy, and on both sides of the Ohio River, is a huge barge staging area that rivals the intensity of Pittsburgh for barge traffic. Most of the tows are coal barges, and there's a strong whiff of coal dust in the air. The Big Sandy River ranks third, behind only the Ohio and the Monongahela Rivers, in terms of coal shipments.
        The Big Sandy flows generally northward for close to 30 miles, and we observed several small deadheads and branches in this river, making this an uneasy transit for recreational boats. he very muddy-colored and unappealing Big Sandy is supposedly navigable for 23 miles, and primarily carries coal barges out of the region. There are nearly two dozen, mostly coal, terminals in the first nine miles of the river. This river has very little to offer recreational boaters. Near Louisa (Kentucky) and Fort Gay (West Virginia), the Levisa Fork and Tug Fork join to form the Big Sandy. The Tug Fork, the more eastern fork, continues to be the boundary between West Virginia and Kentucky.
        One of the most notorious family feuds occurred in the Tug Valley during the late 19th Century between the Hatfields of West Virginia and the McCoys of Kentucky. Both families made money off moonshine. The feud escalated into minor warfare between Kentucky and West Virginia, and lasted over a decade. More than a dozen lives were taken. Eventually, authorities from both states had to step-in to quell the violence.

**ASHLAND, KY** (mile 321-323, LDB):
        In 1786, the Poage family from Virginia's Shenandoah Valley settled in Ashland. They arrived in Kentucky, not by water, but via the Cumberland Gap, more than 150 miles to the south. The area was first called Poage's Landing. In 1854, the name was changed to Ashland in honor of Kentuckian Henry Clay's home estate near Lexington. That estate was named for the many ash trees on Clay's property.
        Along with Ironton and Hanging Rock Ohio, Ashland's growth was also spurred by early iron furnaces. In 1924, a small oil refinery in nearby Catlettsburg became Ashland Oil. In the late 1990s Ashland combined many of its assets with Marathon Oil. In the 1910s, the American Rolling Mill Company (later to become Armco Steel), established its second plant in Ashland. In the late 1980s, feeling the pressure from international competition, Armco joined Kawasaki Steel Corporation and became AK Steel. Today, the Catlettsburg Marathon Oil Refinery and AK Steel are pillars of the Ashland economy.

**IRONTON-HANGING ROCK, OH** (mile 325-330, RDB):

Lawrence County was founded in 1816, and named for Naval Officer James Lawrence, famous for his line "don't give up the ship." The county seat, Ironton, founded in 1849 was chosen for its position on the river, along with its ability to move heavy raw materials to the river and then ship the finished goods down the Ohio. In 1862, noted abolitionist John Rankin moved to Ironton after his wife died in Ripley. During the latter half of the 19th Century, Ironton was one of the foremost producers of pig iron in the world. Twenty iron furnaces were operating at one point. Ironton's pig iron was used in English, French, and Russian battleships. The Detroit, Toledo, and Ironton Railroad (DT&I) connected Ironton with Detroit. Another railroad, the Iron Railroad Company, was established to transport pig iron and manufactured goods from outlying towns to the steamboats parked at the Ironton wharf. With its remarkable growth, Ironton also became a Mecca for vice. Ironton attracted many saloons, brothels, and a racetrack. It was said that glitzy Ironton was the 19th Century Las Vegas. Quick and quiet marriages could also be arranged in Ironton.

By the early 20th Century, Ironton's painful demise had started. Thanks to advancement in steel production, the market for pig iron had drastically changed. Two major floods (1917 and 1937) and the Great Depression further destabilized the area. As the iron industry tanked, this labor-oriented town tried to attract other heavy industries. In the 1930s, the Allied Corporation (now Honeywell) and the Alpha Portland Cement built factories. But by the 1960s, the cement plant had closed, and by the early 21st Century, a roofing materials and an iron foundry had also closed. Another 1,000 jobs were lost. There were fewer people living in the entire county, than had lived in the city of Ironton a mere 110 years ago.

Today, there are still many old homes built during Ironton's days of opulence dating from the mid-19th Century. One can take a self-guided tour of these old houses. Ironton, like other Ohio River towns, has some picturesque seawall murals, reminding us of its rich past. Outside the seawall, right on the river, there's also a caboose and the Fuzzy Duck Restaurant.

**GREENUP, KY** (mile 336, LDB):

In 1751, Christopher Gist –the trailblazer who often preceded George Washington, was likely the first white person in the Greenup area. In 1803, the county was founded, with Greenup as the seat. This part of Kentucky was no slouch when it came to pig iron production. The northeastern Kentucky pig iron industry was started in 1791. By the 1830s, Kentucky was the third leading iron-producing state.

In October 1862, one of the more masterful retreats of the Civil War ended in Greenup Kentucky. The Cumberland Gap, where Kentucky, Virginia and Tennessee meet, was considered pivotal during the war. General Ulysses S Grant called the Cumberland Gap, "the Gibraltar of America." In 1861, the Confederates controlled The Gap. By the summer of 1862, Union General George W. Morgan controlled The Gap. But the Confederates were soon able to severe Morgan's supply lines. Morgan's Union troops were nearly surrounded, and in real danger of being overrun. General George Morgan smartly withdrew with about 8,000 men, and covered over 200 miles, to reach Greenup Kentucky and the relative safety of the Ohio River in just 16 days. During this 'masterful retreat,' General George Morgan's troops were harassed by Confederate General John Hunt Morgan's Raiders. In 1863 Union General Ambrose Burnside retook The Gap.

The town and county were named for early Kentucky politician, Christopher Greenup. Greenup was a Revolutionary War officer, a US Representative from Kentucky as well as the third governor of the state. Today, there are many modestly-nice homes along the Ohio River in Greenup.

**LITTLE SANDY RIVER, KY** (mile 336.3, LDB):

The Little Sandy River generally flows north-northeast for about 90 miles before dumping into the Ohio River at Greenup Kentucky.

**FRANKLIN FURNACE, OH** (mile 339, RDB):

Franklin Furnace is the first Ohio town in Scioto County. There is a nearby bridge over the Ohio River that crosses into Greenup County Kentucky. If you're traveling down the river, one of the only full-service marinas, between Huntington West Virginia and Aberdeen Ohio (i.e., in about a 100-mile stretch of river) can be found on Ginat Creek in Franklin Furnace.

**PORTSMOUTH, OH** (mile 355-356, RDB):

In the late 1790s, Alexandria, on the banks of the Scioto and Ohio Rivers, was founded by Revolutionary War veteran Colonel Thomas Parker. In 1803, an area adjacent to Alexandria was laid-out, and named Portsmouth for Portsmouth Virginia. By 1808, frequent floods influenced many residents of Alexandria to move to the higher ground just upriver –to Portsmouth. By 1814, as its population surpassed Alexandria's, Portsmouth became the Scioto County seat. Today, Alexandria Point Park sits on the high point on the LDB of the Scioto River and RDB of the Ohio River at the western edge of Portsmouth.

In the 1840s, Portsmouth was the southern terminus of the Ohio and Erie Canal. In the 1870s, Portsmouth developed a sizeable shoe-making industry and soon also had a steel mill. Local industries continued to grow with two more steel mills, lumber mills, brick ovens, and stone quarries. But as things sadly often go on this river, those industries were mostly defunct by the 1980s. In 1986, Shawnee State University, with currently nearly 4,000 students, was established. Shawnee State is Ohio's newest four-year undergraduate university.

In 1908, the first Portsmouth seawall was constructed, but it failed during the 1937 flood. The seawall was rebuilt and strengthened. The seawall murals were inspired by those at Steubenville. This ongoing mural project was started in 1993. The historic Bonneyfiddle District sits just beyond the murals and seawall close to the Ohio River. A Ramada Inn, hardware store, grocer, post office, and several downtown restaurants are near this area. The bridge near the center of Portsmouth over the Ohio carries US Route 23. US Route 23, in Kentucky, is also known as the 'Country Music Highway.' Portsmouth hosts its annual 'River Days Festival' at the Landing over Labor Day Weekend.

Clean-cut cowboy Roy Rogers and innovative and theatrical baseball executive Branch Rickey are two of Portsmouth's favorite sons. Branch Rickey had a colorful career, and revolutionized professional baseball in ways that were long overdue –by creating a framework for the modern minor league farm system, signing the first African American player –Jackie Robinson in 1947, and drafting the first Hispanic player –Roberto Clemente in 1955.

**SCIOTO RIVER, OH** (mile 356.5, RDB)

Scioto is a Native American word for 'deer.' The Scioto River had long provided access to the heart of Shawnee Country in southern and central Ohio. No less than two major Shawnee villages were once located on the Scioto River –one here at its confluence at the Ohio River, and another about 70 miles upstream near Circleville.

In 1751, intrepid explorer, surveyor, and skilled back-woodsman, Christopher Gist had explored as far westward as the Scioto River. But a few hearty French fur traders were already living with the Shawnees in 'Lower Shawnee Town.' In the fall of 1755, 'Lower Shawnee Town" was also believed to be the location where a kidnapped Mary Ingles, her three children, sister-in-law, and Frau Stumf spent most of their time while in Shawnee captivity.

The Scioto River flows generally south-southeast through Columbus and Chillicothe Ohio. The lowest 80 miles of the Scioto River was once utilized for the short-lived Ohio and Erie

Suspension Bridge, Under Construction, near Portsmouth, Ohio

Canal of the 1840s. The narrow Scioto River has an exceptionally broad flood plain, and from a satellite view, it's very noticeable as it bisects southern Ohio with a north-south ribbon.

**WEST PORTSMOUTH, OH** (mile 363, RDB):

Shawnee State Park and Shawnee State Forest are located about seven miles downriver from Portsmouth. Shawnee State Forest is the largest among Ohio's 20 state forests. Shawnee State Park has cottages, a lodge, tent camping, a golf course, and a nice marina. "Shawnee" in Native American means "those who have silver." The Shawnees conducted much trade in this precious metal. The hilly terrain in this area has often been described as "The Little Smokies" for the blue haze often emanating from these small steep mountains. The blue haze, as it affects the Great Smokey Mountains, comes from moisture in the air which is generated by the thousands of acres of trees.

**VANCEBURG, KY** (mile 378, LDB):

In 1797, Joseph Vance came to the area to make salt from a natural salt well. Vanceburg Kentucky is the only sizeable town on the LDB of the Ohio River between Greenup and Maysville. Vanceburg is the county seat of Lewis County. Lewis County was established in 1807, and named after explorer Meriwether Lewis. The only monument on the south side of the Ohio River ever bestowed to Union soldiers is in Vanceburg Kentucky. This monument is dedicated to the 107 Union troops from Lewis County who died during the Civil War.

**ROME, OH** (mile 384, RDB):

In 1835, Rome was founded by William Stout. The town was a busy river port for the remainder of the 19th Century. William Stout's son, Elijah, was to become a founding father of Omaha Nebraska as well as Denver Colorado. Elijah Stout was born in Rome Ohio.

**MANCHESTER, OH** (mile 397, RDB):

In 1791, Massie's Station was the fourth permanent settlement in Ohio, as well as the first settlement in the post-Revolutionary War 'Virginia Military District.' The Virginia Military District was reserved by the state of Virginia for payment to Virginia's Revolutionary War veterans. After the Revolutionary War, under the Articles of Confederation, Virginia, as well as other states, had to cede most of their western land claims. In 1784, in return for ceding these western land claims, Virginia was granted land in this area to be set aside for the state's war veterans. This Virginia Military District tract of land bordered the Ohio River to the south, the Scioto River to the east, and the Little Miami River to the west. Many Virginia veterans did settle here, even though they had to give up their slaves on account of the provisions of the 1787 Northwest Ordinance. In 1803, when Ohio became a state, the land grant situation became further muddled among Virginia, Ohio, and federal interests.

In 1797, Manchester became the first county seat of Adams County. In 1804, that county seat moved eight miles northeast to the town of West Union. Adams County was named after the second US President –John Adams. Manchester was a busy steamboat port in the mid-19th Century. Manchester has an auto parts store, grocer, laundromat, general store, and a few restaurants.

Vehicle Ferry near Augusta, Kentucky

# CHAPTER 13
# Cincinnati and east ...on the Ohio River, from Maysville KY to the Miami River

We consider this part of the Ohio River to be 'Greater Cincinnati and east.' This chapter includes Hamilton (i.e., Cincinnati), Clermont and Brown Counties of Ohio, and the corresponding Kentucky side. On a weekend, many Cincinnati and Northern Kentucky boaters regularly travel the 60 miles upstream as far as Maysville Kentucky or to many of the other small but very lively Ohio River ports between Cincinnati and Maysville. There is only one lock and dam –the Captain Anthony Meldahl Lock and Dam located about half-way between Cincinnati and Maysville. Compared to the chapter just upriver –Chapter 12 –activities, facilities, and options increase for boaters and river traveler on this section of the Ohio River. Many recreational boats are seen on the river in this, and in the following chapter (i.e., Chapter 14). During the summertime, the river can become very crowded with recreational boats, commercial tows, and jet skis. The river continues to generally flow west-northwest in this chapter, reaching a northern apex at North Bend Ohio –near the western end of Hamilton County.

The following table summarizes the locks and pools on this section of Ohio River with some overlap into adjacent river sections:

**Table 13-A: Locks and Pools on the Ohio River, from Maysville to the Miami River:**

| Lock and Pool Name | Mile | Lock Side | Telephone Number ☎ | Opens for Rec. Vessels | Lift (in ft) | Pool Length (miles) |
|---|---|---|---|---|---|---|
| Capt. Meldahl L&D, (Chilo, OH) | 436.2 | RDB | 513-876-2921 | 24/7 | 30 | 95.2 |
| Markland L&D, (Warsaw, KY) | 531.5 | LDB | 859-567-7661 | 24/7 | 35 | 95.3 |

Dam Gates at Meldahl Lock and Dam, Foster, Kentucky

**MAYSVILLE, KY** (miles 407-409, LDB –Left Descending Bank):

Well before the white settlers arrived, buffalo had been trotting a path between the Ohio River and the salt licks about 20 miles to the southwest toward the heart of Kentucky at what is now Blue Licks. This same path was later used by Native Americans. Later it became part of US Route 68 –the first paved road west of the Appalachian Mountains. This route was also well-traveled by runaway slaves during the time of the Underground Railroad.

In 1773, pioneers discovered a small natural Ohio River harbor at the mouth of Limestone Creek. Frontiersmen Daniel Boone and Simon Kenton were instrumental in founding a settlement here. In 1784, Simon Kenton helped construct the first permanent building. By the late 1780s, several settlers were arriving at the mouth of Limestone Creek. In 1792, 'Limestone Landing' was finished and opened for business.

By 1797, Zane's Trace was completed, providing the first overland route through the Northwest Territories –from Wheeling to Maysville. In 1803, when Merewether Lewis camped in Maysville, John Colter –a young Kentucky sharpshooter, joined the Corps of Discovery. Colter later went on to become a celebrated 'Mountain Man' in the Rocky Mountains.

Throughout the 1830s and 1850s, the Maysville waterfront was a busy place with scores of Ohio River steamboats stopping each month. During the early 19th Century, there were slave holding pens in Maysville. Nonetheless, there was also an active Underground Railroad working toward the opposite goal. The Bierbower House, overlooking the Ohio River, was an Underground Railroad way station.

In 1830, Kentuckian Henry Clay pushed a bill through Congress known as the 'Maysville Road Bill.' The towns of Maysville and Lexington, about 60 miles apart, were to be connected by a road, largely financed by federal dollars. Henry Clay was selling this road project as an extension if the National Road (i.e., from Cumberland Maryland to Wheeling) and Zane's Trace (from Wheeling to Maysville). Congress passed the bill, but President Andrew Jackson vetoed it, arguing that federal money should not be spent solely on a 'one state' project. Among many other things espoused, Henry Clay was a strong advocate for public works projects funded with federal assistance. When President Jackson's veto was upheld, several other similar expansion projects (e.g., roads, canals, and other infrastructure) were also derailed. Henry Clay and his vision of federalism suffered a major political blow.

Maysville is the county seat of Mason County. Mason County was formed in 1788, and named after far-sighted Virginian George Mason, a major author of the US Bill of Rights. Confederate Civil War General Albert Sidney Johnston, who was killed at the *Battle of Shiloh*, was born near Maysville. Singer and actress Rosemary Clooney was also born here.

Today, Maysville has a sizeable historic district and a mural floodwall project that began in 1998. The old landing has become Maysville Riverfront Park and Fishing Pier. The Bierbower House has been turned into an Underground Railroad Museum. In downtown, besides a helpful Visitor's Center, Maysville has the educational Kentucky Gateway Museum (☎ 606-564-8535).

**ABERDEEN, OH** (mile 409, RDB –Right Descending Bank):

In 1786, Colonel Benjamin Logan, a veteran of Lord Dunmore's and the Revolutionary Wars crossed the Ohio River from Kentucky with the local militia and other troops in a retaliatory raid to pursue Indians deep into Ohio. In the early 1800s, Zane's Trace was not much more than a rudimentary path, but it did reach Aberdeen. In 1816, Aberdeen was founded at the southern terminus of the Trace, on the north shore of the Ohio River. A ferry was soon crossing the river to Maysville. Aberdeen's annual River Festival is held during the first weekend in October. Aberdeen, less touristy than Maysville –its partner town across the river, offers less of a show, but it also offers less expensive motels and restaurants.

134

# Sketch 13-A: The Ohio River –from Maysville, Kentucky to California, Ohio

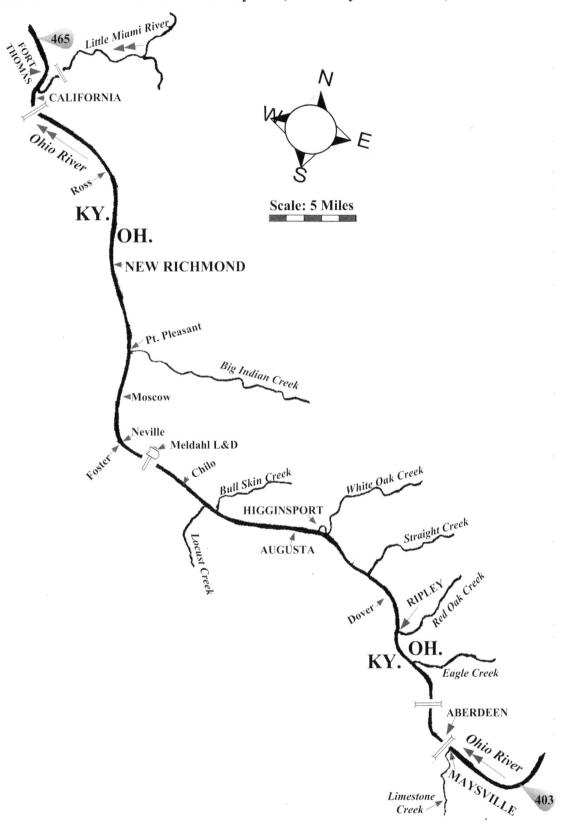

465

Little Miami River

FORT THOMAS

CALIFORNIA

N
W E
S

Ohio River

Ross

Scale: 5 Miles

KY.

OH.

NEW RICHMOND

Pt. Pleasant

Big Indian Creek

Moscow

Neville

Meldahl L&D

Foster

Chilo

Bull Skin Creek

White Oak Creek

HIGGINSPORT

Straight Creek

Locust Creek

AUGUSTA

RIPLEY

Dover

Red Oak Creek

KY.

OH.

Eagle Creek

ABERDEEN

Ohio River

MAYSVILLE

403

Limestone Creek

**RIPLEY, OH** (mile 417, RDB):

It's hard to argue that Ripley was not the heart of the Underground Railroad movement on the Ohio River. In the early and middle 19th Century, John Rankin, with his convincing abolitionist ways, lent Ripley this distinction and its solid place in American History. To many slave-owning Kentuckians, this town was known as a 'black, dirty abolitionist hellhole.'

In 1812, Revolutionary War veteran, Colonel James Poage founded Ripley. He had been granted a sizeable tract of land within the Virginia Military District. He freed his Virginia slaves upon arriving here. The area was originally named Staunton for Poage's hometown in Virginia. In 1816, the town was renamed in honor of War of 1812 General Eleazar Ripley. In the early 1800s, Ripley became an important pork butchering and packing center. Tobacco, flour, lumber, a winery and ship-building also spurred Ripley's early economy. Ripley was once the third largest boat-building city in Ohio, specializing in flat boats. Regular steamboat service linked Ripley to Pittsburgh upriver, and St. Louis and New Orleans downriver.

In 1822, after finding mostly hostile audiences in Tennessee and Kentucky, abolitionist Presbyterian Minister John Rankin and his family moved to Ripley. Rankin soon organized the Ripley Anti-Slavery Society. His first home was right on the Ohio River, hoping that to be the best location to abet runaways. In 1828, he smartly moved to another house high atop a hill, and about a half mile from the river. That house could be seen from Kentucky and well across the river. At night, a lantern left on in the attic was a signal to runaways. It's believed that most of the 2,000 runaway slaves that passed through Ripley stayed, at one time or another, with the Rankins. All of Rankin's 13 children had roles in the Underground Railroad.

In 1831, a slave named Tice Davis swam across the Ohio River. His master was on his heels chasing him in a boat. Nonetheless, when Davis reached the Ripley shore, only minutes ahead of his pursuer, he was able to successfully 'disappear.' After arriving in Ripley, the frustrated and irate slave owner sardonically exclaimed something like, 'he must have found an underground railroad' –thereby coining a new lexicon in our vocabulary. Harriet Beecher Stowe set her great novel *Uncle Tom's Cabin* in Ripley.

Civil War Raider, General John Hunt Morgan vowed to burn that "damned abolitionist hellhole to the ground." Morgan never made it to Ripley, but he did wreak havoc in nearby Georgetown Ohio –Union General Ulysses Grant's boyhood home about 10 miles to the northwest. In Georgetown, Morgan's men usurped horses, food, and other supplies, and robbed a local bank. The local militias in Ripley and Brown County were known as 'the squirrel hunters.' They were good marksmen that supposedly never had to shoot at the same squirrel twice. Brown County contributed more than 1,300 'squirrel hunters' for the defense of southern Ohio during the Civil War, and more than any other county in Ohio.

Today, one can still retrace a few of those steps runaway slaves made through Ripley Ohio. The Rankin House/Museum (☎ 937-392-1627) is open to visitors from Memorial Day through Labor Day, about five days/week. The John Parker House sits right on the river, and is located at 330 Front Street. Besides Parker's and Rankin's homes, there are no less than another half-dozen other houses in Ripley that have been recognized as crucial locations for the local Underground Railroad. Many of these and other local attractions can be visited with the help of a self-guided 'Freedom's Landing Brochure,' available at many places in town.

Ripley is also home to 'The Ripley Museum' and 'The Ohio Tobacco Museum.' The Tobacco Museum (☎ 937-392-9410) is also located at 703 S. Second Street and is generally open on the weekends during the spring, summer, and fall. Ripley host is annual Ohio Tobacco Festival during the last weekend in August. Ripley has several taverns, a nice diner, and a pharmacy.

**DOVER, KY** (mile 419, LDB):

In the 1830s, Dover was one of the largest tobacco ports on the Ohio River.

Summer fun at boat ramp in Ripley, Ohio

**HIGGINSPORT, OH** (mile 425, RDB):

Higginsport was founded in 1816, by Revolutionary War Colonel Robert Higgins who received this particular land grant. Higginsport's heydays were during the 1880s, when tobacco warehouses, a shoe factory, lumber and grist mills, and a distillery drove the local economy. In the 19th Century, steamboats were also built in Higginsport, and in nearby Levanna and Ripley. Today, Vonderhaar's Manufacturing makes hand-crafted billiard tables in Higginsport.

**AUGUSTA, KY** (mile 427, LDB):

In 1786, Augusta was founded as an Ohio River trading post. The town was named after Augusta County in Virginia. In the early 19th Century, Augusta became the seat of Bracken County. The ferryboat service between Augusta and the Ohio side has been in operation since the early 1800s. In 1833, great American songwriter Stephen C Foster routinely visited his uncle, who was the president of nearby Augusta College. Foster often heard melodious voices emanating from an old Negro church atop a hill float softly over Augusta. Undoubtedly this influenced Foster's music, and many of his now familiar songs reflect the doleful melodies that originated from these African American spirituals. During the earlier years of the Civil War, Union troops were stationed in Augusta. By late 1862, they were temporarily driven out by Confederate Raiders  Augusta prides itself as a haven for many runaways during the Underground Railroad days. Portions of the Hollywood films "Centennial" and "Huck Finn" were filmed here. There are several Bed and Breakfasts, antiques shops, and a general store in quaint Augusta. Augusta hosts its annual 'Sternwheel Regatta' during the last weekend of June.

# Roebling Suspension Bridge into downtown Cincinnati

**CHILO, OH** (mile 434, RDB):

. The Lock House from old lock #34 is still very functional. It's been turned into a river museum –Chilo Lock #34 Park Visitor Center and Museum (☎513-876-9013). There are models and exhibits of wicket dams, towboats, and more. The Crooked Run Nature Preserve is also tied to this property.

**POINT PLEASANT, OH** (445.2, RDB):

Point Pleasant sits at the confluence, and on the RDB of Big Indian Creek. In 1822, Hiram Ulysses Grant, one of my favorite generals, was born in Point Pleasant. He spent most of his youth in nearby Georgetown Ohio about 20 miles to the east. Right on the Ohio River, there's a roadside picnic area. The Grant Memorial Church and a small museum (open April-October) are across the street.

**NEW RICHMOND, OH** (mile 450, RDB):

In 1814, New Richmond was founded. The town is named for Richmond Virginia. In 1828, New Richmond and the neighboring town of Susanna were incorporated. In 1834, James Birney found a receptive audience for his abolitionist paper, *The Philanthropist*. Previously, Birney could find no supporters across the river in Kentucky. The paper soon moved to the larger nearby Cincinnati market. But in Cincinnati, hostile mobs repeatedly destroyed his presses and personally threatened Birney.

During much of the 19th Century, New Richmond was a busy port for packet boats. In March 1997, New Richmond was devastated by an Ohio River flood. Some houses were covered by nine feet of water. There's a hardware store, grocers, and several restaurants in town. New Richmond hosts their annual River Days (☎ 513-684-1253) in mid-August. During this three-day festival, the town has a cardboard canoe regatta, and boat and helicopter rides.

# Sketch 13-B: The Ohio River –from the Lit. Miami River to the Great Miami River

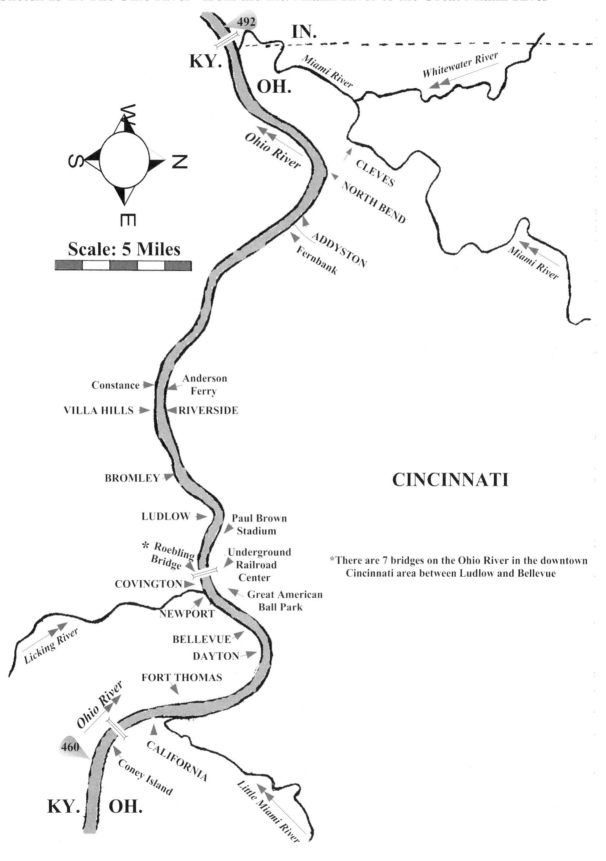

IN.

KY.

OH.

492

Miami River

Whitewater River

Ohio River

CLEVES

NORTH BEND

ADDYSTON

Fernbank

Miami River

W

S          N

E

Scale: 5 Miles

Constance

Anderson Ferry

VILLA HILLS          RIVERSIDE

BROMLEY

CINCINNATI

LUDLOW

Paul Brown Stadium

* Roebling Bridge

Underground Railroad Center

*There are 7 bridges on the Ohio River in the downtown Cincinnati area between Ludlow and Bellevue

COVINGTON

Great American Ball Park

NEWPORT

Licking River

BELLEVUE

DAYTON

FORT THOMAS

Ohio River

CALIFORNIA

460

Coney Island

Little Miami River

KY.          OH.

## Bustling Riverfront between Cincinnati and Covington, Kentucky

## Seawall-Landing in Augusta, Kentucky

**CALIFORNIA, OH** (mile 463, RDB):

California Ohio is an area in the eastern part of Cincinnati. It has been often labeled 'Cincinnati's Playland' because of three local recreation destinations along the Ohio River. These three large complexes are: Coney Island Amusement Center (☎ 513-232-8230, www.coneyislandpark.com), Riverbend Music Center (☎ 513-232-6220, www.riverbend-music.com), and River Downs Horse Racing Track (☎ 513-232-8000, www.riverdowns.com). Besides the huge marina complexes on the Ohio River west of California, there are also a handful of smaller, specialized marine service stores, and repair facilities west of the Little Miami River along Kellogg Avenue.

**LITTLE MIAMI RIVER, OH** (mile 464, RDB)

The Little Miami River flows southwestward starting from northeast of Xenia Ohio. The river is named for an Algonquin-speaking tribe. It forms the western boundary of the Virginia Military District. The Little Miami River has been designated a National Wild and Scenic River. Going downriver on the Ohio River, the mouth of the Little Miami River is easy to miss. The Little Miami River can be choked with debris.

**FORT THOMAS-DAYTON-BELLEVUE, KY** (miles 464-469, LDB):

This part of Northern Kentucky is also a part of 'Greater Cincinnati.' The City of Fort Thomas was named after Union Civil War General George Thomas. At the onset of the Civil War, Thomas was ostracized and forever spurned by his Virginia family because he chose to support the Union, and not the Confederacy. He proved himself a most distinguished Union officer, and rose to the rank of Brigadier General. In August 1863, during the 'Second Battle of Chattanooga,' Thomas was able to hold a precarious Union line together and deservedly earned the nickname 'the Rock of Chickamauga.' In early 1880s, Army Chief of Staff, General William Tecumseh Sherman decided to relocate Newport Barracks to higher ground upriver in order to avoid the constant Ohio River flooding that occurs in Newport. Sherman named this new fort, after courageous General Thomas.

Downtown Cincinnati and Great American Ballpark, from Licking River

**CINCINNATI, OH** (downtown, miles 469-471, RDB):

In 1788, a small settlement called Losantiville was founded on the Ohio River opposite the mouth of the Licking River. This name meant 'the place opposite the Licking River.' In 1789, Fort Washington was built in response to the Indian hostilities in the area. The first governor of the Northwest Territories, Arthur St. Clair, made the village his seat, and changed the named to Cincinnati The Society of Cincinnati was an organization of ex-American Revolutionary War officers aspiring to the noble ideals of Roman citizen-soldier Lucius Quintus Cincinnatus. Cincinnati became the county seat of Hamilton County –and named after Alexander Hamilton.

In 1790 from Fort Washington, General Josiah Harmar launched an unsuccessful expedition against Chief Little Turtle in northwestern Ohio. In 1793, General "Mad" Anthony Wayne with better trained troops, and a more thought-out plan, departed Fort Washington. This time, Wayne's 3,000 Americans were able to defeat Chief Little Turtle and Chief Blue Jacket along with 1,500 Shawnees, and Miamis, in the *Battle of Fallen Timbers* near present-day Toledo. In 1803, Fort Washington was replaced by the Newport Barracks across the Ohio River.

With the Indians subdued at the *Battle of Fallen Timbers*, Cincinnati and most of present-day Ohio and Indiana were secured for future growth. In 1803, Meriwether Lewis and his portion of the Corps of Discovery stopped in Cincinnati. They likely camped in the area that is now the baseball park. After the War of 1812, when steamboats became prevalent on the Ohio, Cincinnati started to become an important commercial center. In 1827, the Miami Canal added to the city's strategic importance. Cincinnati became a major point of embarkation for settlers forging west.

In the early 19th Century, mostly due to its geographic position in the country, Cincinnati reflected the ongoing national debate over slavery. Before and during the Civil War, Cincinnati was a stronghold of Copperhead political activity. Copperheads were Northerners sympathetic to the Southern cause. On the other hand, in the 1830s, abolitionist James G. Birney published his newspaper, *The Philanthropist*. For much of the 1830s and 40s, Harriet Beecher Stowe lived in Cincinnati where she wrote her best seller –*Uncle Tom's Cabin*. Cincinnati had its first African American church by 1809, and an African American school by 1825. In 2004, the five-story National Underground Railroad Freedom Center (☎ 513-333-7500, www.freedomcenter.org) opened on the riverfront at 50 East Freedom Way. A visit here may very well be the highlight of any day spent in Cincinnati. This is an excellent downtown venue, with four thought-filled theatres offering visitors moving enlightenment about events and a time in American history that we should never forget.

By the 1850s, Cincinnati's economy was booming. It was the pork-packing capital of the world, and also called, 'Porkopolis.' Other nicknames Cincinnati had include, 'the Queen of the West,' 'the Queen City,' 'the Blue Chip City,' and 'the City of Seven Hills.' Many considered Cincinnati to be America's first major 'boomtown' –expanding rapidly in the heart of the country. In the 1850s, as many as 8,000 steamboats per year were parking along the Cincinnati waterfront. Soon, Cincinnati had become our nation's largest inland port, and there was a need to connect Cincinnati with Kentucky. In 1856, John Roebling started constructing the 'Covington-Cincinnati Suspension Bridge.' Roebling was a German immigrant educated in philosophy and engineering. Work on this bridge was interrupted by the Civil War. In 1866, when this Ohio River bridge was finally completed, it had the world's longest suspension span. This bridge, later renamed the John Roebling Bridge, held this distinction until 1883, when another John Roebling designed bridge –New York's Brooklyn Bridge broke the record. The Brooklyn Bridge was supervised by son, Washington Roebling.

Immediately after the Civil War, Cincinnati continued to prosper. However, near the end of the 19th Century, growth had begun to slow. In the 1870s, river traffic started declining. It's been said that Cincinnati weathered the Great Depression better than other cities of its size, because it was able to fall back on river trade.

Today, Cincinnati is Ohio's second largest metropolitan area –barely behind Cleveland. There is a significant German heritage in Cincinnati's cultural life. The city's 21$^{st}$ Century economy is diverse. Machinery and machine tools, jet engines, electronic equipment and components, packaged meat, banking and finance are a few pillars of Cincinnati's modern economy.

The Cincinnati Reds (i.e., Red Stockings) are America's oldest professional baseball team. The Reds started in 1866, and became a professional team three years later. The Great American Ballpark, opened in 2003, is their new home. On the river side of this ballpark, a 60-ton red paddlewheel, positioned atop two three-story towers, is a replica of the steamboat *American Queen's* paddlewheel. This is part of the National Steamboat Monument, which has many other interesting plaques and exhibits. Paul Brown Stadium, opened in 2000, sits downriver from the National Underground Railroad Freedom Center, and is the home of the Cincinnati Bengals.

In 1988, as part of its bicentennial celebration, the Port of Cincinnati hosted its first Tall Stacks Festival. That year, about 700,000 folks and fourteen riverboats, including the *Delta Queen* and *Belle of Louisville* showed up for the party. This festival has been since held in October every three or four years. In 2003, a five-day festival drew 19 riverboats, and about 150 bands – including many celebrity entertainers, along with 900,000 visitors. The most recent festival was held in October 2006. For more information on the next riverfront gala, visit: (www.tallstacks.com, or phone ☎ 513-721-0104).

Today, there may be over a score of, mostly upscale, restaurants on the Ohio River waterfront. Many of these restaurants are on the Kentucky side in 'Covington Landing,' 'Newport on the Levee,' and upriver from these two areas. A few of these restaurants are in massive structures floating on the Ohio River –Hooters, the Beer Sellars, the Waterfront Restaurant, and Mike Finks. The legendary Mike Fink used to call himself the 'king of the keelboaters.' Fink was a loud hard-drinking, brawler and braggart. He and 'friends' would amuse themselves by shooting cups of whiskey off each others heads. Davy Crockett called Fink 'half horse and half alligator.' In 1823, Fink was deliberately killed by a gunshot wound. It was provoked by either an argument over a woman or in retaliation for his killing of another by a 'missed low' shot aimed at a whiskey cup atop the head of a 'friend.'

**NEWPORT, KY** (mile 470, LDB):

In the mid-1790s, Newport started to be settled. The village was named for Christopher Newport, the commander of the *Susan Constant* –one of the first English ships to arrive in Jamestown Virginia in 1607. In 1803, the main fort on the other side of the Ohio River, Fort Washington, was moved here and became Newport Barracks. The fort was busy during the War of 1812 and throughout the Civil War. After the Civil War, the fort's days were numbered. Periodic Ohio River flooding often jeopardized the barracks, as did new military policies to build larger installations. By the early 1890s, the operations at Newport Barracks had been transferred to a site on higher ground in nearby Fort Thomas. During the days of prohibition, Newport became a gambling center.

Today, 'Newport On The Levee' (☎ 866-538-3359), www.newportonthelevee.com) has about 10 acres on the Ohio River, that include, among other things, shopping, 12 dinning venues, movies, and a comedy club. Just about every weekend during the summer, there's a major happening at 'Newport On The Levee.' The 100,000-square foot Newport Aquarium (☎ 859-261-7444, www.newportaquarium.com) is situated near the downriver end of 'Newport On The Levee.'

**THE LICKING RIVER, KY** (mile 470.1 LDB):

In August 1782, one of the last major battles of the Revolutionary War was a decisive British and Indian victory on the Licking River. This disastrous Revolutionary War Battle of Blue Licks occurred about 70 miles upstream –and only about 20 overland miles from Maysville. About 1000 British and Indian allies, heading south from Detroit, initially had planned to attack Wheeling. They changed their plans and decided to attack the less fortified settlements in northern Kentucky. After a diversionary attack on a small Kentucky outpost, near Lexington, a contingent of retreating Indians was used as a decoy. A group of about 180 Kentuckians from Lexington followed this 'easy trail' to pursue the 'retreating' Indians. But Virginia militia Lieutenant Colonel Daniel Boone was wary and feared a trap. Boone's commander overruled, and called Boone a coward. As the Kentuckians were crossing a ravine near the Licking River, a full force of British regulars and Indian allies ambushed them. Seventy-two of the 180 Kentuckians were killed, including the commander and Daniel Boone's son, Israel. Daniel Boone was able to retreat what-was-left of his force across the Licking River and back toward Lexington. In November 1782, Daniel Boone, George Rogers Clark, Simon Kenton, and Benjamin Logan reassembled their forces at the mouth of the Licking River to plan a retaliatory attack. This may have been the only time that all four of these great frontiersmen ever met. Their forces reached the Shawnee village near Circleville, and found that it and many other nearby settlements had already been deserted.

Today, the Licking River separates Newport (i.e., on the RDB) and Covington (i.e., on the LDB) Kentucky. The captain of the excursion boat *River Queen* informed me that a boat can easily travel about five miles upstream to the route I-275 Bridge, "after that, the river gets pretty shallow." There is a quasi-industrial flavor on the lowest three miles of the Licking River.

**COVINGTON, KY** (mile 471, LDB):

During the late 18th Century, this area was called 'The Point' and 'Kennedy's Ferry.' In 1815, Covington was incorporated and named for General Leonard Covington, a competent Marylander who was killed during the *War of 1812*. Today near the Licking and Ohio Rivers, Covington has its upscale 'Licking River Historic District.' Covington Landing, like 'Newport On The Levee,' is that city's entertainment center on the Ohio River. The Northern Kentucky Convention Center is nearby, as are several nice hotels and restaurants including a Marriott and a TGIFridays.

**LUDLOW-BROMLEY, KY** (miles 473-474, LDB):

In the late 18th Century, a few settlers started arriving in the Ludlow area. In 1846, the land was sold to Israel Ludlow, and the area was soon incorporated. Celebration Riverboats (☎ 859-931-6752) and RiverCity Charters (in Villa Hills ☎ 859-341-8221) park their boats in the Ohio River near Bromley. In 1880, the center of US population was about four miles southwest of this town.

**NORTH BEND-CLEVES, OH** (mile 486, RDB):

After 1841, it was a tradition for Ohio River steamboats to blow a low whistle when passing North Bend as a tribute to President William Henry Harrison. Harrison, the ninth US President is buried here, after spending only 31 days in that office. Twenty-third US President Benjamin Harrison, born in North Bend, was the grandson of William Henry Harrison. Ohio is the birthplace of seven US presidents –these seven served between 1869 and 1923. At the time these presidents were born, Ohio was a rough-hewn frontier. That positive surviving-in-the-frontier attitude may have tempered these men for future greatness? Ohio claims eight US presidents: William Henry Harrison (the 9th US President and born in Virginia), Grant (the 18th), Hayes, Garfield, Benjamin Harrison, McKinley, Taft and Harding (the 29th). Besides William Henry Harrison, three other Ohio presidents also have died while serving in office.

North Bend is the northernmost point on the Ohio River in its lowest 780 miles (i.e., all but the 200 miles just below Pittsburgh).  The confluence of the Great Miami River is fives miles downriver on the Ohio from North Bend.   However at North Bend, the Miami River is only about one mile away as the crow flies.  In 1843, there was a 1,782-foot brick-lined canal tunnel connecting the Ohio River with the Miami and Whitewater Rivers northwest of Cleves.  This canal tunnel bore through the ridge between North Bend and Cleves.  This 24-foot wide and 20-foot high 'Cincinnati and Whitewater Canal' tunnel was the first canal tunnel in Ohio.  But by 1856, the canal had gone defunct.  Six workers died during the canal's construction.

**MIAMI RIVER, OH** (mile 491, RDB):

The Great Miami River (i.e., or the Miami River) flows south-southwest for about 160 miles, while going through Middleton and Dayton Ohio.  In the 1830s, the Miami and Erie Canal connected the Ohio River with Lake Erie.  Work on the Miami [and Erie] Canal was begun at Middleton in 1825.   Unlike the Ohio and Erie Canal, the Miami [and Erie Canal] was not originally conceived as being a water route connecting Lake Erie to the Ohio River.  By 1830, the Miami Canal had been completed to Dayton.  In 1845, a 250-mile canal was opened from Lake Erie to the Ohio River.  But by the 1850s, the canal was deemed uneconomical and soon obsolete.

Today, a sinewy fairly deep channel goes back and forth across the wide (i.e., it's difficult to ascertain the channel's location in such a wide river) lower Miami River, and there are no channel markers.  The river is also loaded with sandbars and debris.  The shoreline is rather unappealing with no trees and eroded grasslands.

Ohio River from bluffs, near Hanover, Indiana

Dock in Westport, Kentucky

# CHAPTER 14
## Louisville and east …on the Ohio River, from Lawrenceburg IN to the Salt River, KY, including the Kentucky River and Harrods Creek

This 135-mile section of the Ohio River is the busy corridor between Cincinnati and Louisville, including all of Louisville. River borne traffic is about as heavy as in the previous chapter when we were near Cincinnati. There's one lock and dam between Louisville and Cincinnati, the Markland Lock and Dam, about 70 miles upriver from Louisville. In this chapter, the river here generally flows southwest. Several of the small Indiana towns along the river have flashy casinos on the water. We will also make a side trip in this chapter. We'll explore the Kentucky River for about 70 miles as far as Frankfort Kentucky.

**Table 14-A: Locks and Pools on the Ohio River, from Lawrenceburg, IN to the Salt River:**

| Lock and Pool Name | Mile | Lock Side | Telephone Number ☎ | Opens for Rec. Vessels | Lift (in ft) | Pool Length (miles) |
|---|---|---|---|---|---|---|
| Markland L&D (Warsaw, KY) | 531.5 | LDB | 859-567-7661 | 24/7 | 35 | 95.3 |
| McAlpine L&D (Louisville KY) | 606.8 | LDB | 502-774-3514 | 24/7 | 37 | 75.3 |
| Cannelton L&D (Cannelton, IN) | 720.7 | RDB | 812-547-2962 | 24/7 | 25 | 113.9 |

**LAWRENCEBURG, IN** (mile 493, RDB –Right Descending Bank):
Heading down the Ohio, Lawrenceburg is the first city in Indiana. Lawrenceburg is home to the Argosy Casino Boat, and the Lawrenceville Speedway (☎ 859-581-8759). Besides a casino, there's a nice hotel and several motels. Lawrenceburg has a pleasant Riverwalk along the levee for about one-mile. Lawrenceburg is the seat of Dearborn County.

**PETERSBURG, KY** (mile 495, LDB –Left Descending Bank):
In 1789, Tanner's Station, the first settlement in Boone County, was established. Today quaint Petersburg Kentucky has a general store and a boat ramp at the end of Market Street.

**AURORA, IN** (mile 497, RDB):
In 1819, Aurora was established. Aurora is a picturesque river town with many travelers' amenities, as well as several Ohio River marinas. It's also one of the few sizeable river towns in this portion of Indiana that does Not support a Riverside casino or casino boat. Downtown Aurora has a grocer, several restaurants (both upscale and downward), a laundromat, and a nearby gas station.

**RISING SUN, IN** (mile 506, RDB):
In the early 1800s settlers from the East began arriving here. In much of the 20th Century, the J.W. Whitlock Company was the major employer, building fine furniture. The higher end furniture was milled from local walnut. Mr. J.W. Whitlock was also an avid boat racer. In 19 years of racing, Whitlock lost only two races. Whitlock built and raced his famous *Hoosier Boy* race boats in the early 1900s. In 1924, the *Hoosier Boy* set a speed record on the Ohio River –racing roundtrip from Cincinnati to Louisville and back (267 miles) in just under 268 minutes. Whitlock's record is safe because: a) gasoline prices will never be as low as 22¢ per gallon again, and b) the Markland Lock and Dam – was not blocking the river in 1924.

Until 1962, there was a ferry service between Rising Sun and Rabbit Hash Kentucky. Today, the Grand Victoria Casino and Resort fuels the economy. The Empire House historic waterfront hotel, several cafés and restaurants, gift shops, a grocer, general store, auto parts store,

# Sketch 14-A: The Ohio River –from Lawrenceburg, Indiana to Westport, Kentucky, plus the Kentucky River to Frankfort

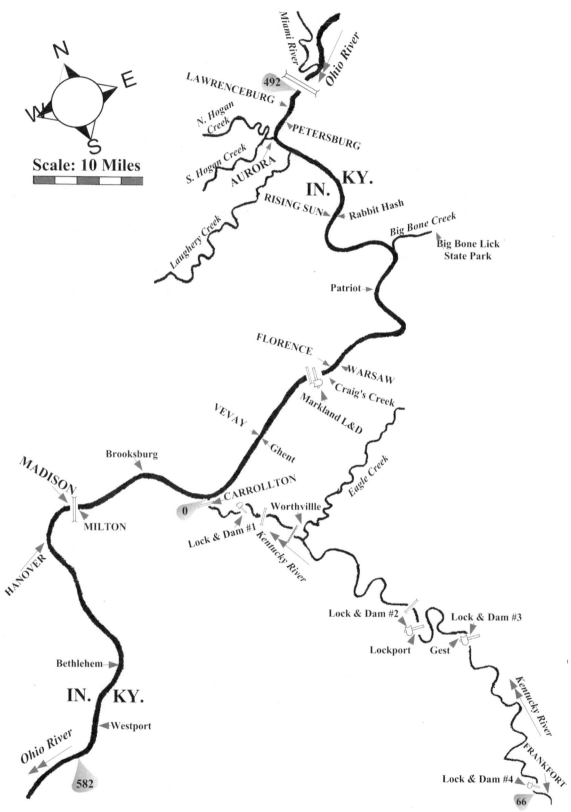

an historical museum, a library, and a post office are all within walking distance from the Ohio River. The oldest Indiana courthouse in continuous operation and the Pendleton Art Center (☎ 812-438-9900) are also nearby. Rising Sun is the seat of Ohio County.

## RABBIT HASH, KY (mile 506, LDB):

Where did that name come from? Supposedly, at one time, townsfolk used the local rabbit population as cuisine. The Rabbit Hash General Store, built in 1831, is one of the better known and preserved country stores in Kentucky. In 1998, and again in 2004, a dog was 'elected' as the unofficial mayor.

## BIG BONE LICK, KY (mile 517, LDB):

About 15,000 to 20,000 years ago, an ice sheet covered much of North America. Near the southern edge of this ice sheet, herds of mastodons, wooly mammoths and bison, as well as ground sloths were attracted by, and would congregate at, the warm salt and sulfur springs at Big Bone Lick. But many creatures became trapped in the jelly-like consistency of the ground, and perished. Over time, their bones, tusks, and teeth fossilized.

In 1739, Big Bone Lick was discovered by French explorers, and the ancient fossils were discovered. In 1755, Mary Ingles and Frau Stumf began their escape from the Shawnees Indians and their two French trapper allies. The larger group was on a salt-making expedition from the Scioto River to Big Bone Lick. Ingles' and Stumf's amazing successful escape back to Virginia is chronicled in the outdoor play, 'The Long Way Home' and in James Thom's embellished book account 'Follow the River.' Their return trip to Virginia, staying on the Kentucky and West Virginia side of the Ohio River, and later the Kanawha River (i.e., always on the LDB side), was made during the late fall. Neither woman could swim, so whenever they came to a tributary that they couldn't wade across, they had to follow it upstream to a point where they could cross it. This lengthened a 450-mile hike to an arduous 800-mile trek. When the two women made it back to Draper Meadow Virginia, six weeks later, winter was settling in. Both were close to death. They had survived by eating berries and insects.

In 1803, Meriwether Lewis stopped at Big Bone Lick to obtain fossils for President Jefferson. By 1812, more efficient salt-extraction methods became common, and Big Bone Lick salt-making heyday was over. Nonetheless, the health curative powers of mineral waters were discovered. In the early 19th Century, this area became a playground for wealthy southerners with health spas and resorts. The Civil War ended this era of a rich southerner's playground.

Today, Big Bone Lick State Park (☎ 859-384-3522, www.parks.ky.gov/bigbone.htm) has a museum, gift shop, miniature golf course, groceries, camping and hiking. The museum and gift shop are loaded with local fossils. About three miles away, on Big Bone Creek, there's a nicely-maintained Big Bone Landing Marina and Jane's Saddlebag (☎ 859-384-6617) –a grill and a friendly country store.

## WARSAW, KY (mile 528, LDB):

Warsaw is a fair-size river town with a couple of motels, restaurants, a grocer, a hardware store, and a Radio Shack. The popular Kentucky Motor Speedway, in Sparta Kentucky, is about seven miles from Warsaw. This town is the seat of Gallatin County.

## GHENT, KY (mile 538, LDB):

In 1794, settlers began visiting this area and called it McCool's Creek. Legend states that in 1816, Kentuckian Henry Clay suggested the name Ghent, on account of the Treaty of Ghent. That treaty ended the War of 1812. Clay was a signer to that treaty. Ghent hosts its annual 'Riverboat Fest' during the second weekend in August.

**VEVAY, IN** (mile 538, RDB):

Vevay was settled in 1802 by Swiss immigrants from Vevay Switzerland. They made the local economy viable by growing and using grapes for the first commercial winery in the United States. Vevay supposedly has the oldest continuous business sitting on its original site? Danner's Hardware was established in 1838. The Switzerland County Courthouse was built in 1864. Today, the Belterra Casino Resort drives the local economy. In Vevay, there's also a general store, grocer, a River History Museum, laundromat, antique shops, several Bed and Breakfasts, and the Ogle Haus Inn.

**CARROLLTON, KY** (mile 545, LDB):

In 1763, a few settlers started arriving here. In 1785, Virginian Charles Scott built a blockhouse to protect settlers from hostile Indians. Scott later became the fourth governor of Kentucky from 1808 to 1812. In 1794, Port William was established at the confluence of the Kentucky River. In 1838, the area was renamed Carrollton. That change was made to honor the last surviving signer of the Declaration of Independence –Charles Carroll of Maryland. Carrollton, the seat of Carroll County, has a very tastefully done central district with a hotel, several restaurants, a gas station, an auto parts store, and an interesting courthouse. General Butler State Resort Park (☎ 502-732-4384) located just outside Carrollton, has dinning, a lodge and a golf course, and honors a prominent Kentucky military family. Carrolton's moniker is 'Where Rivers and People Meet.'

## Louisville Waterworks

# Sketch 14-B: The Lower Ohio River Region –from Madison, IN to the Mississippi River

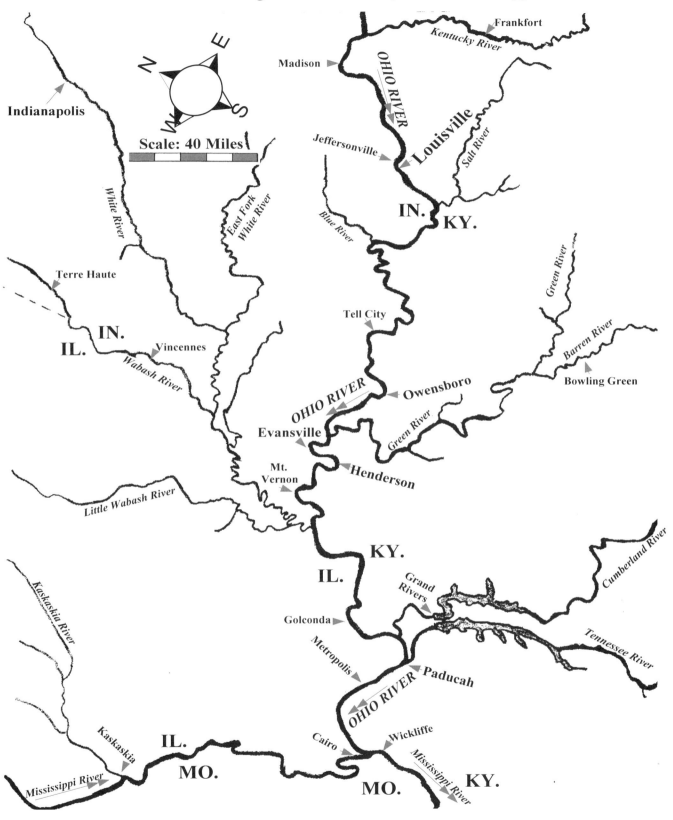

**KENTUCKY RIVER, KY** (mile 546, RDB):

At one time there were 14 working locks and dams on the northwest-flowing Kentucky River. This river was navigable for about 255 miles from the Ohio River at Carrollton to Beattyville. However, this maintained river was never profitable. There has never been enough commercial freight to justify the locks and dams. In the best of conditions (i.e., when the locks were all operational and there was no flooding) a 255-mile trip took three days (versus a one day trip by rail). From Beattyville to Carrollton, the Kentucky River drops 226 feet.

Between 1836 and 1842, the Commonwealth of Kentucky built the first five locks (i.e., from Carrollton to above Clifton), and operated them until the Civil War. In the 1880s, the Corps of Engineers (i.e., the federal government) took over the river. By 1917, the Corps had completed another nine locks and dams (i.e., Locks and Dams #6 through #14) as well as refurbished the lowest five locks and dams. Navigation had been extended to a confluence area of the 'three forks' near Beattyville. The plan was to ship coal and timber out of the region. Even coal shipments were sporadic, as only a couple of coal towboats and steamships worked the Kentucky River in the early 20th Century. This system couldn't compete with rail transport, and by the 1970s, coal and aggregate tows were completely absent from the upper river.

In the 1980s, the Corps of Engineers, handed the uppermost 10 lock and dams to the State Kentucky River Authority. Today, these upper ten locks remained closed, and the Kentucky River Authority (☎ 502-564-2866, www.finance.ky.gov/ourcabinet/attached+agencies/kra) manages only the lowest four locks. Locks #1 through #4 operate only on the weekends from Memorial Day to Labor Day, and even then, there are serious limitations. In 2005, Lock #3 was closed nearly all year. In 2006, Lock #3 only opened on holiday weekends. Hence in the summertime, a trip from the Ohio River at Carrollton to charming Frankfort Kentucky may not be possible depending on the condition of the locks.

Perhaps one could take a one-way 42-mile boat trip on the Kentucky River from Carrollton as far as the lower end of Lock #3, near Gest Kentucky during the summer months, and on the weekend? But even before trying that venture, contact the Kentucky River Authority first. If all four lower locks should be operational, a boater could travel about 80 miles (i.e., close to non-operational Lock and Dam #5) –from Carrollton to beyond Frankfort Kentucky. Frankfort, in Pool #4, is 65 Kentucky River miles from the Ohio River. There are a couple of boating facilities and many recreational vessels in the Frankfort Pool. But oftentimes, the boats in this pool find themselves 'land-locked.'

Fort Boonesborough, the second oldest settlement in Kentucky, is about 175 miles up the Kentucky River. Fort Boonesborough State park has an interesting river museum, and varied recreational activities, including a campground, miniature golf course, museum, pool, and picnic shelters. The fort is located just downriver from old Lock and Dam # 10. The first settler was killed here when he was trying to build a ferry across the Kentucky River.

The following table summarizes the locks and pools on the Kentucky River:

**Table 14-E: Locks and Pools on the Navigable Kentucky River:**

| Lock and Pool Name | Mile | Lock Side | Telephone Number ☎ | Opens for Rec. Vessels | Lift (in ft) | Pool Length (miles) |
|---|---|---|---|---|---|---|
| McAlpine L&D (Louisville, KY) | -61 mi. on Oh. | LDB | 502-774-3514 | 24/7 | 37 | 65.0 |
| L &D # 1 (Carrollton, KY) | 4.0 | RDB | 502-564-2866 | Limited | 8 | 27.0 |
| L &D #2 (Lockport, KY) | 31.0 | RDB | 502-564-2866 | Limited | 14 | 11.0 |
| L & Dam #3 (Gest, KY) | 42.0 | LDB | 502-564-2866 | Very Ltd. | 14 | 23.0 |
| L & D #4 (Frankford, KY) | 65.0 | LDB | 502-564-2866 | Limited | 14 | ≈17.0 |
| L & D #5 (Tyrone, KY) | 82.2 | LDB | 502-564-2866 | Closed | 14 | NA |

**FRANKFORT, KY** (mile 65-67, L & RDB, Kentucky River):

Charming Frankfort, one of our nation's smallest capitals, is Kentucky's capital. The state capitol building was completed in 1910. Daniel and Rebecca Boone's graves are in Frankfort, reburied here in 1845. They died, and they were first buried in Missouri. Frankfort's sister city is San Pedro de Macoris in the Dominican Republic. Baseball fans might recognize San Pedro de Macoris as the home to scores of professional major league baseball players. There's a bridge over the Kentucky River that 'sings' as vehicles drive over it. The Frankfort Boat Club is just downstream from this singing bridge. Frankfort holds its annual Kentucky River Fest around the 4th of July.

**MADISON, IN** (mile 558, RDB):

In 1809, Madison was established. The advent of the steamboat, during the next decade, gave the small town a shot in the arm. Madison became an entry point into the Indiana Territory. The Indiana Territory was created in 1800, and was the first new territory carved from the lands of the Northwest Territory. This territory included all of present-day Indiana, Illinois, Wisconsin, and portions of Michigan and Minnesota. In 1816, the 19th state of Indiana was admitted into the Union.

By 1832, The 'Old Michigan Road' was being extended from Madison northward to Lake Michigan near Michigan City Indiana. Indiana's first railroad, the Madison-Indianapolis Railroad was built between 1836 and 1847, and Madison prospered. But a later railroad line connecting Cincinnati, Indianapolis and Louisville bypassed Madison, and then the steamboat traffic started declining.

In 1848, Eleutherian College (☎ 812-273-9434, www.eleutherian.us), outside Madison, was established. This far-sighted college was founded by abolitionists to support education for all races and genders. Hanover College (www.hanover.edu), founded in 1827, and also outside Madison, is the oldest private four-year college in the state. Most of this beautiful campus sits on a 630-acre bluff overlooking the Ohio River about four miles downstream from Madison. Hanover College also has a 'Rivers Institute' (www.riversinstitute.org). The mission of the 'Rivers Institute' is to enhance understanding of the culture, economics, and science of river systems. Clifty Falls State Park (☎ 812-273-8885) sits between Madison and Hanover College. This pretty state park has four sizeable waterfalls, several canyons, a pool and 14 miles of trails.

Near the boat landing in Madison, there's a grocery store, hardware store, auto parts store, a few taverns, a handful of restaurants, and three motels. Madison, the seat of Jefferson County, hosts its annual 'Ribberfest' in mid-August.

**WESTPORT, KY** (mile 580, LDB):

In 1780s, the village of Liberty was first settled here. By 1800, a ferryboat was working the river. In the early 19th Century, Westport was seen as a link to the Illinois County –and the Ohio River's 'Port to the West.' The Westport General Store advertises dinning and cocktails.

**UTICA, IN** (mile 596, RDB):

During the first quarter of the 19th Century, Utica Indiana was a popular Ohio River ferry crossing to Kentucky. Located about ten miles upstream from the 'Falls of the Ohio,' this ferry was considered to be at a 'safe enough' distance from those falls.

**HARRODS CREEK, KY** (mile 596, LDB):

Harrods Creek is a neighborhood at the upper northeastern end of Louisville along the Ohio River, about ten miles from downtown. In 1923, entrepreneur James Taylor began developing the Harrods Creek area as the nucleus for a flourishing local African-American community. Narrow Harrods Creek is navigable for about two miles and is chock-full of marinas as well as a few restaurants.

# Sketch 14-C: The Ohio River –the Greater Louisville Area

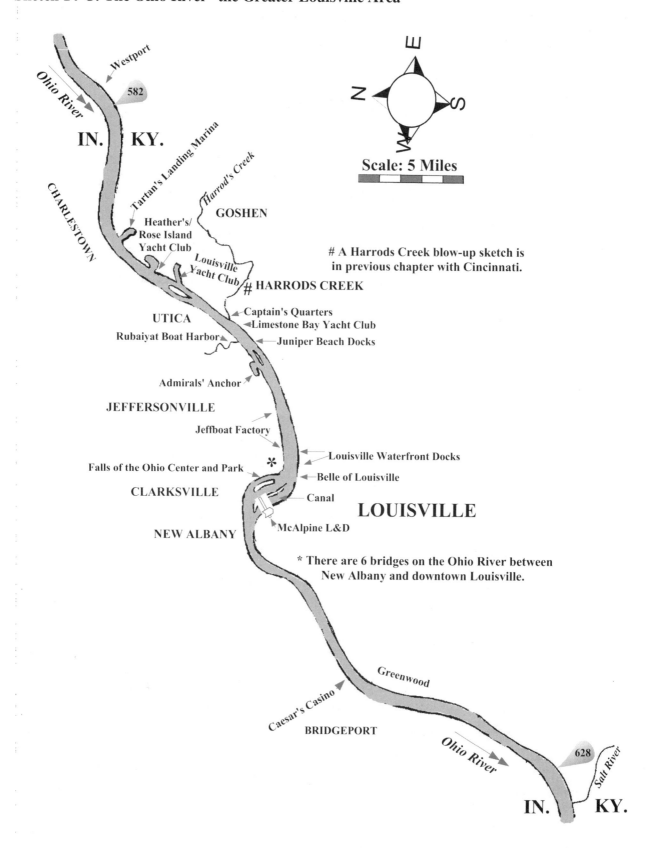

Westport

Ohio River

582

IN.   KY.

CHARLESTOWN

Tartan's Landing Marina

Harrod's Creek

GOSHEN

Heather's/
Rose Island
Yacht Club

Louisville
Yacht Club

# HARRODS CREEK

# A Harrods Creek blow-up sketch is
in previous chapter with Cincinnati.

UTICA

Captain's Quarters
Limestone Bay Yacht Club

Rubaiyat Boat Harbor

Juniper Beach Docks

Admirals' Anchor

JEFFERSONVILLE

Jeffboat Factory

Louisville Waterfront Docks

Falls of the Ohio Center and Park

*

Belle of Louisville

CLARKSVILLE

Canal

LOUISVILLE

NEW ALBANY

McAlpine L&D

* There are 6 bridges on the Ohio River between
New Albany and downtown Louisville.

Greenwood

Caesar's Casino

BRIDGEPORT

Ohio River

628

Salt River

IN.   KY.

Scale: 5 Miles

154

**LOUISVILLE, KY** (miles 598-610, LDB):

In 1778, and as part of his successful exploits in winning the West during the American Revolution, George Rogers Clark assembled his 150 men and built a fort on Corn Island (near the 'Falls of the Ohio'). By 1780, Clark was detailing a plan for a new city to be built near his Corn Island outpost. This outpost would become Louisville, and would be named after King Louis XVI of France in appreciation for his assistance during the American Revolution.

In 1785, William Clark, George Rogers Clark's 18-year younger brother, first came to this area. In 1803, William Clark was about to make history when he teamed-up with his old military friend, Meriwether Lewis, leading 'The Corps of Discovery.' One of the newer members of that Corps recruited nearby was Charles Floyd. Floyd was from St. Matthews Kentucky. Popular Floyd was promoted to be one of the Corps few sergeants. But Floyd had the unenviable distinction of being the only member of the Corps to die during the journey –probably from acute appendicitis. Another member of the Corps of Discovery, a Clark family slave and the only African American in the Corps, was the legendary York. In 1816, ten years after the Corps retuned, York was finally granted his freedom. York then settled in Louisville with his family to work as a wagon-driver.

Louisville's early economy was boosted by being strategically located near the 'Falls of the Ohio,' in addition to the advent of steamboats. In autumn 1811, the first Ohio River Steamboat, the *New Orleans* passed through Louisville. Soon six local steamboat lines were in operation and hundreds more steamboats were being constructed in town. In the late 1810s and early 1820s, Louisville's economy was thriving on river businesses. By 1830, the Louisville and Portland Canal was completed, and the entire Ohio River –from Pittsburgh to Cairo –and thus all of the way to New Orleans or St. Louis, became 'navigable,' during any season. Today, the Portland Museum (☎ 502-776-7678) celebrates this 'Falls of the Ohio' river heritage.

In 1819, near financial ruin, James J. Audubon moved from Henderson Kentucky to Louisville. Before long, Audubon's luck had changed, and he was establishing himself as one of the foremost naturalists of the 19th Century. By 1830, Louisville had secured its place as the largest city in Kentucky. During the Civil War, Louisville was a crucial base of operations for Union forces. After the war, the city continued to grow. The Louisville and Nashville Railroad also became a critical transportation link between industrialized northern cities and the South.

The twelfth president of the United States, Zachary Taylor, is buried in Louisville. Taylor was the last veteran of the War of 1812 to serve as president. General Taylor distinguished himself in the Mexican American War (1846-48). Taylor died in office, after only 16 months, probably as the result of complications from heatstroke. Before being elected president Taylor had never held a public office. He preferred old rumpled clothing lending to his nickname 'Old Rough and Ready.' Taylor was a Virginia-born aristocrat and a southern slave owner. During the presidential election of 1848, Taylor was able to appeal to southerners, as well as northerners who were impressed with his long military resume. Under Taylor's administration, the US Department of Interior was organized.

After Prohibition (1919-1933) was repealed, Joseph Seagram and his sons opened the world's largest distillery in Louisville during the mid-1930s. In 1942, during the early part of World War II, and like Charleston West Virginia on the Kanawha River, Louisville became an important location for the development of synthetic rubber. Several chemical companies established factories in 'Rubbertown' near the western end of Louisville.

Today, the Louisville Metropolitan area, with about 1.2 million people, is the third largest metropolis on the Ohio River, ranked behind only Pittsburgh (at about 2.4 million) and Cincinnati (at about 2.1 million). Louisville is still the largest city in Kentucky. The steamboat *Belle of Louisville* (☎502-574-2992, www.belleoflouisville.org), the oldest operating steam-driven paddlewheeler in the country, is a National Historic Landmark. The *Belle*, at 191 feet long with two steam engines, can accompany 650 passengers. The nearby *Spirit of Jefferson* is also parked at the Port of Louisville. The Louisville Science Center, Kentucky Museum of Arts and Crafts, the Greater Louisville Convention and Visitor's Bureau (☎ 888-568-4784, www.gotolouisville.com), and the Louisville Slugger Museum are also in downtown Louisville, and within a couple of blocks from the river. Louisville Slugger Baseball Bats (☎ 502-588-7228, www.sluggermuseum.org), established in 1884, makes over a million bats per year. Beside the museum, Louisville Slugger offers factory tours.

The Muhammad Ali Center (☎ 502-584-9254), in downtown Louisville, opened in November 2005 and is one of the newer attractions. In Louisville, in October 1960, Cassius Clay (later to rename himself Muhammad Ali) won his first professional fight. Ali, born in Louisville, won six Golden Glove tournaments in Kentucky. In February 1964, Ali beat Sonny Liston for his first, of three, World Heavyweight Boxing Champion Titles. In 1981 at age 39, Ali permanently retired with a career record of 56 wins (37 by knockout) and five losses. In 1999, *Sports Illustrated* magazine crowned Muhammad Ali 'Sportsman of the Century.'

World famous Churchill Downs (☎ 800-283-3729, www.kentuckyderby.com) is about five miles from the Ohio River. Churchill Downs, established in 1874, is the oldest continually operating horse racing track in the United States. The Kentucky Derby, now held on the first Saturday in May, was first run in 1875. There's a Kentucky Derby Museum (☎ 502-637-7097, www.derbymuseum.org) located near Churchill Downs. Some say the Kentucky Derby is the most exciting two minutes in any sport. 'Thunder Over Louisville,' an annual event held in late April since 1990, kicks-off Kentucky Derby Week. The Ohio River is chock-full of boats and both river banks are lined with tens of thousands. There is an aircraft show, a fireworks display, and all sorts of other festivities up and down the Ohio River.

**JEFFERSONVILLE, IN** (miles 598-603, RDB):

In Indiana, the cities of Jeffersonville, Clarksville, and New Albany all sit on the Ohio River across from sprawling Louisville. New Albany sits below 'The Falls of the Ohio.' The smallest of the three cities, Clarksville, sits at 'The Falls.' Jeffersonville, the upriver most city, is situated above 'The Falls of the Ohio.' In 1786, Fort Finney was established about a half mile above the 'Falls of the Ohio.' In 1789, this garrison was renamed Fort Steuben. Early settlers congregated near the garrison to take refuge from hostile Indians. This fort was the beginning of Jeffersonville –the seat of Clark County. This city is the only one designed by Thomas Jefferson, and so named in his honor.

The local economy, in large part, is supported by JeffBoat. Located on the Ohio River, JeffBoat is the largest inland shipbuilder, and second-largest barge builder in the United States. In late 2006, JeffBoat was constructing an average of about eight barges per week! JeffBoat was originally the Howard Shipyard. After the Great Depression, in 1942, the US Navy bought-out the failing Howard Shipyard. During World War II, a new shipyard company, Jefferson Boat and Machine Company, was formed. During the war, that company –later to become JeffBoat, built LSTs and submarine chasers, along with many other Naval vessels. After the war, JeffBoat was specializing in barge and towboat construction. Today, the four-story Howard Steamboat Museum (☎ 812-283-3728, www.steamboatmuseum.org) has models of the *Robert E. Lee* and a few of the other old steamboats. The excursion boat, *Star of Louisville* (☎ 812-218-1565), parks on the Jeffersonville waterfront, across from downtown Louisville.

**CLARKSVILLE, IN** (miles 605-606, RDB):

In 1778, George Rogers Clark established an outpost on Corn Island. In 1781, the land was granted to Clark and his men for their Revolutionary War services. By 1784, tracts were occupied, and the town was named Clarksville. In early October 1803, Clark's younger brother, William Clark joined with Meriwether Lewis, and the Corps of Discovery became a reality. For about 12 days, Lewis and Clark, and their men, re-provisioned and traveled between Clarksville and Louisville, before eventually heading down the Ohio River. Three years later, in November

1806, after having trekked across and explored the continent, Lewis and Clark returned to Clarksville.

The 'Falls of the Ohio' State Park has an Interpretive Center (☎ 812-280-9970, www.fallsoftheohio.org) and is a most interesting stop. This center has a bit of everything –from geologic, to Native American, to Colonial history; from early wicket dam to present-day fish and wildlife displays. This worthwhile education center addresses the local prehistoric fossil beds dating as far back as 386 million years ago. The George Rogers Clark home site is located near 'The Falls of the Ohio' State Park.

**NEW ALBANY, IN** (miles 608-609, RDB):

In 1813, New Albany was founded by three brothers from New York who named the new town after their New York capital. By 1819, New Albany became the seat of Floyd County. By the mid-19th Century, steamboat construction was driving the economy. With its location Below 'The Falls of the Ohio,' New Albany had a transportation advantage over neighboring towns. No less than a half-dozen steamship builders were busy in New Albany. Between 1818 and 1867, more than 350 steamships were constructed in town. By 1850, New Albany was the largest city in Indiana. In 1866, the famed steamship, *Robert E Lee*, was built at the Riverfront Shipyard. By the middle of the 20th Century, hardwood plywood and veneer had replaced steamship construction. Before long, New Albany was one of the top world producers for hardwood plywood and veneer.

Downtown Louisville

# Marina, Brandenburg, Kentucky

Sternwheeler *Belle of Louisville*

# CHAPTER 15
## The Evansville-Henderson-Owensboro Area ...on the Ohio River, from West Point KY to Mount Vernon IN, including the Green River

This chapter corresponds to a 225-mile section of the Ohio River downstream from Greater Louisville.  A few modest-size cities dot the river –Evansville, Indiana, and Owensboro and Henderson in Kentucky, as well as many smaller enchanting towns –Mount Vernon, Newburgh, Tell City, Cannelton, Rockport, and Leavenworth in Indiana, and Brandenburg, West Point, Hawesville, and Cloverport in Kentucky.  However, river access to these and other smaller towns can be limited.  Evansville has a few first class marinas.  Most of the other towns along the Ohio River have boat ramps, and a few may even have a public or a seasonal dock as in Mount Vernon and Henderson.

The non-transiting 'small boat traffic,' like that seen around Louisville and Cincinnati, virtually disappears.  Along the river, one may have this section all to oneself, except for the towboats.  Of course, there are the tows, but there are fewer towboat terminals here than on other more industrial and more urban portions of the Ohio River.  With this diminished intensity of recreational vessels and towboat traffic, we found traveling along this portion of the river more relaxing and enjoyable than many other portions –if you prefer having the river more to yourself.  The gently rolling landscape also adds to the allure of the Ohio River.  Somewhere between Leavenworth and Cloverport –in the Hoosier National Forest, the riverside topography changes from high hills to low hills.  Our mountains, and even large hills, are upstream and behind us.

We also made a 72-mile one-way side trip up the Green River.  The Green River is maintained by the Corps of Engineers for slightly more than 100 miles from the Ohio River.  Lock and Dam #3, downriver from Rochester, near mile 109, has been dismantled and even a small boat cannot travel any farther up the Green River without being pulled out of the water.  There are two locks and dams (near Spottsville and Calhoun) as well as two towns –Calhoun and Livermore –on the navigable Green River.

**Table 15-A: Locks and Pools on the Ohio River, from West Point, KY to the Wabash River:**

| Lock and Pool Name | Mile | Lock Side | Telephone Number ☎ | Opens for Rec. Vessels | Lift (in ft) | Pool Length (miles) |
|---|---|---|---|---|---|---|
| Cannelton L&D  (Cannelton, IN) | 720.7 | RDB | 812-547-2962 | 24/7 | 25 | 113.9 |
| Newburgh L&D  (Newburgh IN) | 776.1 | RDB | 812-853-8470 | 24/7 | 16 | 55.4 |
| J. Myers L&D (Mt. Vernon, IN) | 846.0 | RDB | 812-838-5836 | 24/7 | 18 | 69.9 |

**WEST POINT, KY** (mile 630, LDB –Left Descending Bank):
In 1789, West Point, Kentucky was founded when James Young built a cabin on the site. The town sits at the confluence of the Salt and Ohio Rivers.  The Salt River flows west-northwestward for about 140 miles.  Kentucky's first settlement, Harrodsburg, is situated about 130 miles up the Salt River.  In 1803, when Lewis and Clark stopped at West Point, they recruited John Shields.  At 34 years old, Shields was the oldest member of the Corps, but he was a skilled carpenter, blacksmith and gunsmith.  Brothers Joseph and Reubin Field also joined the Corps at West Point.  Both were excellent marksmen.

Nearby, Fort Knox is the home of the US Army Armor School, the General George S. Patton Museum, and the US Gold Bullion Depository.

# Sketch 15-A: The Ohio River –from West Point, Kentucky to Troy, Indiana

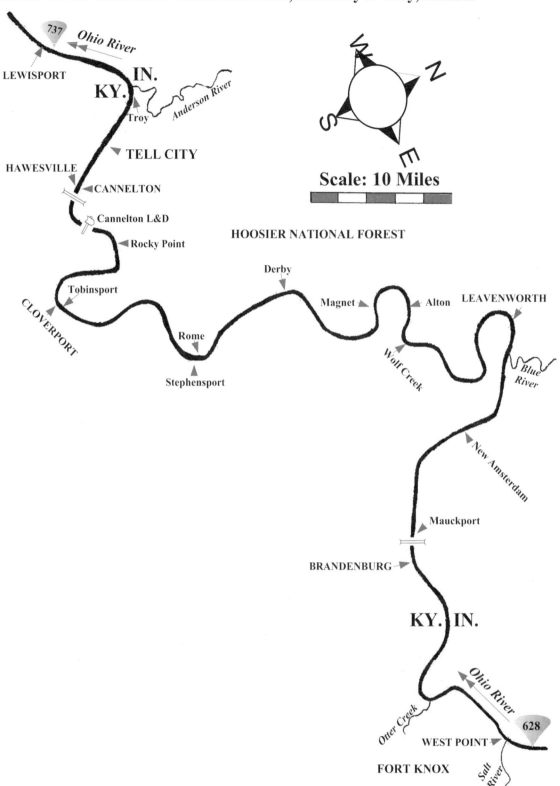

737

*Ohio River*

LEWISPORT

IN.

KY.

Troy

*Anderson River*

TELL CITY

HAWESVILLE

CANNELTON

Cannelton L&D

Rocky Point

Scale: 10 Miles

HOOSIER NATIONAL FOREST

Derby

Tobinsport

Magnet

Alton

LEAVENWORTH

CLOVERPORT

Rome

*Wolf Creek*

*Blue River*

Stephensport

*New Amsterdam*

Mauckport

BRANDENBURG

KY. IN.

*Ohio River*

*Otter Creek*

628

WEST POINT

FORT KNOX

*Salt River*

**BRANDENBURG, KY** (mile 646, LDB):

In the 1780s, pioneers started visiting Meade County.  In the 1790s, a few permanent settlements had sprung-up along the Ohio River.  In 1804, Brandenburg became a ferry crossing, as was so until 1966.  In the 1820s, Brandenburg became the seat of Meade County.

From July 7th through 9th 1863, during the Civil War, Confederate Raider John Hunt Morgan assembled more than 2,000 cavalrymen in Brandenburg with a grand scheme to cross the Ohio River and wreak havoc in Indiana and Ohio.  On July 7th, the unsuspecting mail streamer, *John T. Combs* docked in Brandenburg.  This vessel was quickly seized by the Confederate Raiders.  The Confederates then ordered the captain of the *Combs* to send a distress signal to another unsuspecting passing-by vessel, the *Alice Dean*.  The *Alice Dean,* a luxury passenger side-wheel steamer bound for Louisville, was deceived in coming to the aid of the *Combs*. Passengers from both steamers were put ashore in Brandenburg, and warned not to raise an alarm. During the next 17 hours, using the two steamers, Morgan's Raiders and their horses ferried themselves to Indiana.  An Indiana Home Guard cannon across the river, along with the small Union gunboat *Springfield* unsuccessfully tried to thwart the Confederate crossing.  On July 9th, after the ferry crossing was completed, the *Alice Dean* was set ablaze and left to drift helplessly down the river.  The *Combs* fate wasn't as bad.  The captain of the *Combs*, being an old friend of one of the Confederate Raider colonels, was allowed to take the *Combs* upriver to Louisville where it couldn't be used to pursue the Rebels.

On April 3, 1974, with hardly any prior warning, dozens of tornados touched down in a six-state area, claiming 120 lives and over a billion dollars in property damage.  Brandenburg was one small town particularly hard hit.  When an F-5 tornado touched-down in Brandenburg, 28 folks lost their lives, 150 were injured, and more than half the homes in Brandenburg were either destroyed or severely damaged.  Property damage in Brandenburg was estimated at $22 million.

**Looking down at Ohio River, from bluffs hundreds of feet above, near Leavenworth, Indiana**

**MAUCKPORT, IN** (mile 648, RDB –Right Descending Bank):

In 1790, brothers Squire and Daniel Boone discovered a cave about four miles north of Mauckport. In 1804, Squire Boone settled near Buck Creek Indiana. The nearby cave would become Squire Boone's Caverns (☎ 812-732-4381, www.squireboonecaverns.com). Today, besides a cavern tour, there's a pioneer log cabin village.

In July 1863, after Confederate Raider John Hunt crossed the Ohio River he quickly looted Mauckport. After Mauckport, Morgan's Raiders traveled 15 miles inland to raid Indiana's old capital –Corydon. In 1813, the capital of the Indiana Territory had been moved from Vincennes to Corydon. In the early 1820s, the Indiana state capital finally moved from Corydon to Indianapolis. Today historic Corydon, the seat of Harrison County, is loaded with tourists' attractions.

**BLUE RIVER, IN** (mile 663, RDB):

The Blue River goes through the heart of Indiana's 'Cave County.' The Blue River passes through limestone bluffs, by numerous springs, and past several caves (on private property). Saltpeter (for gunpowder), chert, and aragonite were also mined in this cave area. The Blue River is very popular among canoeist during the spring and summer. Cave Country Canoes (☎ 812-365-2705, www.cavecountrycanoes.com) accommodates this market niche by offering one-half to two day canoe excursions on the Blue River.

**LEAVENWORTH, IN** (mile 664, RDB):

Leavenworth, established in the 1810s, may be one of the most scenic Indiana towns on the Ohio River. It's located near the base of a bluff on a horseshoe bend in the river. Just beyond Leavenworth, the river changes its direction from flowing northwestward to eastward (for about a three-mile stretch). In the late 19th Century, Leavenworth was a center of boat building, and for buttons made from the shells of Ohio River mollusks. From 1843 until 1895, Leavenworth was the seat of Crawford County. In 1937, after that horrible Ohio River flood, parts of Leavenworth were moved to higher ground, slightly downriver, and up towards the bluff.

Quaint Leavenworth supports a handful of bed and breakfasts, and antique shops. The Dock Restaurant (☎ 812-739-4449) sits along the river's edge near central Leavenworth. The Overlook Restaurant (☎812-739-4264, www.theoverlook.com), about one mile downstream and outside of Leavenworth, is situated on a breath-taking bluff overlooking the Ohio River. Still in Indiana's 'Cave Country,' Wyandotte Caves (☎ 888-702-2837, www.wyandottecaves.com) and Marengo Cave are located near Leavenworth.

**TIME ZONE CHANGE, KY** (mile 689 LDB, and mile 732 RDB):

On the Kentucky side (i.e., LDB), about 25 miles downriver from Leavenworth, at the Meade-Breckinridge County line, we switch from Eastern to Central Time. However, that imaginary time zone line goes right down the Ohio River for another 43 miles. On the Indiana side (i.e., RDB), that time zone line will head north once again when it reaches the Perry-Spencer County line, west of Troy Indiana.

**HOOSIER NATIONAL FOREST, IN** (miles 677-708, LDB):

The Hoosier National Forest (☎ 812-547-7051, www.fs.fed.us/r9/hoosier/) has about 200,000 acres comprising four large tracts located in two districts, in southern Indiana. The largest tract runs along the Ohio River for more than 30 miles. National Forests are managed for multiple uses –from wildlife, to all sorts of recreational activities, to limited sensible timber harvesting.

**MAGNET-DERBY AREA, IN** (miles 683-693, RDB):

There are no less than four log cabin sites for rent on the Ohio River in this area. In Magnet, contact Colucci Log Cabins on the Ohio River (☎ 812-843-5607, www.coluccirivercabins.com) or Vinnie's Ohio River Log Cabin (☎ 812-843-4848). In Derby, contact Ohio River Cabins (☎ 812-836-2289, www.ohiorivercabins.com) or Forgotten Time Log Cabins (☎ 812-836-2447, www.perrycountyindiana.org). Some of these cabins on the Ohio River have docks.

**ROME, IN** (mile 701, RDB):

Rome was first established as Washington, then Franklin, and finally Rome in 1819. From 1819 until 1859, Rome was also the second county seat of Perry County. The Perry County Court House was built to echo the design of the first Indiana Capital in nearby Corydon. This two-story court house still stands today.

**CLOVERPORT, KY** (mile 711 LDB):

In 1803, Cloverport was founded at the mouth of Clover Creek. In 1816, when Abraham Lincoln and his family moved from Kentucky to Indiana, a Cloverport ferryboat operator piloted the Lincoln family across the Ohio River. Abraham Lincoln's father didn't have much –a horse, a cart, one milk cow, a dog, and a few household goods. Before the age of plastics, a factory in Cloverport manufactured buttons from Ohio River mollusks. Cloverport also has a small museum with artifacts and photos from the town's steamboat days.

**ROCKY POINT, IN** (mile 719, RDB):

During 1824-25, Revolutionary War hero and Frenchman, Marquis de Lafayette was making his American farewell tour from New Orleans to Boston. Lafayette often traveled aboard steamboats up many inland rivers, including the Ohio. In May 1925, his steamer, *Mechanic,* struck an Ohio River rock and sank. The steamer and all personal property were lost; however, all of the passengers were rescued. For two days, Lafayette was treated to local Indiana hospitality before a new steamer, *Paragon,* picked him up and continued his journey upstream toward Louisville.

**HAWESVILLE, KY** (mile 724, LDB):

During the 1910s, the train station was a fairly large embarkation point for soldiers heading off to World War I. In 1948, Harry Truman made a whistle stop here during his campaign for US president. Hawesville is the seat of Hancock County.

**CANNELTON, IN** (mile 724, RDB):

Many early settlers in the area mined a brightly burning bituminous coal that was known as cannel coal. In 1827, the site was named Coal Haven. The American Cannel Coal Company was formed, and cannel coal was exported afar aboard steamboats. Steamboats also started using this coal over wood as fuel. In 1841, the site became known as Cannelsburg, and by 1844 known as Cannelton. By the late 1840s, the large coal conglomerate integrated with a new cotton mill, Indiana Cotton Mills, to keep the local work force employed. By the 1850s, cotton and textiles had become more profitable than coal. During the Civil War, this cotton mill churned out uniforms for the Union army. In the mid 19th Century, the Cannelton Cotton Mill was once the largest industry west of the Appalachian Mountains. But by 1954, the Cannelton Cotton Mill had to close it doors. In 1991, this old five-story cotton mill, with its twin towers facing the Ohio River, became a National Historic Landmark. From 1859 until 1994, Cannelton was the third county seat of Perry County.

**Sketch 15-B: The Ohio River –from Lewisport, Kentucky to the John Myers Lock & Dam, plus the Green River to Rockport**

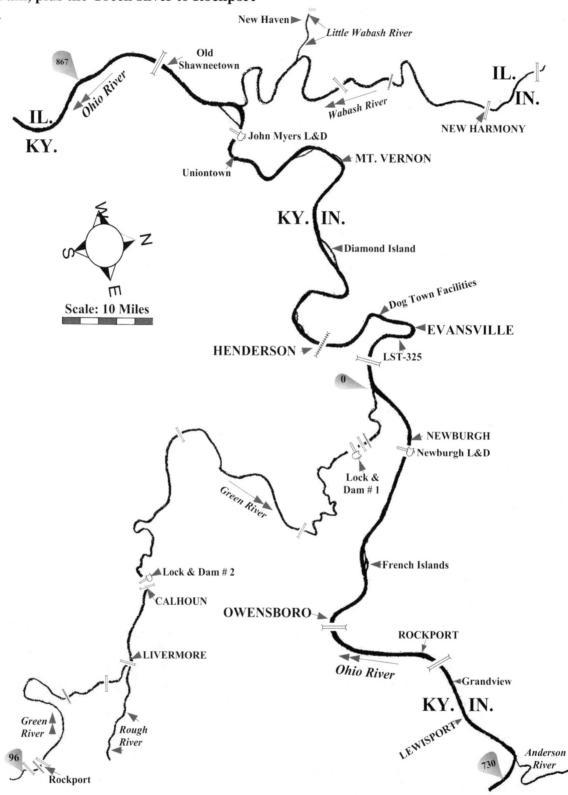

New Haven

*Little Wabash River*

Old Shawneetown

867

*Ohio River*

*Wabash River*

IL.

IN.

NEW HARMONY

IL.

KY.

John Myers L&D

Uniontown

MT. VERNON

KY. IN.

W

N

S

E

Scale: 10 Miles

Diamond Island

Dog Town Facilities

EVANSVILLE

HENDERSON

LST-325

0

NEWBURGH

Newburgh L&D

Lock & Dam # 1

*Green River*

French Islands

Lock & Dam # 2

CALHOUN

OWENSBORO

ROCKPORT

*Ohio River*

Grandview

LIVERMORE

KY. IN.

*Green River*

*Rough River*

96

LEWISPORT

730

*Anderson River*

Rockport

**TELL CITY, IN** (mile 727, RDB):

    In 1856, a group of Swiss and German immigrants met in Cincinnati. Their purpose was to find an affordable homestead for mechanics, shopkeepers, factory workers and small farmers as well as to establish a diverse economy devoid of slavery. In 1857, this 'Swiss Colonization Society' purchased a tract of land on the Ohio River. By 1858, settlers started arriving, and the new town was initially named 'Helvetia.' The name was soon changed to the more Anglo-sounding 'Tell City,' named in honor of legendary Swiss liberator and archery hero William Tell. Tell City's founders designed wide streets, and named them after contemporary Swiss and American heroes. Although the Swiss named the town, the Germans were in the majority. Tell City, helped by its progressive industries, soon became the largest town in Perry County. Since 1994, Tell City has been the seat of Perry County. In Tell City near the river access, there's a hardware store, a few cafés, and a gas station. Away from the river, a mile or so distant, there are shopping centers, motels, and several restaurants.

**TROY, IN** (mile 731, RDB):

    In 1803, Troy was established. From 1814 until 1819, Troy was the first seat of Perry County. Perry County was named for Commodore Oliver Hazard Perry, who defeated the British on Lake Erie in 1813, during the *War of 1812*. In 1825, a young Abraham Lincoln operated a ferry boat across the nearby Anderson River. The town of Troy has a grocer, diner, gas station, and a small tavern.

**LEWISPORT, KY** (mile 738, LDB):

    The town was originally called 'Little Yellow Bank,' and renamed Lewisport in 1839. During the latter part of the Civil War, in December 1864, a Union steamboat was overrun and captured by Confederate guerillas. Passengers were robbed, and three Union soldiers were killed.

**GRANDVIEW, IN** (mile 742, RDB):

    Grandview likely received its name because of its 'grand view' of the Ohio River. This is also the most likely location where Josiah Henson of Harriet's Beecher's Stowe's *Uncle Tom's Cabin* made his daring escape with his entire family from slavery in Kentucky to his eventual freedom. Henson led a very productive latter life in Canada, including assisting others in the Underground Railroad.

**ROCKPORT, IN** (mile 747, RDB):

    Rockport, much of it sitting on a high river bluff, is the seat of Spencer County. In 1844, Abraham Lincoln, 14 years after he moved from Indiana to Illinois, returned to Spender County to give a speech in support of presidential candidate and Kentuckian Henry Clay. Whig Party candidate Clay lost the 1844 presidential election to James Polk, in large part, due to Polk's more popular and aggressive stand on westward expansion (later to be called 'Manifest Destiny'). The four-lane William H. Natcher Suspension Bridge on US Highway Route 231, completed in 2002, connects Rockport with Kentucky, about seven miles north of Owensboro.

**OWENSBORO, KY** (miles 755-758, LDB):

    Before the European's arrival, buffalo herds were pounding a trail from the southeast to the Ohio River at present-day Owensboro. In the 1797, the first settlers used this same trail to arrive in the Owensboro area. This area was first called 'Yellow Banks,' due to the coloration of the high banks along the Ohio River. These 'high banks' protected Owensboro from much of the devastation that fell on other river towns during the great flood of 1937.

    In 1815, Daviess County was formed, and named after Colonel and US attorney Joseph H. Daviess. In 1806, at the behest of President Thomas Jefferson, Daviess unsuccessfully prosecuted Aaron Burr. In 1811, Daviess died during General William Henry Harrison's successful *Battle of Tippecanoe*. In 1812, Thomas Clay, the father of the great Kentucky statesman Henry Clay, settled here. During the Civil War, Owensboro, like most Kentucky towns on the Ohio River, was occupied by a small Union force. However, in September 1862, a Confederate force was able to take control of much of Owensboro. The Unions troops hunkered down at the old fairgrounds and refused to surrender. One Union soldier was able to make his way to the Ohio River, swim across it, and summon for reinforcements in Indiana. The next day, the Indiana Home Guards were able to dislodge the Confederates from Owensboro.

The Cannelton Cotton Mill, Cannelton, Indiana

Evansville, Indiana from the Ohio

Owensboro's heyday was after the Civil War, and between 1870 and 1910. In the 1870s, the Owensboro and Russellville Railroad had reached the city. During the 1880s, showboats, circuses, entertainers and even evangelists regularly paid visits to Owensboro. Much local commerce was engaged in exporting tobacco and sour-mash whiskey.

Today, Owensboro, with a population of 110,000, is the third largest city in Kentucky, behind only Louisville and Lexington. Owensboro is also known as 'Kentucky's Festival City' as 20 different festivals are scheduled annually. Owensboro calls itself 'The BBQ Capital of the World,' and holds its annual BBQ festival and competition during the second weekend of May. Owensboro has a Convention Center/Hotel, the 'Owensboro Museum of Fine Arts' (☎ 270-685-3181, the Museum of Science and History (☎ 270-687-2732), and the International Bluegrass Music Museum (☎ 270-926-7891). The Bluegrass Museum is one block from the Ohio River near River Park Center. For more information on local happenings in Owensboro, contact the Owensboro-Daviess County Tourist Commission at (☎ 270-926-1100, www.visitowensboro.com).

## NEWBURGH, IN (mile 778, RDB):

In 1803, John Sprinkle arrived and started a settlement originally called Sprinklesburg. By 1837, Newburgh became perhaps the largest river port on the lower Ohio River. In 1850, the first deep mine coal shaft in Indiana was sunk near Newburgh. During the early Civil War, in 1862, Newburgh was the first 'northern town' captured by the Confederates. A small guerrilla band had crossed the Ohio River and successfully confiscated supplies and munitions without firing a shot.

Today, historic Newburgh (☎ 812-853-3578, www.newburgh.org) has four blocks listed on the National Register of Historic Places. A riverfront walk and a handful of parks, along with many antique stores, cafés, and specialty shops dot the quaint business district along the Ohio River. Newburgh hosts its annual Summerfest during the second weekend of June.

## EVANSVILLE, IN (mile 792-794, RDB):

Evansville Indiana sits in another one of those broad gentle Ohio River horseshoe bends. The river's gradual 180-degree change of directions here takes over two miles. In 1809, a cabin was built in the area. By 1812, a ferry landing was founded. In 1817, a town was laid out and named in honor of Robert Evans. Evans, one of the town's founders, was also an officer under General William Henry Harrison during the *War of 1812*. The town quickly grew. By 1850, the Evansville and Crawfordsville Railroad was built. In 1853, Evansville was the terminus for the short-lived Wabash and Erie Canal –another economically nonviable dream to connect the Great Lakes with the Ohio River. By 1890, Evansville was the 56th largest urban area in America. In the early 1900s, German immigrants shaped the city into a furniture and cigar manufacturing center, and added two breweries. After a bad experience with the 1937 flood, a system of levees and pump stations were built to protect the city.

In 1932, a bridge across the Ohio River connected Evansville with Henderson, Kentucky. Prior to 1932, only two vehicle bridges crossed the Ohio River below Louisville. Today, US Route 41 runs over this bridge. US Route 41 extends from the northern peninsula of Michigan all of the way to Miami, through Milwaukee, Chicago, Nashville, Chattanooga, Atlanta, and Tampa. A second bridge span was constructed in 1965.

During World War II, factories in Evansville started cranking out P-47 Thunderbolt single-engine fighter airplanes as well as tank landing ships (LST's). LST's are amphibious vessels/vehicles designed to land manned combat-ready tanks and troops on occupied enemy beaches. A typical LST could hold as many as 20 Sherman Tanks. In the early 1940s, with 60,000 factory workers, Evansville became the largest inland producer of LST's, and churned out 167 such ships for the war effort. Through the tireless efforts of an aging group of World War II veterans, one particular LST recently made it back to Evansville. LST-325 was launched in

October 1942. In 1943, LST-325 saw action in the Mediterranean and made three beachhead trips to Salerno Italy. In 2000, LST-325 was about to be turned into scrap in a Greek shipyard. But in 2001, after some major repairs, LST-325 made it back to the United States. By 2005, she became a proud part of the LST Ship Memorial on the Ohio River near the Evansville's riverfront. With her new homeport in Evansville, LST-325 has plans to become a waterborne war-history museum for all to appreciate. During her first 11 months in Evansville, LST-325 (☎ 800-433-3025, www.lstmemorial.org) has already had 30,000 visitors.

In December 1977, a DC-3 charter airplane, carrying the University of Evansville basketball team, crashed shortly after take-off, killing all 29 aboard. The weather conditions were driving rain and dense fog, but the National Transportation Safety Board determined the cause of the accident was due, in part to, improper weight balance.

In late 20th Century Evansville gradually transformed itself into a commercial, medical and service hub, attracting such international heavyweights as Bristol-Myers-Squibb, Whirlpool, Toyota, AK Steel, and the Aztar Casino. The Aztar Casino Boat parks on the Evansville riverfront. The Pigeon Creek Greenway also extends for about 1½ miles along the downtown waterfront. The Evansville Museum of Arts, History and Science and the Evansville Visitor's Center –in the pagoda-like building upstream from downtown are along the greenway. The Museum of Arts, History and Science (☎ 812-425-2406, www.emuseum.org) addresses river life, early river transportation, Native American cultures, and has a planetarium, a steam railroad exhibit, and hands-on science exhibits. The Reitz Home Museum (☎ 812-426-1871, www.reitzhome.evansville.net) is also near downtown. The Reitz Home Museum is a Victorian House Museum noted as one of the country's finest examples of French Second Empire architecture. Across the Ohio River from Evansville, there is nothing but undeveloped farmland in Kentucky.

Ellis Park Horse Race Track (☎ 812-425-1456, www.ellisparkracing.com) is on the Ohio River's RDB, but is actually in Kentucky. How can this be? In 1793, the Indiana-Kentucky border had been defined by the low-water mark on the north bank of the Ohio River –the Indiana shoreline. In 1812, the New Madrid Earthquake created Reelfoot Lake in northwestern Tennessee, as well as causing the Ohio River to change its course. As a result of that earthquake, a portion of Henderson County Kentucky (four miles long by one mile wide) jumped from the Ohio River's LDB to its RDB. In 1922, Ellis Park, constructed to resemble New York's Saratoga Track, was built on this unique portion of 'Kentucky real estate.'

Angel Mounds State Historic Site (☎ 812-853-3956, www.angelmounds.org) is about three miles upstream from Ellis Park Race Track. Angel Mounds, near the Ohio River, is an archaeological dig with an interpretive center/museum addressing Native Americans who lived in the area from 1100 to 1500 AD. There are eleven Indian mounds, a town plaza, and the remnants of a village area that once held 1,000 inhabitants.

During the wee hours of the morning on November 6, 2005, a tornado, traveling northeastward, crossed the Ohio River in the Henderson-Evansville-Newburgh area on no less than three separate occasions. There were 25 fatalities and about $85 million in property losses – mostly in the southeastern side of Evansville. At the Ellis Park Track, 22 of its 38 barns were badly damaged or completely destroyed, and several race horses became fatalities. The tornado was a high-end F-3, with 200 MPH winds. This monster cut a fairly straight-line swath, 400 yards wide by about 41 miles long. When this happened, I was in my boat, on the Ohio River, slightly less than 90 miles downriver from Evansville. Seeing ominous clouds the day before, I dutifully listened to NOAA weather radio. Before I went into my bunk for the night, I recollect NOAA weather radio mentioning that a strong cold front with severe weather would be passing through; but I didn't recollect NOAA weather radio predicting an impending tornado? Lesson learned: NOAA weather reports are helpful, but not infallible.

Marina, Downriver from Evansville, Indiana

Today, Evansville, with a population of over 120,000, is the largest city in the lower Ohio River Valley, as well as being Indiana's third largest city, behind only Indianapolis and Fort Wayne. Evansville, the seat of Vanderburg County, has as its moniker, 'River City.' During the last week in June, Evansville hosts its annual 'Evansville Freedom Festival' (☎ 812-421-1120, www.evansvillefreedomfestival.org), with many river events, including a hydroplane race on the Ohio River.

**HENDERSON, KY** (miles 802-805, LDB):

The Native Americans called this area 'Red Banks' because of the reddish clay soil found on the high Ohio River banks. In 1797, Henderson was founded. By the early 1800s, the region's 'dark tobacco' was being exported to markets afar. This tobacco-exporting economy soon made Henderson one of the richest per-capita towns in America. The local economy was also spurred along by being an early transportation hub and a ship-building center.

In 1810, James J. Audubon and his wife settled, and opened a general store in Henderson. By the time Audubon left Henderson for Louisville, he had failed in several business enterprises – that general store, a liquor store, grist and saw mills, and steamboat ownership. His only financial success was 'selling' his steamship, the *Pike*. Nevertheless, while in Henderson, Audubon also studied and painted birds and other wildlife, and started the groundwork for his *Birds of America*. Perhaps his several business ventures had failed because, they were not his real life's passion? In 1819, Audubon moved to Louisville, and began establishing himself as one of the great ornithologists and naturalists of the 19th Century. The John J. Audubon State Park and Museum (☎ 270-826-2247, www.parks.ky.gov/stateparks/au), at the north end of Henderson, houses the world's largest collection of Audubon memorabilia.

In 1885, the first Henderson Railroad Bridge across the Ohio was completed. As late as 1889, this was the only river bridge downstream from Louisville. This railroad bridge was an early link between St. Louis and the Gulf Coast. The present double-track bridge was built in 1932. Audubon Mill Park, near the base of the railroad bridge, is on a scenic vista overlooking the Ohio River. This was the site of Audubon's Grist Mill.

From 1892 to 1903, 'the father of the Blues' William Christopher Handy lived in Henderson. In W.C. Handy's autobiography, he wrote, "I didn't write any songs in Henderson, but it was there I realized that experiences I had had…could be set down in a kind of music characteristic of my race. There I learned to appreciate the music of my people –then, the Blues were born." After leaving Henderson, Handy became part of the Blues scene in Clarksdale Mississippi, and later in Memphis. Every year, Handy is remembered when Henderson hosts a large free outdoor week-long concert –the W.C. Handy Blues and Barbecue Festival. This festival is held during the middle of June.

Four Kentucky governors hail from Henderson, including one who later became a 'Commissioner of Baseball' –Benjamin 'Happy' Chandler. During the horrible 1937 flood, Henderson, the seat of Henderson County, came up with its unofficial motto, 'On the Ohio, but never in it.' Even though the Ohio River crested at 54 feet, much of Henderson was spared because it still stood above this cresting water.

The Henderson Visitors Center (☎ 270-826-3128, www.hendersonky.org), in 'the Depot,' building is near the downriver end of enchanting Audubon Mill Park. Vibrant downtown Henderson, a few blocks away, has many restaurants, a hardware store, a library, post office, and a farmers market. The more commercial section of Henderson is northeast of downtown and fairly close to John J. Audubon State Park. The industrial part of Henderson is downriver.

## MOUNT VERNON, IN (miles 828-830, RDB):

In 1806, the early settlement on a 90-degree Ohio River bend became known as McFadin's Bluff. In 1816, a town was named after George Washington's Plantation, Mount Vernon Virginia on the Potomac River. Mount Vernon is the southernmost town in Indiana, and situated in the state's southwest corner.

Mount Vernon is also one of only three of Indiana's ports –the other two being Jeffersonville on the Ohio River and Burns Harbor on Lake Michigan. Midwestern grain and farm products are shipped aboard barges from Mount Vernon to markets all over the world. The Port of Mount Vernon is known as the Southwinds Maritime Center. The Center is connected to the river, rail and highways, as well as being home to a Foreign Trade Zone. Foreign Trade Zones encourage greater Local participation in the global marketplace by side-stepping import duties and streamlining certain production assemblies and paperwork.

The Ohio River Channel is on the LDB side of Mount Vernon Towhead Island. The Southwinds Maritime Center is on the RDB side of this island. There is about a 50-foot free courtesy boat dock at Sherburne Park, just off downtown. Friendly Mount Vernon has several restaurants and taverns, a grocer, a hardware store, an auto parts store, a laundromat, and a post office. Mount Vernon, our last city in Indiana, is the seat of Posey County.

## GREEN RIVER, KY (mile 784.4, LDB of Ohio River):

The Green River, in total, is around 300 miles long, and flows westward from the center of Kentucky. About 200 miles from the Ohio River, the Green River flows through Mammoth Cave, and drains much of that enormous cave system. During the late 19th and early 20th Centuries, the Green and Barren Rivers were navigable for 180 miles from the Ohio River, all of the way to Bowling Green Kentucky –on the Barren River. In 1828, the tiny shallow-draft steamboat, *United States* made the trip from the Ohio River arriving in Bowling Green Kentucky. Channel improvements continued throughout the 1830s. By 1842, the state of Kentucky had canalized a waterway to Bowling Green, and the town was connected to New Orleans and Pittsburgh. Steamboats exported locally produced tobacco, livestock, timber, and hides, while bringing in sugar, coffee, flour, and other foodstuffs. Bowling Green became the commercial center of south-central Kentucky. During this waterway's heyday, there were a total of five locks and dams –four on the Green River and one on the Barren River.

In September 1861, during the early Civil War, Confederates overran Bowling Green. The city was perceived strategically important because of the Green-Barren Rivers waterway as well as the north-south Louisville and Nashville Railroad. The Confederates occupied the city for about five months before withdrawing south.  Soon after, the Union Army occupied the port for the remainder of the war.

In 1888, the federal government (i.e. Corps of Engineers) took over the management of the Green River from the state of Kentucky.  In the 1900s, two more locks and dams were opened on the Green River, allowing river traffic to reach Mammoth Cave.  But by the 1930s, the small steamboats had vanished.  In 1941, Mammoth Cave National Park was established, and the latest two upper locks and dams were closed by 1950.  In 1957, the Corps deepened the lowest 103 miles of the Green River to nine feet.  In 1965, Lock and Dam #4 at Woodbury, Kentucky failed.  By 1981, Lock # 3 was decommissioned.  To date, only the lowermost two Green River locks operate.  Nonetheless, the Corps of Engineers maintains the Green River for about 103 miles, and to about six miles below the river-wide obstruction at old Lock and Dam #3.

For its uppermost 25 or so navigable miles, on its LDB, the Green River flows through Kentucky's Muhlenberg County.  Muhlenberg County was once the largest coal-producing county in the country.  In 2002, more than 10 million tons of coal, coke, and ore were shipped out of the area aboard small towboats operating on the Green River.  Daily, as many as a half-dozen towboats, most of them pushing two-by-twos, ply the Green River.  Like many other working tributaries of the Ohio River, the banks near the mouth of the Green River are laden with barges that are being readied for 'tow building' (i.e., assembling an array of barges to be pushed by a tow).  Sufficient water depths should not be an issue for any recreational vessel, except very near the shore.

The following table summarizes the locks and pools on the navigable portion of the Green River:

**Table 15-E: Navigable Locks and Pools on the Green River:**

| Lock and Pool Name | Mile | Lock Side | Telephone Number ☎ | Opens for Rec. Vessels | Lift (in ft) | Pool Length (miles) |
|---|---|---|---|---|---|---|
| John. Myers Lock & Dam  (Mt. Vernon, IN) | -(62) Ohio Riv | RDB | 812-838-5836 | 24/7 | 18 | 71.1 |
| L & D #1 (Reed, KY) | 9.1 | RDB | 270-826-2048 | 24/7 | 7.5 | 54.0 |
| L & D #2 (Calhoun, KY) | 63.1 | RDB | 270-273-3107 | 24/7 | 14 | ≈45 |
| L&D #3 (Rochester KY) | 108.5 | Both | | Prm. Obs | NA | ≈40 |

**CALHOUN, KY** (mile 63.5, RDB):

In the 1700s, Fort Vienna was founded in order to protect a bend of the Green River.  The area later was named Calhoun and became the seat of McLean County.  Calhoun has the Lighthouse Restaurant on the Green River, a grocer, a drug store, a general store, an auto part store, a laundromat, and a few gas stations.  Rumsey is an even smaller town on the opposite bank (i.e. the LDB) of the Green River.

**LIVERMORE, KY** (mile 71.5, RDB):

Livermore has a nice city park on the Green River, along with a few restaurants –the Copper Skillet and Tony's Pizza, plus a drug store, a grocer, a general store, and a laundromat.  During the last weekend in August, Livermore hosts the annual 'Livermore Boat Races,' on the Green River.  The food and festivities are mostly provided by the local Lion's Club.

**ROCKPORT, KY** (mile 95, RDB)

In 1870, Rockport Kentucky was established on the Green River.  Today, there is only a steep ramp, with no dock, for traveling boaters.  Rockport has a post office, and nothing else commercial.

Courtesy Dock, Sherburne Park, Mount Vernon, Indiana

'End of the Line,' on the Green River, near Rochester, Kentucky

# CHAPTER 16
## The Paducah Area ...on the Ohio River from the Wabash to the Mississippi River, including the Wabash River to Terre Haute, IN

This is our last regional chapter, covering about 140 miles of the lowest Ohio River from the Wabash River (i.e., the Indiana-Illinois state line) to the Ohio's confluence with the Mississippi near Cairo Illinois. This is perhaps the least developed section of the entire Ohio River –competing with sections of the previous chapter. The terrain is definitely not mountainous, but not flat either. In many places, there are bluffs, many over 200 feet high, hovering above the banks of the Ohio River. There is only one sizeable city –Paducah Kentucky, located along this section of river. A handful of enchanting smaller towns usually have docks for river access –Metropolis, Rosiclare, Elizabethtown and Golconda in Illinois. A few other towns, like Old Shawneetown and Cave-in-Rock are worthwhile visits, but without any permanent docks. Cairo and Mound City Illinois have only steep boat ramps and offer very little for the traveling river visitors behind their levees. Wickliffe Kentucky, on the Mississippi River, slightly less than three miles downriver from Fort Defiance (i.e., where the Ohio and Mississippi River join at Cairo), is a pleasant town with much nicer amenities than Cairo.

Currently, there are three Ohio River Locks and Dams. However, the lowest two, Lock and Dams # 52 and # 53, should eventually be replaced by one –the Olmstead Lock and Dam, which is being constructed two miles below Lock and Dam # 53. Lock and Dams # 52 and 53, are the only old-style wicket dams still seen on the Ohio. In time of high water, the wickets may be lowered, and boats can bypass the locking chambers passing right over the lowered dam. There is significantly more towboat traffic on this lowest portion of the Ohio River, than in the preceding chapter. From this area, commercial river traffic can spread-out onto any one of three navigable rivers. Tows are also bigger here too. We have spotted a couple 'four by fives' (i.e., a tow pushing four barges wide by five barges deep). Around Paducah, there are major towboat repair facilities.

Three Ohio River tributaries are also discussed in this chapter –the Wabash, Cumberland and Tennessee Rivers. By boat, we've only explored the lowest portion of these three rivers. The Tennessee River is navigable by a vessel for more than 650 miles, with nine tall locks and dams that raise/lower the Tennessee River level by more than 500 feet. Knoxville and Chattanooga Tennessee as well as Florence and Decatur Alabama are situated on the navigable Tennessee River. The Cumberland River is navigable by boat for about 380 miles from the Ohio River. There are four locks and dams on the navigable Cumberland River that raise/lower this river by about 200 feet. The Cumberland River flows through the Tennessee cities of Nashville, Clarksville, Carthage and Celina. The Wabash River, at over 400 miles long, is the longest unimpeded river (i.e., with no locks or dams) in the United State east of the Mississippi River. Unlike the Cumberland or Tennessee Rivers, the Corps of Engineers does not maintain the Wabash; it is non-navigable by large boat. When the Indiana cities of Vincennes, Terre Haute, and Lafayette were established, the Wabash River was a major trading artery.

**Table 16-A: Locks and Pools on the Ohio River, from the Wabash to the Mississippi River:**

| Lock and Pool Name | Mile | Lock Side | Telephone Number ☎ | Opns f. R. Ves. | Lift (in ft) | Pool Length (miles) |
|---|---|---|---|---|---|---|
| J. Myers L&D, (Mt. Vernon, IN) | 846.0 | RDB | 812-838-5836 | 24/7 | 18 | 69.9 |
| Smithland L&D, (Hamletsburg IL) | 918.5 | RDB | 618-564-2315 | 24/7 | 22 | 72.5 |
| Lock & Dam # 52, (Brookport, IL) | 938.9 | RDB | 618-564-3151 | 24/7 | 12 | 20.4 |
| Lock & D # 53, (Grand Chain, IL) | 962.6 | RDB | 618-742-6213 | 24/7 | ≤17 | 23.7 |
| Olmsted L&D, (Olmsted, IL) | 964.5 | RDB | 618-742-6456 | | ≤30 | 46.0 |

**Sketch 16-A: The Ohio River –from the Wabash River to the Mississippi River, plus 'the Land Between the Lakes,' Kentucky**

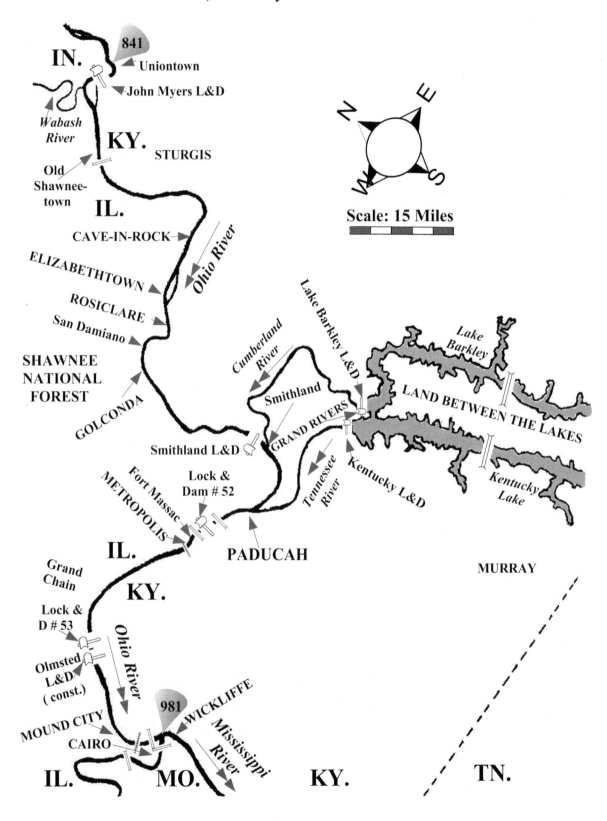

IN.

841

Uniontown

John Myers L&D

*Wabash River*

KY.

STURGIS

Old Shawnee-town

IL.

CAVE-IN-ROCK—

*Ohio River*

ELIZABETHTOWN

ROSICLARE

San Damiano

SHAWNEE NATIONAL FOREST

GOLCONDA

N E W S

Scale: 15 Miles

Lake Barkley L&D

*Cumberland River*

Smithland

GRAND RIVERS

Lake Barkley

LAND BETWEEN THE LAKES

Kentucky Lake

Smithland L&D

Kentucky L&D

*Tennessee River*

Fort Massac

METROPOLIS

Lock & Dam # 52

IL.

KY.

PADUCAH

MURRAY

Grand Chain

Lock & D # 53

*Ohio River*

Olmsted L&D ( const.)

981

WICKLIFFE

MOUND CITY

CAIRO

*Mississippi River*

IL.

MO.

KY.

TN.

174

**OLD SHAWNEETOWN, IL** (mile 858, RDB --Right Descending Bank):

Soon after the American Revolution, Shawneetown became an important administrative center for the new Northwest Territory. Shawneetown shares a distinction with Washington, DC, as being one of only two towns chartered by the US government. In 1813, a federal land office opened in Shawneetown. In 1816, the first bank in Illinois Territory was constructed in Shawneetown. In 1818, Illinois became the 21st state admitted to the Union. In the 1830s, investors approached the Shawneetown Bank, trying to get bonds floated to grow a new Illinois city farther north. The bank refused to help with the financing because they felt that a new town not located on a major river could not succeed. That city turned out to be Chicago! Nevertheless, during the 1840s and 1850s, Shawneetown had thrived as a ferry crossing and one of the major ports between Louisville and the Mississippi River. But Ohio River floods periodically ravaged Shawneetown. The 1937 flood 'broke the camel's back,' and Shawneetown relocated three miles inland to higher ground. Today, only Old Shawneetown sits on the Ohio River, while the 'new' Shawneetown is the seat of Gallatin County. That Old Shawneetown Bank (☎ 618-269-3303) is now a state historic site. Hogdaddy's Saloon (☎ 618-289-4724) and the surrounding area are absurdly packed in mid-July during 'Bike Week' that is centered in Sturgis Kentucky –about 15 miles away. I was told that about 30,000 bikers, from all over the country annually visit the area during this week.

**SHAWNEE NATIONAL FOREST, IL** (mile 861-918, RDB)

Shawnee National Forest (☎618-253-7114, www.fs.fed.us/r9/forests/shawnee/), the third large National Forest along the Ohio River, runs for nearly 60 miles along the river's RDB, with a few gaps around some of the river towns. Contrasting the gently rolling landscape of most of Illinois, the geology of the 277,000-acre Shawnee National Forest is striking. There are many canyons, rocky bluffs and overlooks –some are close to 300 feet higher than the river. The 'Garden of the Gods' includes such rock formations as 'Camel Rock,' Anvil Rock,' and 'Devil's Smokestack.' Besides the many 20-million year old unique geological features, there's quite a diversity in local flora and fauna. The glaciers that once covered much of North America, didn't reach this far south. The geologic processes that formed the unique landscape are also partially responsible for some important minerals found in the area, including lead ore and fluorspar.

**CAVE-IN-ROCK, IL** (mile 881, RDB):

In 1729, a 55-foot wide cave was discovered by French explorers. After the American Revolution, this river cave, a half-mile upstream from the present town, became a lair for some notorious villains. Before the turn of the 19th Century, the Sturdevant Gang of river pirates operated in the area. Later, the Mason Gang used the cave for similar purposes. That gang's leader, Samuel Mason, was once a Revolutionary War officer as well as a judge. Around the turn of the 19th Century, the murderous Harpe Brothers from Kentucky used the cave. Typically, unwary river travelers would be accosted upstream, and then either be enticed or forced into the cave. After they were robbed, most were murdered. Infamous counterfeiters also used the cave. By, the 1830s, most of the cave outlaws and river pirates had been driven away, and travelers could now forge west on the Ohio River making their way safely past Cave-In-Rock.

Around 1816, the town of Cave-In-Rock area was being settled. In the 20th Century, Hollywood made several frontier-western movies near Cave-In-Rock, including "How the West Was Won (1961)," "Davy Crockett and the Keel Boat Race," and "Davy Crockett and the River Pirates." The latter two starred Fess Parker as Davy Crockett.

Today, a 15-car capacity free ferry (☎ 618-289-4599) operates between Cave-In-Rock and Kentucky. Cave-In-Rock State Park (☎ 618-289-4325) is upstream from the ferry crossing and the small town. The town has only a few cafés. The State Park has cabins, a restaurant, a campground, several nice picnic areas, and hiking trails. In September, the town holds its annual Cave-In-Rock Frontier Days.

**ELIZABETHTOWN, IL** (mile 889, RDB):

In the early 1800s, this area was known as McFarlan's Ferry. The town was later named after James McFarlan's wife, Elizabeth. In 1812, the McFarlans completed the first phase of what would become a splendid home on a picturesque Ohio River limestone bluff. Later editions were added to that building –and it became known as McFarlan Tavern/Hotel. In the 19th Century, Elizabethtown was a busy port with salt and pig iron being shipped down the Ohio River, and McFarlan's Hotel had plenty of business. In 1891, the hotel was acquired by Sarah Rose, a worker at the hotel. In 1989, the Illinois Historical Preservation Agency acquired the hotel. Today the Historic Rose Hotel (☎ 618-287-2872, www.rosehotelbb.com), and the oldest hotel in the state of Illinois, operates as an enchanting Bed and Breakfast.

In 1840, Elizabethtown became the seat of Hardin County, as it still is today. Elizabethtown has a laundromat, two small grocers, a service station, and a couple of other Bed and Breakfasts. Hardin County has several entertaining and historical festivals and events throughout the year. Every August, the Heritage Fest and Civil War Reenactment is held here.

**ROSICLARE, IL** (mile 891, RDB):

Around 1807, Ford's Ferry was settled. Near the middle of the 19th Century, lead and fluorspar were discovered in the area. Fluorspar is a combination of two elements –fluorine and calcium. In the late 1880s, the burgeoning steel industry found fluorspar to be a very effective fluxing material in the smelting process. In 1893, the Rosiclare Lead and Fluorspar Mine Company was formed. In 1924, ALCOA purchased that company's property assets. In the early 20th Century, a scientist found a way to utilize fluorspar to greatly improve and revolutionize aluminum production. A derivative of hydrofluoric acid was extracted from fluorspar. This derivative, when used in aluminum production, was able to greatly reduce the cost of finished aluminum. The deepest fluorite mines in the world were located in Hardin County. The Rosiclare area produced three-quarters of all fluorite mined in the United States. The fluorspar industry boomed during the two 20th Century World Wars, as well as boomed and busted a few other times. Fluorspar even had an important role in atomic energy and the first atomic bomb. After World War II, the industry stabilized, and fluorspar found uses in producing glassware, ceramics, and certain plastics. Derivatives of fluorspar are also used in aviation fuel and toothpaste. Sadly today, nearly all fluorspar is imported from overseas. Nonetheless, Rosiclare is home to the American Fluorite Museum (☎ 618-285-3513). The museum features many items from the glory days of the fluorspar mining industry, but this museum has very limited hours – seasonal, weekly, and even daily. Fluorspar is the state mineral of Illinois.

Rosiclare has a grocer, general store, post office, library, and a Visitors' Center –all located near the river. Rosiclare holds it's Fluorspar Festival each October. Along the Ohio River, Rosiclare has a nice one-half mile Riverwalk. The Shawnee Queen River Taxi (☎ 618-285-3342, www.ridesmtd.com) is a 48-seat water taxi departing from Golconda with stops in Rosiclare, Elizabethtown and Cave-In-Rock. This local tour boat, with trips starting at $10, offers two- and four-hour cruises, and permits passengers to alight and board at various other small colorful nearby Ohio River towns.

**SAN DAMIANO RETREAT, IL** (mile 897, RDB):

San Damiano Shrine of the Good Shepard and Retreat (☎ 618-285-3507), opened in 1992, sits on a 225-foot limestone bluff overlooking the Ohio River. The retreat has a 100-seat conference building and workshop rooms, as well as 26 cottages. Shetlerville, one of Illinois first settlements, once sat on this 200-acre site. Shetlerville has been gone since the 1920s, but an old Civil War cemetery remains.

**GOLCONDA, IL** (mile 903, RDB):

In 1796, Major James Lusk and his wife settled here. By 1798, Lusk's Ferry became the first permanent settlement in Pope County. The Illinois town was first named Sarahsville, and later renamed Golconda –after a city in India. By the mid-19th Century, Golconda had become a major shipping point for local timber and produce. Golconda also became the seat of Pope County. The town of Golconda has a grocer, auto parts store, hardware store, library, post office, and a laundromat. In mid-September, Golconda hosts its annual shrimp festival.

In the late 1830s, Golconda was the site where one route of the disgraceful *Trail of Tears* crossed the Ohio River into Illinois. Many eastern Native American's were evicted from their homelands and forced to march west towards Oklahoma. In the late 1820s, white settlers had found small amounts of gold on Cherokee Indian lands in north Georgia, east Tennessee and western North Carolina. By most standards, the Cherokee were quite civil. Many were literate, Christian, and had built roads, schools and churches, as well as adopted many of the 'white man's' mores. The Cherokees had even hoped that the America's legal system would be able to correct the forthcoming egregious injustice. In a favorable US Supreme Court decision, Chief Justice John Marshall ruled that the state of Georgia could not impose laws on Cherokee territory, because only the federal government had that kind of jurisdictional authority in Indian affairs. After that Supreme Court decision, US President Andrew Jackson snickered, "John Marshall has made his decision, now let him [try to] enforce it." Soon President Jackson was using federal troops to round up Cherokees and other Native Americans who were to be shipped to Oklahoma. It's been estimated that 4,000 Native Americans (some estimates are as high as 8,000) out of 17,000 mostly Cherokees perished during this forced relocation. Many Cherokees were dragged from their homes and driven to holding stockades at bayonet point. During their forced march to Oklahoma, the luckless Native Americans were often fleeced by landowners, who extracted tolls when the Native Americans 'passed through' a white man's land.

Looking out at the Ohio River from Cave-in-Rock

**THE WABASH RIVER, IN-IL BORDER** (mile 848.1, RDB):

The Wabash River, originating in the western part of the state of Ohio, is nearly 500 miles long. In the northern half of Indiana, the Wabash River completely bisects Indiana on an east-west axis before becoming the Indiana-Illinois state line along the lower western portion of Indiana. From the mid-17th Century to the mid-19th Century, the Wabash River was a major trading artery that linked the Great Lakes to the Mississippi River. The name comes from Miami Indian, meaning something like 'bright white river.' Southwest of present-day Fort Wayne, Native Americans noted the clarity of the river as the waters reflected off the white limestone river bottom. The French spelled that Native American name 'Ouabache.' Later that name was anglicized to 'Wabash.' Today, there are a few small oil wells in both Illinois and Indiana in the lower Wabash River region.

In February 1779, as George Rogers Clark was about to win the American Revolution in the west, he directed an artillery and supply laden ship, the *Willing*, from Fort Kaskaskia –down the Mississippi River then up the Ohio and finally up the Wabash Rivers to Vincennes. The *Willing* arrived near Vincennes on the Wabash River two days late, and after Clark and his men had already trodden through the southern Illinois marshes and taken Fort Sackville and Vincennes. In 1791, on the banks of the Wabash River near the present-day Indiana-Ohio state line at Fort Recovery, Major General Arthur St. Clair was badly defeated by an Indian force commanded by Chief Little Turtle. In 1811, near Prophetstown (i.e., near present-day Battle Ground Indiana) and the Tippecanoe River (a Wabash tributary), General William Henry Harrison won the costly *Battle of Tippecanoe* over the Indians, less than two miles from the Wabash River.

In 1913, the song 'On the banks of the Wabash, Far Away' became the official Indiana state song. 'The Wabash Cannonball' was a folk song that originated near the end of the 19th Century. It very well may have had its origins from the songs of hobos after they had invented a mythical train taking them to their 'just reward.' Later, The Wabash Railroad, named its express run from Detroit to St. Louis, 'the Wabash Cannonball.'

With a dam (no lock) on the Wabash River, located nearly 411 miles away from the Ohio River near Huntington Indiana, the Wabash River is the longest unimpeded river east of the Mississippi River. It's one of the longest 'non-navigable' rivers in the entire country. The cities of Vincennes, Terre Haute, and Lafayette were established when the Wabash was once a major trading artery. In the 1820s, plans were forged to connect a waterway from Lake Erie (near Toledo) to the Ohio River (near Evansville) utilizing the Maumee River from Fort Wayne to Toledo, and the Wabash River from southwest of Fort Wayne to near Evansville. In 1832, ground was broken. At the northern end of the canal, in the 1830s and 1840s, canal construction spurred the growth of the Indiana cities of Fort Wayne, Huntington, Wabash, Peru, Logansport, and Lafayette. By 1853, the Wabash and Erie Canal was completed to near Evansville. At 635 miles, this canal was the longest in the world. But less than a decade later, about the time of the Civil War, the canal had become uneconomical. By 1874, the last boat was gone. Once again, the railroads, with a much more efficient form of freight and people movement, had doomed another promise-filled 19th Century canal.

Today, boating on the non-maintained Wabash River is a bit tricky. From the Ohio River, I was able to go about 16 miles up the Wabash River, and that was plenty before turning around and heading back down to the relative safety of the Ohio. The river is loaded with sandbars, deadheads, stumps, and other floating debris. Navigating a boat in the muddy Wabash River is not for the faint-hearted.

In the lowest 16 miles of the Wabash River, during two weekdays in late fall, I did encounter one other 'underway' vessel on this river. This vessel was manned by two commercial fishermen in an open trailerable boat. Their quarry was hackleback (or shovelnose) sturgeon. The black eggs, or roe, of this fish has a nutty sweet taste similar to that of exquisite Russian Sevruga caviar. Sturgeons have been wandering the planet since the days of the dinosaurs. The hackleback is one of nine species of sturgeon found in the United States. These hearty fishermen were from near Corydon Indiana, and have occasionally trailered their boat to as far as the Allegheny River to fish. The sturgeon season here is during the coldest and most uncomfortable months of the year –from October to May.

**NEW HARMONY, IN** (mile 45, LDB):

In 1804, a group of Harmonists from Germany established a religious community north of Pittsburgh in Butler County Pennsylvania. These Harmonists pursued Christian perfection in their daily lives, and believed that the second coming of Christ was imminent. In 1814, this group purchased land on the left bank of the Wabash River. By 1824, their new self-sufficient community was well established with 180 log cabins and brick homes. But in 1825, the leader of the Harmonist sold the town lock, stock, and barrel to an industrialist and social reformer from Scotland. The new owner also wanted to establish a utopian community whereby social equality, education, and enlightenment would flourish. Many contemporary scholars were attracted to New Harmony. But by 1827, this social experiment 'Community of Equality' had dissolved when labor and agricultural disputes could not be resolved. Nevertheless in 1827, many inhabitants of New Harmony choose to remain in this less-than-perfect village. During the mid-19th Century, the town remained at the intellectual forefront of geology and publishing. By the time of the Civil War, New Harmony's scientific and scholarly pursuits had gone by the wayside.

Today, the New Harmony Visitor's Center (☎ 800-231-2168) offers tours of these earlier times. The town has a museum, several cafés and restaurants, and a few bed and breakfasts. New Harmonie State Park (☎ 812-682-4821) is about three miles downriver from New Harmony on the Wabash River's LDB. During the first weekend of August, New Harmony is the terminus for the Wabash Heritage Paddlefest (☎812-682-4488, www.canoeevansville.com) that begins in Grayville, IL   As many as 500 canoes travel the nearly 10 miles from Grayville to New Harmony.

Wabash Cannonball Bridge,
near St. Francisville, Illinois

**Sketch 16-B: The Wabash River –from the Ohio River to Terre Haute, Indiana**

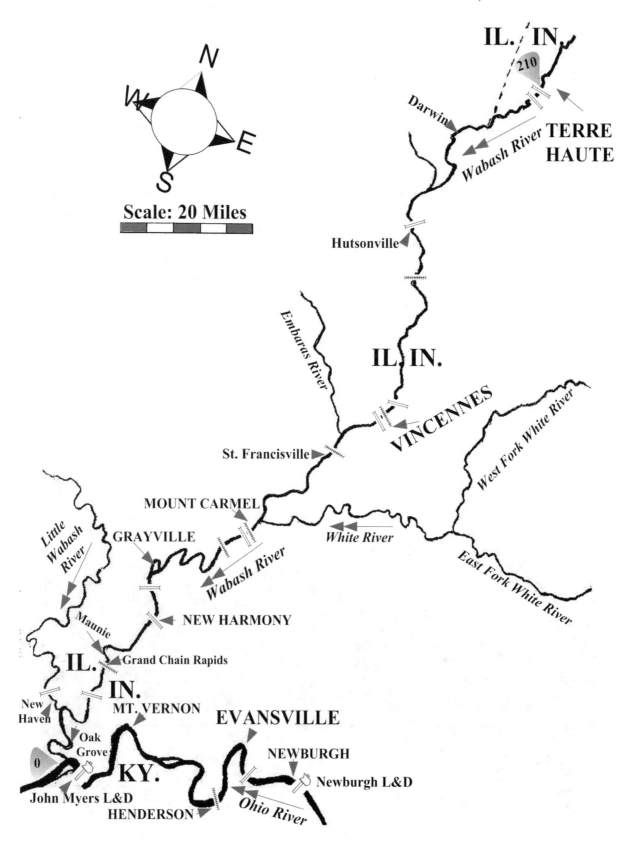

Wabash River, near
St. Francisville, Illinois

Vigo County Courthouse,
Terre Haute, Indiana

**GRAYVILLE, IL** (mile 56, RDB):

Grayville is on the RDB of a hairpin bend in the Wabash River. Recent aerial photographs have revealed that this hairpin bend has been pinched-off. The main channel of the Wabash River now bypasses Grayville (this is not shown on maps), leaving Grayville on an almost closed 'oxbow lake.' This oxbow lake still has some shallow water, but is it accessible to the main Wabash River channel? Like on the Mississippi River, there are many oxbow lakes just beyond the banks of the Wabash River. Over time, the main river channel bypasses, and thus leaves behind these oxbow lakes. In 1830, the Wabash House Hotel was built to provide food and lodging for boat travelers on the river. Today, Grayville has a campground, few restaurants, an auto parts store, and a laundromat.

**MOUNT CARMEL, IL** (mile 87, RDB):

Mount Carmel, the largest city, thus far, on the Wabash River, has a couple of motels and several restaurants. The town is protected from the Wabash River by a floodwall. The Mount Carmel truss bridge over the Wabash River was opened to traffic in 1932. Mount Carmel is the seat of Wabash County Illinois.

**ST. FRANCISVILLE, IL** (mile 108, RDB):

In February 1779, George Rogers Clark and his men camped here before crossing the Wabash River toward their goal of Vincennes. The Port of St. Francisville was established in 1812, and is one of the oldest communities in Illinois. Today, two miles northeast of town, there's the unique 'Wabash Cannonball Bridge' over the river. This bridge once carried a railroad and could swing open allowing boats to pass beneath. In 1968, the bridge was sold to a private source that used it to haul grain over the river. In 1996, the bridge became public when the city of St. Francisville purchased it. Today, vehicles can cross this unique, old, wooden-deck, one-lane bridge over the Wabash River for a fare of only 50¢.

**VINCENNES, IN** (mile 119-121, LDB):

In 1732, Vincennes was founded as a French fur trading outpost. This is also the oldest city in Indiana. After losing the French and Indian War, and since 1763, the local French inhabitants had to tolerate the British as their new landlords. In the summer of 1778, with encouragement from a French priest, Father Pierre Gibault, and spurred on by George Rogers Clark recent victory in Kaskaskia, the French had an uprising against their British occupiers. But in the fall of 1778, a British force from Fort Detroit, coming down the Wabash River, put down this French insurrection, and fortified their local outpost – Fort Sackville. This fort was about 35 feet from the Wabash River.

In February 1779, George Rogers Clark and about 170 men marched overland 180 miles from Kaskaskia on the Mississippi River through the cold and sodden Illinois sloughs to retake Vincennes for the Americans, once and for all. Before taking Fort Sackville and Vincennes, Clark had adroitly neutralized the local Native Americans –who were earlier allied with the British. Clark also developed a reputation for being even-handed when dealing with the local French settlers. After a two-day siege, the British commander at Fort Sackville, knew he had no chance without the support of the local French inhabitants of Vincennes, and smartly surrendered to Clark. Clark renamed the fort, Fort Patrick Henry after the Virginia Governor. Clark's unique combination of boldness, even-handedness, and diplomacy lead to the largest land conquest of the entire Revolutionary War! In 1878, the deteriorated Fort Sackville was rebuilt as Fort Knox. Today, Vincennes is the seat of Knox County

In 1800, when the Indiana Territory was created, Vincennes was the first capital. In 1803, the capital moved to Corydon. From 1803 to 1812, territorial governor, William Henry Harrison lived in Vincennes at his estate in Grouseland. Vincennes University, founded in 1801, is older than the state of Indiana, and it is located on the Wabash River. In 1833, when Abraham Lincoln left Indiana for business dreams in Illinois, he crossed the Wabash River in Vincennes.

During the 20th Century, the US Navy named four ships in honor of Vincennes. The last one was an Aegis guided missile cruiser launched in 1984. Today the George Rogers Clark National Historic Park (☎ 812-882-1776, www.nps.gov/gero) is on the Wabash River at the site of old Fort Sackville. The Cathedral and Basilica of St Francis Xavier, built in 1826, is across from this historic park. The Ouabache Trails County Park (☎ 812-882-4316) is about three miles north of Vincennes on the Wabash River. This park has a campground, RV sites, cabins, picnic areas, and four miles of hiking trails. For more info on historic Vincennes, call: (☎ 800-886-6443, www.vincennescvb.org)

## HUTSONVILLE, IL (mile 167, RDB):

Hutsonville was named for Isaac Hutson. In 1813, Hutson's family was massacred by Indians. Today, Hutsonville has a small grocer in town and a nice picnic area on the river.

## TERRE HAUTE, IN (mile 209-211, LDB):

'Terre Haute,' means 'high land' in French. Early 18th Century French explorers described the strategic plateau-like rise on the left descending bank of the Wabash River as such. No less than one long-standing Native American village of Wea Indians was also camping nearby. By 1809, many of the Wea were forced to cede their lands. In 1811, en route to the *Battle of Tippecanoe,* General William Henry Harrison constructed Fort Harrison on the Wabash River. In 1812, Captain Zachary Taylor successfully defended Fort Harrison from a Native American attack. In 1816, a town slightly south of Fort Harrison was platted. By 1824, the last of the Wea's male warriors were forced to leave, and they left behind their wives and young children. An enterprising Wea chief placed an ad in the newspaper imploring the local populace, 'not to mistreat the remaining Wea women and children,' as he and his men were forced west.

In the 1820s and 1830s, steamboats regularly plied the Wabash River. Pork and other agricultural products were shipped downriver from Terre Haute. In the late 1830s, Terre Haute was the center for the construction of the National Road. Terre Haute (and even the entire state of Indiana) has sometimes been called 'the Crossroads of America' because the National Road (i.e., present-day US Route 40) intersected US Route 41 (the route from northern Michigan to Florida).

From 1847 until 1876, Terre Haute was the headquarters of the short-lived Wabash and Erie Canal. By 1849, this canal, being constructed southward, had reached Terre Haute. By the 1850s, the railroad also reached Terre Haute, and the city was gaining a reputation as a transportation hub. After the Civil War, Terre Haute became an industrial and mining center with iron furnaces, and steel mills. Today, pleasant Fairbanks Park, near the downriver end of Terre Haute has a boat ramp, a 150-foot dock, an amphitheatre, and covered picnic pavilions.

Terre Haute is the seat of Vigo County. The county was named for one of George Rogers Clark's critical frontier financers. In the late 1760s, Italian-born Francis Vigo found his way to the new world serving in a Spanish regiment stationed out of New Orleans. After being discharged by the Spanish, Vigo became a financially successful fur trader in St. Louis. In 1778, After George Rogers Clark had taken Kaskaskia, Vigo made a fateful decision to support Clark (and not the British). He soon proved himself to be a very reliable American patriot. Two months before Clark advanced on Vincennes, Vigo was taken prisoner there. The British didn't realize how deeply connected Vigo was to the American cause, and released him within days. A month later, Vigo was in Kaskaskia providing Clark with nearly 'real time' intelligence on the state of affairs in Vincennes. This intelligence report by Vigo greatly enabled Clark to make his successful march and capture of Fort Sackville and Vincennes.

# Restaurant Dock in Elizabethtown, Illinois

# River Traffic, near Cave-in-Rock State Park, Illinois

**SMITHLAND, KY** (mile 920, LDB –Left Descending Bank):

In 1780, the Gower House was built in Smithland to accommodate the many river travelers who passed through to spend the night. The Gower House remained a busy place for the next century. In the winter of 1838-1839, during the forced *Trail of Tears*, before the Native Americans crossed the Ohio River, many had spent a brutally cold winter camped in Smithland – and they surely didn't lodge at the Gower House. In September 1861, Union General Ulysses Grant moved to Smithland and constructed Fort Smith to protect the mouth of the Cumberland River. The fort was manned by several Union detachments, including one composed of African-America soldiers near the end of the Civil War. Today, Smithland is the seat of Livingston County.

One of the widest portions of the entire Ohio River, at nearly one mile wide, is just upstream from the Smithland Lock and Dam. Both of the locking chambers at the Smithland Lock are 1,200 feet long (i.e., there is no smaller chamber). As expected, this newest lock and dam on the lowest part of the Ohio River handles considerable towboat traffic.

**PADUCAH, KY** (mile 935, LDB):

In 1795 the federal government awarded nearly 74,000 acres of land, including the area around present-day Paducah, to George Rogers Clark, and more than 15 years after his invaluable Revolutionary War Service. In the meantime, a settlement called Pekin sprung up at the confluence of the Tennessee River. There's a loose legend that a friendly Chickasaw Indian Chief, Paduke, would welcome flat boat travelers to his small Native American community. In 1822, Captain Valentine Owen, started an Ohio River ferry service from that Kentucky settlement to Illinois. Today, the island at the mouth of the Tennessee River is named for Owen.

In 1827, William Clark –the younger brother of George Rogers Clark, after some legal wrangling, acquired the deed to his then deceased older brother's land around Chief Paduke's settlement. William Clark platted the area. Clark already had a noteworthy career as a western explorer, military officer, territorial governor of Missouri, and superintendent of Indian Affairs. In 1830, the town of Paducah, named for the chief, was incorporated.

Paducah's location, near four great navigable rivers, as well as being the northernmost ice-free port, proved ideal for steamboat traffic. By the 1850s, Paducah had established itself as a serious boat-building center in the Ohio and Tennessee Rivers region. To this day, 20 river towboat companies operate in Paducah, and there are many repair facilities as well as dry docks.

By the 1850s, railroad lines also linked Paducah to many southern cities. The Illinois Central Railroad knitted Wisconsin, Iowa, Illinois and Missouri, with a network that tapered into a north-south trunk line near Paducah, before servicing the southern states along the Gulf of Mexico. Besides the steamboats and trains, brick ovens and foundries for rail and locomotive components further spurred Paducah's economy. In the late 1920s, the Illinois Central Railroad built one of the largest railroad factories in the world, and employed around 1,800 in Paducah.

In September 1861, during the Civil War, after having trained his men at Fort Defiance in Cairo, Union General Grant arrived in Paducah by gunboat. Grant's men soon built a pontoon float bridge across the Ohio River that allowed thousands more Union troops to enter into Kentucky. Grant also constructed Fort Anderson. Fort Anderson was named after Union Major Robert Anderson, who commanded Fort Sumter South Carolina. For four months before the Civil War, Anderson walked a diplomatic tightrope at Fort Sumter. At the onset of the Civil War, when Fort Sumter was bombarded for 34 hours by several Confederate garrisons, Anderson, a loyal Union solider born in Louisville, refrained from returning fire on the civilians in Charleston.

In March 1864, Confederate General Nathan Bedford Forrest raided Paducah with about 3,000 cavalrymen. About 650 Union soldiers were hunkered-down at Fort Anderson. During this *Battle of Paducah*, Forrest's command burned the wharf and took what they wanted – supplies, horses, mules, and destroyed much of what was left, so that it would be unusable to the Union. After Forrest had left Paducah, a local newspaper reported that Forrest's troops had missed more than 100 fine horses hidden in a foundry during the raid. Within weeks, one of Forrest subordinates returned to the foundry that the newspaper described, and successfully seized these renowned horses.

During the 20<sup>th</sup> Century, before floodwalls were built, Paducah experience two awful floods. In 1913, The Ohio River crested at over 54 feet. But in January-February 1937, it was even worse. The Ohio River rose nearly 61 feet, and the river was supposedly seven miles wide. Ninety percent of Paducah was inundated and about 27,000 residents were forced to flee. Many downtown buildings bear plaques showing the 1937 high water mark. Now, Paducah is protected by floodwalls. And wow, has this city done a nice job painting some great historical scenes on these floodwalls. This ongoing floodwall mural painting project began in 1996.

Paducah's two favorite sons are Ervin Cobb and Alben Barkley. In 1901, Barkley started his law practice in Paducah. Barkley became a Kentucky Congressman and Senator before becoming Harry Truman's Vice President in 1949. During his time as VP, the nickname 'Veep' came about. His young grandson couldn't pronounce the complete title, so two e's were sandwiched between the V and the P. Irvin Cobb was a humorist, columnist and author, who wrote over 60 books and 300 short stories. Cobb also covered World War I for the *Saturday Evening Post*. Cobb said of Paducah, "…an agreeable blend of western kindliness and northern enterprise superimposed upon a southern background."

There are many attractions in downtown Paducah, within blocks of the Ohio River. Several Bed and Breakfasts are located near the river. For the latest performing arts, visit the Luther Carson Four Rivers Center (☎ 270-443-9932). Nearby, the Paducah Railroad Museum (☎ 270-519-7377, www.paducahrr.org) offers many rich local history lessons. The William Clark Market House Museum (☎ 270-443-7759) has many artifacts displaying Paducah's rich past. The Museum of American Quilters' (☎ 270-442-8856, www.quiltmuseum.org) is the largest quilt museum in the world. Every late April, quilt enthusiasts flock to Paducah for the annual quilter's show held at the convention center. The outstanding, four-year old Paducah River Heritage Museum (☎ 270-575-9958, www.riverheritagemuseum.org) has a little bit of everything –from river habitat to recreation to locking. There are many interactive exhibits including a lock and dam, with a flood table. This very multi-faceted educational museum is located in Paducah's oldest standing building.

One of three centers for Maritime Education (the others are in New York and Houston) is located in Paducah (☎ 270-575-1005). This excellent training center enhances the professional competency of merchant mariners with support and practical training. A high-tech portion of this training utilizes real-life towboat bridge simulators. All of the major towboat companies support this fine operation. The Maritime Center also supports the meaningful Seamen's Church Institute (www.seamenschurch.org).

Over the Fourth of July, Paducah hosts its riverfront concert and fireworks. In late July, Paducah hosts its one-week Paducah Summer Festival with many events along the river, including a *Sand in the City* event where sculpting teams make sand sculptures in the Farmers Market parking lot. During the last weekend of September, Paducah hosts its 'Old Market Days, Barbeque on the River, and Marine Industry Days' along the riverfront. For more information on happenings in Paducah, the seat of McCracken County, please visit (www.paducah-tourism.org).

**METROPOLIS, IL** (mile 943, RDB):

Before the Americans, the Metropolis area had three European flags flown over the region. The Spanish loosely held the area for two centuries –the 16<sup>th</sup> and 17<sup>th</sup>. For most of the 18<sup>th</sup> Century, the French controlled the area, and built a trading post and a mission. In 1757, during the French and Indian War, the French constructed Fort De L'Ascension. The fort was later rebuilt, and renamed it Fort Massiac. In the early 1760s, after the French and Indian War, Indians burned the fort to the ground. Afterward, the British controlled the area, but didn't re-garrison the fort. In 1778, when George Rogers Clark and his 'Long Knives' arrived, they expected a British confrontation. But when Clark's men arrived aboard their boats, they auspiciously found the British fort abandoned. From Fort Massac, Clark's men marched overland through Illinois Territory, to take Fort Kaskaskia on the Mississippi River, by surprise on July 4, 1778.

In 1794, after the American Revolution, President George Washington, had the fort rebuilt as a defensive point against the encroaching Spanish –only 60 miles to the west. In the fall of 1803, Lewis and Clark's Corps of Discovery stopped at Massac Village. There they enlisted civilian George Drouillard for their Corps. Drouillard, with a French father and a Shawnee Indian mother, proved invaluable. Besides being a highly skilled woodsman and an excellent marksman, Drouillard could communicate in several Native American dialects. In 1805, reckless adventurer Aaron Burr went to Fort Massac, to further his plans to start a new nation in the American Southwest. In 1814, the fort was abandoned, and the nearby inhabitants dismantled the fort's logs for local construction projects. During the early years of the Civil War, the site served briefly as a Union training camp. In 1908, Fort Massac became Illinois' first state park through the efforts of the local Daughters of the American Revolution.

Around 1839, about one mile downriver from the fort, the city of Metropolis was platted. In 1917, the Metropolis Railroad Bridge, connecting Metropolis with Kentucky opened. In 1972, the Illinois State legislature declared Metropolis Illinois the 'the hometown' of comic book hero 'Superman.' There once was a large water tower with a Superman painting facing the Ohio River. That tower is now gone. But in town, there still is a large Superman statue, a small Superman museum. The local newspaper is called the 'Metropolis Planet.' Metropolis is the seat of Massac County.

Harrah's Riverboat Casino, made to look like a three-story paddle-wheeler, is one and a half miles downriver from Fort Massac. This attraction annually brings about two million visitors to Metropolis. In late May, at Fort Massac, there's a French and Indian War re-enactment on the Ohio River. A Superman Celebration is held during the second weekend of June. That annual Superman festival has attracted Hollywood celebrities that have had any type of association with 'Hollywood Superman.' During the third weekend of October, Metropolis also holds 'The Encampment' festival at Fort Massac.

## GRAND CHAIN-OLMSTED, IL (mile 960-965, RDB):

In 1803, when the Corps of Discovery passed this area, it was noted that, "there was a 'great chain' of rocks stretching in an oblique manner across the Ohio River." Present-day Lock and Dam #53 now sit near this site. Nearby, upriver, the Grand Chain Lodge and Campground (☎ 618-634-9411, www.grandchainlodge.com) has a restaurant, boat ramp, and RV park.

In the early-mid 1990s, the Olmstead Lock and Dam project was started. Many of the lock and dam components are being fabricated off-site, and then floated to the construction site aboard barges. The latest multi-year (and multi-decade) price-tag is around $1.4 billion. Over the last decade, congressional funding for the Olmstead project has been 'year by year.' Completion of the Olmsted Lock and Dam is behind its original schedule, and probably not slated for opening until sometime in the middle of the next decade…hopefully?

In August 2005, there was a drought, the Ohio River level became very low, and dredging operations were needed to keep towboat traffic barely moving through the area. Sixteen-hour river traffic delays were commonplace. At one point, 40 towboats were backed-up and waiting to get through this area. Had the Olmsted Lock and Dam been completed, this wouldn't have been a problem.

Paducah Floodwall Murals

The Ohio River, from the end of Broadway, Paducah, Kentucky

**MOUND CITY, IL** (mile 973, RDB):

During the Civil War, Mound City was a very busy place. The keels of three Union iron-clad gunboats were laid at the local shipyard. A portion of the Union's western river fleet was based in Mound City. In 1861, a Civil War Hospital was built. By 1862, after the *Battle of Shiloh*, this hospital treated 2,200 wounded Union as well as Confederate soldiers. In 1864, near the end of the Civil War, the Mound City National Cemetery (☎ 800-248-4373) was opened. Both Union and Confederate soldiers are buried here. Mound City is the seat of Pulaski County.

**CAIRO, IL** (mile 979, RDB):

In the early 18th Century, the French believed that the confluence of the Mississippi and Ohio Rivers would be an important strategic point for a fortification and a settlement. In November 1803, Lewis and Clark's Corps of Discovery spent six days in the area honing their celestial navigation skills, before heading up the Mississippi River. As early as 1818, the site was a moorage area for boats and had a lumber yard. Great things were expected to happen at the confluence of these two great rivers. A port was expected to surpass St. Louis, Louisville, and Cincinnati. So, in 1837, a town was founded.

However, in 1841, when Charles Dickens visited Cairo [pronounced as 'Kay-Row'] on a steamboat, he stated, "We arrived at a spot so much more desolate than any yet beheld...a place without any single quality, in earth, air, or water...such is this dismal Cairo." By 1843, Cairo had constructed its needed levees. During the 1850s, Cairo had several hundred inhabitants, many of whom lived on wharf boats. During that decade, Cairo was becoming an important steamboat port. In 1854, Congress made Cairo a US Customs port. Customs officials inspected goods and collected fees after vessels had passed through a point of entry near New Orleans. In 1872, the three-story Cairo Customs House was finished. During the Civil War, within ten days after the bombardment of Fort Sumter South Carolina, Union troops started occupying Cairo. Fort Defiance –the point at the south end of town where the Mississippi and Ohio Rivers converge – was strategically important to the Union. In 1861, General Ulysses Grant trained a Midwestern regiment at Fort Defiance.

After the Civil War, much of the usual commerce that went through the area became more routed in an east-west orientation (versus a north-south orientation), and Cairo was losing ground. In the 1884 novel *Adventures of Huckleberry Finn,* Mark Twain had as a goal for Huck and his slave friend Jim to reach Cairo. After reaching Cairo, Huck and Jim had planned to catch a steamboat up the Ohio River. In 1889, the Illinois Central Railroad opened a bridge over the Ohio River. This bridge replaced a ferryboat taking trains across the river. At that time, this bridge was the longest metal bridge in the world. That Cairo Railroad Bridge was rebuilt in 1952, and many of the original piers were reused.

Since the 1920s, Cairo has regressed and the population has declined every decade. In the late 1960s, racial tensions were high, and the National Guard had to be called-in to quell the threat of violence. For many years, much of Cairo has had the air of the worst part of a large 'inner city' –liquor stores were about the only establishments regularly open and even the laundromats were boarded-up. In the 2005 music album, *Greetings from Cairo*, Stace England chronicles Cairo's dismal history. On the western edge of town, Cairo does have a neighborhood of grand houses, dating from its more prosperous days in the late 19th and early 20th Centuries. But even many of these older homes are in a state of decay. The old Cairo Customs House has been converted into a museum, and this may be the only tourist draw to dreary Cairo. Cairo is the seat of Alexander County.

Near Cairo, the states of Kentucky and Missouri are the only two bordering states that do not connect via a direct highway. That Kentucky-Missouri connection carrying US Routes 60 and 62 (over the Mississippi and Ohio Rivers) goes through Cairo Illinois. The connecting Ohio River highway bridge, near Fort Defiance now carrying US Routes 51, 62, and 62, was built in 1837, and refurbished in 1979.

**WICKLIFFE, KY** (two miles below the Ohio River, and the LDB of the Mississippi River):

Wickliffe Kentucky, the seat of Ballard County, sits two miles below the mouth of the Ohio River, on the LDB of the lower Mississippi River. Sixty percent of the river water flowing past Wickliffe comes from the Ohio River, while only 40 percent comes from the upper Mississippi River. By boat, Wickliffe may be only slightly more accessible than Cairo or Mound City Illinois. Nevertheless, this town is a much more pleasant stopover than Cairo.

Native American mound builders lived here from about 1100 to 1350 AD. Wickliffe Mounds State Historic Site (☎ 270-335-3681), just north of town, was a Native American Village of mound builders.

In 1682, when LaSalle sailed down the length of the Mississippi River, he stopped in present-day Wickliffe, and claimed the area for France. In about 1780, George Rogers Clark named the site for Virginia's new governor, Thomas Jefferson. Fort Jefferson was soon constructed three miles below the mouth of the Ohio River. All other areas nearby were prone to flood. During the early Civil War, this fort was one of four river forts in the area used by Union troops operating in the western theatre. Today, a 95-foot tall memorial cross rises on this highest point near the confluence of the two great rivers. The grounds around this cross, completed in 1999, have been used for many ceremonies –weddings, memorials, candle light vigils, Easter Sunrise services and even a 9/11 service. The town of Wickliffe has gas stations, an auto-parts store, a few good value restaurants and a motel.

Rainbow in background of Fort Jefferson
Memorial, Wickliffe, Kentucky

House, gazebo, and dock on river near Elizabethtown, Illinois

Fort Massac State Park, Metropolis, Illinois

## ON THE CUMBERLAND AND TENNESSEE RIVERS:

We have already talked about how many important cities that eventually became large are situated on major navigable rivers. In the state of Tennessee alone, the five largest cities are located on either the Mississippi River or on one of two Ohio River tributaries coming from the state of Tennessee. Tennessee's largest city, Memphis, is on the Mississippi River. Nashville and Clarksville, Tennessee's 2nd and 5th largest cities, are situated on the Cumberland River, while Knoxville and Chattanooga (the state's 3rd and 4th largest cities) are on the Tennessee River.

It is nearly 1,000 miles from the Ohio River, at Cairo Illinois, to the Gulf of Mexico near New Orleans. But from the Ohio River, at Paducah, it's slightly less than 700 miles to the Gulf of Mexico outside Mobile Bay. This shorter trip would involve running up the Tennessee River (for about 215 miles) and then down the Tenn-Tom Waterway (for about 450 miles). This is almost a 300-mile shortcut from the Ohio River to the Gulf of Mexico. And without any doubt, that 'Tennessee River and Tenn-Tom Waterway' offers many more services and amenities for boaters and other travelers than anything possibly found along the Mississippi River. Like the Tennessee River, the Cumberland River is another pleasant mid-south river. But after the free-flowing canal, about 33 miles up the Cumberland River, that connects the Cumberland to the Tennessee River in the 'Land Between the Lakes' area, the Cumberland River, has no other navigable outlet.

The Land Between the Lakes, an idea of the Kennedy Administration, was created in the mid-1960s, after the Cumberland River was dammed to create Lake Barkley. For over 40 miles the Cumberland and Tennessee Rivers closely parallel each other, and are only about five-to-eight miles apart. That narrow strip of land between these two rivers –actually between the two dammed lakes on these two rivers –comprises the 'Land Between the Lakes.' After boating down the Ohio River, and then entering either one of the two lakes –Kentucky Lake on the Tennessee River or Lake Barkley on the Cumberland River –there's a whole different 'feel' or change of pace. The Ohio River *felt* more historical, more hardscrabble, more 'you're on your own,' or maybe just more blue-collar. These two rivers –the two lakes *–feel* more 'resort-collar.'

A canal connects Lake Barkley with Kentucky Lake 33 miles from the Cumberland River's mouth on the Ohio and 25 miles from the Tennessee River's mouth on the Ohio. This one-mile long, free-flowing canal (i.e., no lock or dam) allows boaters to travel between the two lakes without having to go all of the way down to the Ohio River.

The following table summarizes the locks & pools on lowest Cumberland and Tennessee Rivers:
**Table 16-F: Locks and Pools on the Lowest Cumberland and the Lowest Tennessee Rivers**

| Lock and Pool Name | Mile | Lock Side | Telephone Number ☎ | Opens for Rec V. | Lift (in ft) | Pool Lgth (mi.) |
|---|---|---|---|---|---|---|
| Lock & Dam # 52 (Brookport, IL) | 938.9 | RDB | 618-564-3151 | 24/7 | 12 | 46.6 |
| Lake Barkley L & D, Cumberland River, (Grand Rivers, KY) | 30.6 | LDB | 270-362-9131 | 24/7 | 57 | 118.1 |
| Kentucky Lock & Dam, Tennessee River (Grand Rivers, KY) | 22.4 | RDB | 270-362-4226 | 24/7 | 57 | 185.2 |

**CUMBERLAND RIVER, KY** (mile 923 Ohio River, LDB):
The Cumberland River flows about 700 miles generally westward to the Ohio River. Its tributaries begin near the Kentucky-Virginia state line on the Cumberland Plateau. In the early 1750s, when Dr. Thomas Walker found and named the 'Cumberland Gap' he also discovered and named the river. The river flows through Kentucky's Daniel Boone National Forest.

In 1924, near the end of the steamboat era, there were fifteen working locks and dams on the Cumberland River. Today, these locks have been replaced by four modern locks and hydroelectric dams that were built between the late 1950s and early 1970s. The Cumberland River is commercially navigable for about 380 miles from the Ohio River, or about 190 miles upriver from Nashville.

That free-flowing canal (i.e., with no lock nor dam) connects the Cumberland River with the Tennessee River. Before this **one-mile** long canal was dredged in the mid-1960s, a boat trip from the Cumberland River side to the Tennessee River side of Grand Rivers Kentucky was 68 miles –via 10 miles of Ohio River.

**TENNESSEE RIVER, KY** (mile 934.5 Ohio River, LDB):

The Tennessee River, the largest tributary of the Ohio River, begins in the foothills of the Great Smokey Mountains. Outside Knoxville, French Broad and the Holston River join to form the Tennessee River. The Clinch River and Little Tennessee River also feed the great Tennessee near its headwaters. The Clinch and the Holston Rivers originate in the rugged Appalachian Mountains of southwestern Virginia. The French Broad River, another one of the oldest rivers in the world, originates in western North Carolina, and flows through Asheville. The Little Tennessee River goes through the Cherokee and the Nantahala National Forests, and has tributaries extending into northeastern Georgia.

From its origin in the foothills of the Smokey Mountains, the [Great] Tennessee River forms a broad flat horseshoe, traveling southwesterly, then westerly, and finally northerly, before dumping into the Ohio River at Paducah. The Tennessee River and its tributaries flow from seven southern states, including Alabama, and Mississippi. The Tennessee River is navigable its entire length, or for 650 miles all the way to Knoxville Tennessee. About 215 miles from the Ohio River, in Pickwick Landing Lake, one LDB arm of the Tennessee River, Yellow Creek, is the beginning of the Tennessee Tombigbee Waterway (or Tenn-Tom). The Tenn-Tom, an ambitious and worthwhile project, opened in 1985. Before the Tenn-Tom was built, a boat trip from Paducah Kentucky to the Gulf of Mexico, via the Ohio and Mississippi River ending near New Orleans was about 915 miles. After the Tenn-Tom, a trip from Paducah to the Gulf of Mexico via the Tennessee River, the Tenn-Tom Waterway ending near Mobile, Alabama was reduced to 665 miles, or by about 250 miles.

By the end of World War II, the navigable Tennessee River had become the nation's largest electricity supplier. Unlike the Ohio River, the ten dams with locks on the Tennessee River system (as well as the four dams with locks on the Cumberland River) are also used to produce hydroelectric power. The 20 lock and dams on the Ohio River are used solely for navigation purposes. When a dam is managed for hydroelectricity, great amounts of water are sometimes 'stored' behind that dam. The release of that stored water is timed to coincide with times of peak electricity demand. The river currents below hydroelectric dams have been known to strengthen or weaken greatly during the course of a 24-hour day. On the Tennessee River, I've heard first-hand panic stories of a boat trying to make its way upstream, **below** and against 'a releasing' hydroelectric dam's current. And I've heard of a boat parking overnight in a small tributary **below** a hydroelectric dam, and then finding itself high and dry the next morning, after the normal flow of water through the dam had been curbed for the night. If you operate or park a small boat close to, and **below,** any hydroelectric dam, please be especially mindful, and take potential current and water level fluctuation variables into consideration.

**GRAND RIVERS, KY** (mile 24, RDB of the Tennessee River, AND mile 32, LDB of the Cumberland River):

In the early and mid 19th Century, settlers began arriving here. Iron ore was found in the region and spurred early growth and commerce. On this narrow neck of land, two great rivers, the Tennessee and Cumberland, were barely one mile apart. River transportation, along the two river routes facilitated commerce. But by the early 20th Century, more plentiful iron ore deposits were found in Minnesota's Mesabi Range, and doomed this local industry.

In 1933, during the depths of the Great Depression, the Tennessee Valley Authority (TVA) was established as a part of President Franklin Roosevelt's New Deal. By 1945, ten hydroelectric dams had been built on the Tennessee River offering inexpensive electricity –a feature to help develop local industries. Roosevelt's plan worked. By 1945, the 180-mile long Kentucky Lake on the Tennessee River was created. A pleasant offshoot was a budding tourist industry along the lake. In 1962, a nearby lock and dam on the Cumberland River was completed, creating Lake Barkley. 'The Land Between the Lakes National Recreation Area (LBL)' –and a brainchild of the Kennedy Administration, was a reality. One idea behind the LBL project was to see if an economy based on outdoor recreation could work in an area with limited industrial, agricultural, and forestry resources. This idea also worked. Grand Rivers was, and still is, the town best poised to benefit. A navigable canal sits near the southeastern end of Grand Rivers on the isthmus connecting the Tennessee and Cumberland Rivers.

**Looking-upward from my small boat while inside a deep Locking Pit on the Tenn-Tom Waterway**

# CHAPTER 17
## Commercial Towboat Appreciation

We've saved the best for last. Our country was growing rapidly after the Civil War. There was heightened demand for Appalachian coal, and the need to get that coal downriver. There was also a pressing need to get agricultural commodities grown in the Ohio and Mississippi River Valleys downriver. In the late 19th Century, the US Congress started proposing and funding various 'Rivers and Harbors' Acts. These acts, in turn, assisted the rise of the present-day 'river industry.' Today in the United States, there are about 25,000 miles of inland and intracoastal navigable waterways. About 4,000 towboats work on these waters. This inland river industry contributes $25 billion annually to US exports, while supporting $100 billion annually in interstate commerce. Six of our nation's top ten inland ports, based on trip ton/mile are located in the Ohio River System –Huntington, Pittsburgh, Cincinnati, Louisville, Mount Vernon Indiana, and Guntersville Alabama (on the Tennessee River). The only four 'top ten' ports that are not on the Ohio River are: St. Louis (at #2), Memphis (at # 4), St. Paul (at #6), and Tulsa (at #9). The Inland River Industry along the Ohio and Mississippi Rivers (i.e., a 24-state area) directly supports 70,000 jobs, while indirectly supporting another 800,000 US jobs.

### Freight and Environmental Comparisons

Inland waterway transportation is the most energy efficient mode of transporting raw materials and bulk type products over long distances. The carrying capacity of a 'three by five' tow (i.e., 15 jumbo barges) is the same as that of 870 tractor trailers, or 2¼ 100-car freight trains. That 'three by five' tow is less than one-quarter mile long, whereas the trains would extend for two and three-quarter miles, and a solid line of trucks would stretch out for more than 30 miles – assuming some reasonable traffic separation between the trucks.

A 4,000 horsepower towboat (with twin 2,000 HP engines) pushing a load of cargo on the Ohio River might consume around 4,000 gallons of diesel fuel during a 24-hour day. By truck, one gallon of fuel can ship one ton of cargo only 59 miles. By rail, one gallon of fuel can push one ton of cargo 202 miles. However, aboard an inland barge, one ton of cargo can travel about 800 miles on only one gallon of fuel! If diesel fuel is priced at $3.50 per gallon, the average fuel cost of inland water transportation is about 0.4¢ per ton mile of cargo moved. This compares to nearly 1.7¢ for rail, and 5.9¢ for trucks per ton mile.

River transportation is also the safest and most environmentally friendly method of transporting goods. Nitrous oxide emissions (i.e., pollution) from towboats are between one-third and one-twentieth of comparable emissions from truck or rail. Deaths and injuries associated with truck and rail are in the neighborhood of ten times greater than that for barge transportation.

About a century and a half ago, railroads started to eclipse many small river towns whose livelihood had been dependent on the river, and especially those small towns dependent on canals. In the eastern half of our country, I'm aware of countless examples of newly-built canals having been rendered economically unviable soon after their construction because a newer competing railroad had been constructed. Around the Ohio River Valley, railroads are sometimes better able to provide more direct north-south service via trunk lines than waterborne traffic. But railroads also need a gentle 'railroad grade' to run their tracks and trains . A railroad grade is typically no more than a two percent incline. In nature, the only place this gentle railroad grade can be found (i.e., not requiring an inordinate amount of earth moving) is along the rivers. So the railroads usurped much of the river bottom lands for train tracks and rail yards. As World War I approached, railroads were unable to handle all of the freight traffic, and there was a revitalization of river commerce. In more recent years, a Marshall University study suggests that rail rates have been held down, by 15 to 25 percent, because their primary competition, the towboats, have kept the railroads more competitively priced.

## On The Ohio River

According to the US Department of Commerce, the Ohio River carries 40 percent of the commercial water-borne traffic in the continental United States. In 2006, 241 million tons of cargo was transported on the Ohio River. Coal and other energy products, valued at over $4 billion annually, account for about 60 percent of this tonnage. Most of this is coal destined for one of the 37 or so power plants situated within the Ohio River Basin. Within this region, West Virginia ships out more coal than any other state, while power plants in the state of Ohio accept more coal than any other state. Sand and gravel, grains, chemicals, and iron and steel make up most of the remaining tonnage. About $12 billion worth of goods annually pass through McAlpine Lock, near Louisville.

Sketch 19-A contains two graphs depicting the barge tonnage shipped on the Ohio River by shipment commodity type, from 1997 to 2006 –the latest year of available data. This sketch is divided into two area graphs; one for downbound traffic, and the other for upbound barge traffic. Sketch 19-B shows how the tonnage on the Ohio River and its major tributaries compares with other large navigable national waterways in 2006. This sketch is in bar graph form, and both downbound and upbound tonnage are combined. Although there is more tonnage shipped on the Mississippi than on the Ohio River (e.g., 313 versus 241 million tons), if one compares 'the Mississippi River plus its tributaries' (of course, minus the Ohio) with 'the Ohio River plus its tributaries,' 'the Ohio plus its tributaries' carry more cargo –391 versus 334 million tons. By far, the Ohio and its

tributaries carry more coal than any other river system, while the Mississippi River carries significant amounts of petroleum, chemicals, and farm products. Sketch 19-C depicts the 2006 downbound and upbound tonnage for the Ohio River's six major navigable tributaries–the Tennessee, Cumberland, Big Sandy, Kanawha, Monongahela, and Allegheny Rivers. Sketch 19-C also presents commodity-type information. Downbound shipments on the Big Sandy, Kanawha, and Monongahela Rivers are dominated by coal. Upbound, the 650-mile long navigable Tennessee River dominates river traffic with a variety of commodities. The US Army Corps of Engineers, Waterborne Commerce Statistics Center was the source of the raw data for all three of these sketches.

## Barges

Today, most barges are 35 feet wide by 195 feet long. These are the 'jumbo' barges. You might occasionally see smaller barges, especially in the more upriver areas (e.g., on the Allegheny, Monongahela, upper Ohio and upper Kanawha Rivers). These smaller barges are 175 feet long by 26 feet wide, and they are called 'standard' barges. Over the years, as standard barges were retired, wherever possible, they were replaced with jumbo barges. The latest jumbo barges being constructed are now 35 feet wide by 200 feet long. There are also a handful of customized types and shapes. There are tank barges and deck barges that may not easily fit into any particular size. Tank barges carry bulk liquids such as gasoline, diesel, chemicals, and caustic sodas. Deck barges carry dredges, heavy earth moving machinery, military tanks, and other interesting cargos –like the space shuttle. During the mid-20th Century, many deck barges were customized into 'car carriers' and moved vehicles out of Evansville. Barges generally require nine feet of draft, but if the river levels permit, most companies will load them down to a draft of eleven feet.

196

# Sketch 17-A: Ohio River Waterborne Traffic

## Downbound

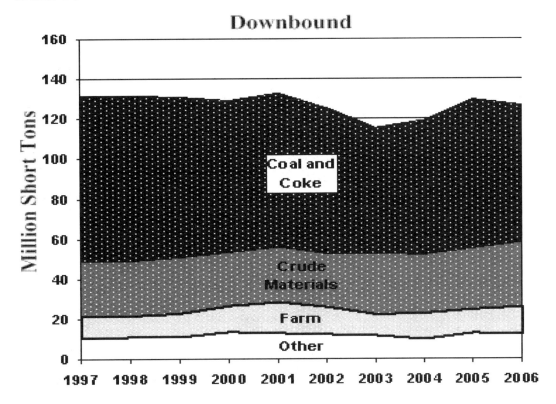

## Upbound

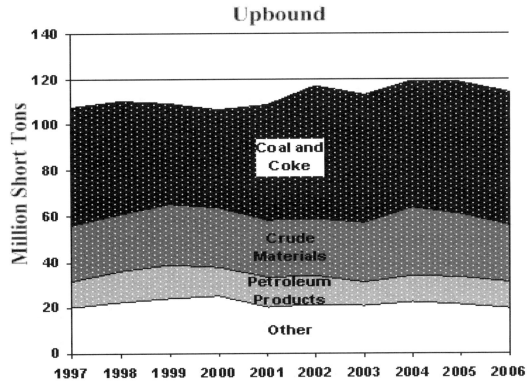

Source: US Army Corps of Engineers,
Waterborne Commerce Statistics Center

197

# Sketch 17-B: Domestic Waterborne Traffic, 2006, by Major US Waterway

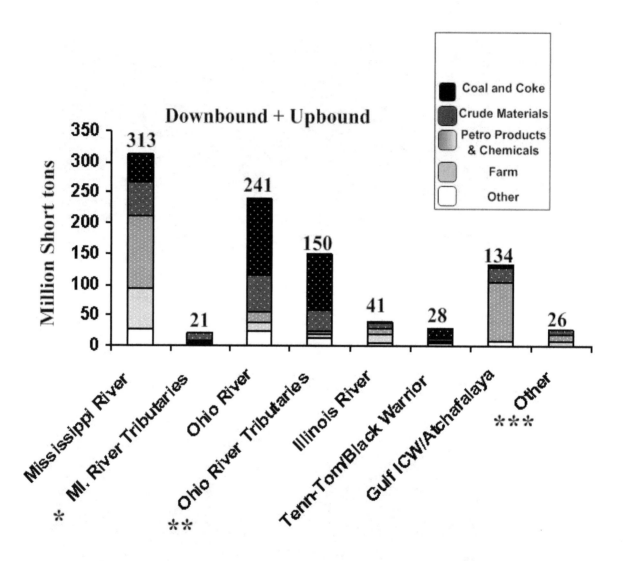

* Includes Arkansas and Missouri Rivers
** Includes Tennessee, Cumberland, Big Sandy,
  Kanawha, Monongahela, and Allegheny Rivers
*** Includes Columbia and Snake Rivers, and Atlantic ICW

**Source: US Army Corps of Engineers,
Waterborne Commerce Statistics Center**

# Sketch 17-C: Ohio River Tributaries, 2006 Waterborne Traffic

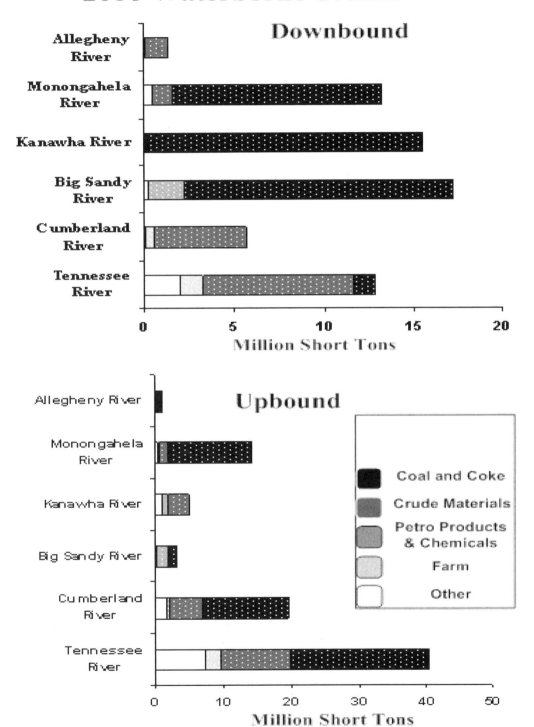

## Downbound

Million Short Tons

## Upbound

Million Short Tons

Legend:
- Coal and Coke
- Crude Materials
- Petro Products & Chemicals
- Farm
- Other

## Source: US Army Corps of Engineers, Waterborne Commerce Statistics Center

Jumbo and standard barges can be 'open hopper' or 'closed hopper.' Open hopper barges carry commodities that don't need protection from the elements –coal gravel, rocks, scrap steel, etc. Closed hopper barges typically carry grain, phosphate, paper, and steel. Some barges have a tapered hull at one end (at the bow and stern), while others barges are squared-off at both ends. The taper is called the 'rake.' When multiple barges are connected 'in line' to form a tow, it's more fuel efficient if the squared-off or boxy ends meet together in the middle of the tow configuration while the raked ends are at the bow and stern.

One jumbo open hopper barge can hold the same amount of contents as 58 tractor trailer trucks. The configuration of multiple barges tied together and pushed by a towboat is known as 'a tow.' When a tow is 'built,' there could be scores of different combinations. One important variable in configuring a tow is the size of the upcoming locking chambers (i.e., the width and the length inside of the locking pits). Tows moving upriver may be longer and narrower (e.g., two wide by five long) than nearly the same number of tows running downstream (e.g., three wide by three long). A 'three-by-three barge' configuration fits tightly, with no room to spare, in a 600-foot long by 110-foot wide locking chamber. But that pit would need to be longer (likely 800 feet) to also accommodate the attached towboat pushing these nine barges. Today, all but the three uppermost Ohio River locks have one large chamber that is 1,200 feet long.

Loaded tows that are five long by three barges wide are fairly common on the lower Ohio and mid-Mississippi Rivers. This typical 15-barge tow on the lower Ohio River can transport the yield from 12,000 acres of corn, or corn from twenty-four 500-acre farms! This tow, including the towboat, may be close to 1,200 feet long. That is longer than any ocean liner afloat! The Panama Canal is only 110 feet wide. That means that a 'four by six' tow (oftentimes seen on the middle and lower Mississippi River) couldn't fit through it. Have you ever seen an unbalanced tow? This could be an empty

barge lashed along the side of the towboat, and it's called a 'hip barge.' A single barge sticking out from the head of the tow is called a 'spike.'

## Towboats

Towboats are the beautifully-engineered and functionally-designed workhorses of ours rivers. Most towboats are between 50 and 200 feet in length. The smaller towboats or tugs, closer to 50 feet long, work around facilities, and move barges around in port areas. Most of the towboats pushing tows up or down these rivers are in the neighborhood of 150 feet long. The horsepower of many towboat engines is in the neighborhood of between 1,000 and 3,000 HP. There are even bigger engines producing 4,000 HP, and upwards! Most towboats have two engines, but a few larger ones have a third engine. A three-engine towboat, providing 3,000 HP per engine, is a 9,000 horsepower towing machine!

Below the waterline, a propeller – often called a wheel, sits inside of a Kort Nozzle. Most propellers are five-bladed, and nine feet in diameter. The Kort Nozzle is a huge rounded housing or shroud surrounding the propeller. A propeller working inside of a Kort Nozzle produces more thrust, especially at low RPMs. If a towboat has two propellers, it will have two Kort Nozzles. A steering rudder is aft of the Kort Nozzle and propeller, while typically two smaller flanking rudders are forward of each Kort Nozzle and propeller. It takes considerable expertise for a pilot to operate a twin-screw towboat with two Kort Nozzles and six rudders. Nevertheless, in the hands of skilled pilots, these vessels have become the wonderful workhorses of our waterways.

Above the waterline, the pilot is steering the entire tow from inside the pilothouse or bridge. This is the highest enclosed structure on the towboat. On some towboats, the entire pilothouse can be hydraulically raised to give the pilot a higher vantage point. Towboats do not have steering wheels. The rudders (as well as the propellers) are controlled by levers in the pilothouse. Unlike a recreational boat, a towboat pilot cannot shift gears (i.e. going from forward to reverse) quickly. The pilot has to wait about 30 seconds or so, for all his machinery to 'calm down' before shifting from forward to reverse, or visa versa. Two large reinforced 'tow knees' are integrated with the bow of the towboat, and built at deck level. These tow knees are the main connection points when pushing barges.

Once an upbound or downbound river tow is underway, it is on a 24/7 schedule. There are two six-hour shifts (i.e., each shift works two six-hour blocks per 24-hour day). Typical work schedules can be: '30 days On, then 30 days Off', or '21 days On, then 21 days Off,' or '28 days On, then 14 days Off.' When it's time for a crew change, the tow could belly-up to the nearest unimproved landing (oftentimes out in the middle of nowhere), while a new crew hops aboard, and the old crew hops off with their luggage. A company van or a waiting taxi drives the departing crew to the nearest airport, so they can return to their homes anywhere in the country. Of course, that unimproved debarking/embarkation point was likely decided upon within the last 24 hours or so. The onboard crew complement is about 9 or 10 seamen. The # 1 person responsible for the vessel's operation is the Captain. He is also known as the Master. The # 2 person is the Pilot. The Pilot operates the vessel and runs the shift when the captain is off duty. The salary for deckhands starts at around $25K per year. Captains can earn about three times that, but they may be on the river, and away from their families, for six months at a time.

The biggest complaint towboat captains have of small recreational vessels (i.e., RVs) is their not knowing, or not abiding by, the 'Rules of the Road.' More specifically, it's those particular rules that pertain to the encounters between large vessels (i.e., towboats) and smaller vessels (i.e., RVs). Towboats are constrained by their draft, and oftentimes *must* operate within confined narrow river channels. An RV has much more room to maneuver with a broader swath of river to work with than a tow.

## Odds and Ends

The iron-hulled towboat *Sprague*, built in 1902, was a paddlewheel steamboat. At 318-feet overall, she may have been the largest towboat ever. She held many records, including pushing 60 standard barges (i.e., 'a twelve by five' configuration of 175-feet by 26-feet empty barges) up the Mississippi and Ohio Rivers to Louisville. Another record was pushing 67,307 tons of coal. The *Sprague* wasn't retired until 1948.

Today, the longest towboat in the United States is the *MV Mississippi* at 241 feet in length. Although at 6,270 HP, there are many other towboats with more horsepower, especially on the lower Mississippi River. The *MV Mississippi* is owned by the US Army Corps of Engineers.

If you don't have your own boat, or don't wish to be hassled with all the details of owning and operating a boat, here's another unique new way to travel on the Ohio River as well as on several other mid-south rivers. Check out the *River Explorer* at 1-888-GO-BARGE, or www.riverbarge.com. The towboat, *Miss Nari* pushes a two-level (plus a sundeck) excursion barge carrying plain folks traveling or just wishing to learn more about our rivers. Round-trip and one-way excursions range from four to ten days, and start at about $1K per person. During the colder winter months the *River Explorer* is operating near New Orleans and the Gulf Coast. From June through October, she might be plying the Ohio or Kanawha Rivers stopping in such ports as Paducah, Louisville, Cincinnati, Marietta, Wheeling, Pittsburgh, or even Charleston West Virginia.

Tow getting ready to make a crew change near Brandenburg, Kentucky

The *River Explorer* on the Kanawha River

# ACKNOWLEDGEMENTS AND DEDICATION

In the late spring of 2005 while contemplating another guidebook project, and before starting a river trip, I queried a few folks. Knowledgeable Ron and Eva Stob generously shared their thoughts and expertise, along with the pros and cons of researching for a guide on several eastern water routes. But without hesitation, Dennis Bruckel suggested "the Ohio!"

Before the researching could begin in earnest, I knew that I would need to be away from my home base in St. Petersburg Florida for more than four months. Several folks back in St. Pete were more than helpful. Edie Christiansen provided a key suggestion regarding how the boating research might still be accomplished, given that my only option was to make a fall start with winter weather fast approaching. While I was away from my home base, Rich Gladd took care of my mail and property. During the writing phase, Pat Hoffman, despite having her own serious physical challenges, often nudged me along with encouragement.

While researching, a few old timers on the rivers gave me hell for not spending more time with them. There is no doubt that they are more knowledgeable about their 'neck-of-the-woods' than I could ever hope to be. But many didn't grasp the fact that I needed to cover the *entire* Ohio River and all its navigable tributaries. As it turned out, working nearly full time on this project – three trips through the area, including a two-month boat trip –took the better part of two years. Having done this type of research several times before, I knew that this Ohio River project was going to be comprehensive, and would require an inordinate amount of time and research. I realized that I didn't have the time or the luxury to sit down for hours and talk with folks who could have greatly enhanced my knowledge of one particular section of river. I honestly wish that I could have done that. But had I taken this more kindly approach, I

don't know when I would have been finished. Afterward, I would have collected even more information. This book might have contained 500 pages, or more. As it was, I had to synthesize more than 40 hours of audio tapes made during my travels. My conundrum was researching about 2,000 miles of rivers, packaging that information into a saleable product, and getting the whole work completed within two years. So, to you more knowledgeable 'river folks,' please accept my apologies for slighting my time spent with you.

A non-fiction work like this requires researching, assimilating, organizing, and verifying huge amounts of material. Obviously, I could not have done this without the help of many. A handful of professionals in the towboat industry were more than helpful in providing important information. These include Captain Larry Giesler of Duffy Ohio, Captain Mike Hosemann and his crew of the *Chattanooga Star,* Captain Kevin Mullen while serving on the *Belle of Louisville,* and especially Captain Robert Taylor at the Center for Maritime Education in Paducah. Captain Taylor improved this work by reviewing, and offering a handful of important suggestions regarding the commercial towboat chapter. Dick Thomas, of Ohio River Trails, Inc in Belpre Ohio, provided a wealth of helpful information on many river sites within the state of Ohio.

Occasionally while underway, I found myself in need of some out-of-the-ordinary services from a few of the lock tenders. I thank Pam Dolan on the Green River, as well as all of the lock tenders on the upper Monongahela River. I'd also like to thank a few boat clubs for their assistance. These clubs include members of the Ripley Boat Club on the Ohio, the River Forest Yacht Club on the Allegheny River, and especially the Ten Mile Yacht Club on the Monongahela River. The management at several marinas generously provided me with some helpful river insights. These include Mike Samples at Hidden Cove on the Kanawha River, Bob Wheeler at Turtle Creek Harbor in Florence Indiana, Dave Howerton at the Owensboro Executive Inn, and especially Captain Ron Riecken at Inland Marina in Evansville. Captain Ron imparted his local knowledge, as well having dug up an old nautical chart of the Wabash River.

I'd also like to thank Ronnie Joyner at Brandenburg Marina in Kentucky, Peggy Baust at Peggy's Harbor in Pittsburgh, and Ron Rowland, Pat Carr, and Ed Butcher at Woods Boat House in Fairmont West Virginia. These folks went out of their way to accommodate me as I was either starting-up or researching 'on the fly.' Peggy effectively allayed my fears one potentially gloomy evening in Pittsburgh. Likewise, the folks at Woods Boat House were equally helpful as my boat was experiencing several start-up problems. In Morgantown West Virginia, Stitch Wilson provided me with a 'base of operations' for a half week while I was working on these matters. A minor mishap plagued me on the Allegheny River, and Tim Connelly of Brackenridge bailed me out with his mechanical expertise and his hospitality. Tim is also a very knowledgeable source on the Allegheny River.

While underway, many helpful local Chambers of Commerce and Visitor Centers were more than generous with their time and resources. There are just too many to mention. Several larger institutions including the National Underground Railroad Freedom Center in Cincinnati, the Carnegie Science Center in Pittsburgh, the Campus Maritus and River Museums in Marietta and the Paducah River Heritage Museum greatly enhanced my local knowledge.

After the field research had been completed, several folks, with specialized local knowledge reviewed and improved this work. In the Pittsburgh area, James Donghia added his insights. Regarding the entire state of West Virginia, historian William 'Stitch' Wilson provided many helpful suggestions. Dave Howard, Emil Pastor, Ray Nickel, and Linda Zucco helped me cull through several hundred photographs in order to select the best ones. Jack Simpson of Little River Books was more than generous sharing his expertise on a few of my prepress questions.

This book was edited by Bill Byrnes. I was most pleasantly surprised at how meticulously, conscientiously, and professionally that Bill's contribution turned out to be. Bill grew up reading Charles Dickens. While attending high school in Queens, New York, Bill flunked three subjects during his junior year because he diverted more of his energies to reading Dickens rather than to his coursework. It proved most fortunate for me as well as for you readers that Bill, our Charles Dickens fan, was thereby able to improve this work.

**DEDICATION:** William E. 'Stitch' Wilson and I go back thirty-six years to our undergraduate days at West Virginia University. During one Christmas Break, my first motor vehicle –a Honda 450 motorcycle broke-down in the middle of Kentucky during what I hoped would have been my first trip to the Gulf Coast. After hitchhiking back to Morgantown, on the next day with no further thoughts or discussion, kindly Stitch took his pick-up truck and retrieved my broken-down cycle. This typifies Stitch. He is always most generous with his time and resources. While researching on my boat for this Ohio River trip, Stitch also stored my boat trailer for six months. Over the past ten years, I have often stayed at Stitch's summer cabin on the Potomac River while promoting my books of that region. Stitch, being an authority on history, has also helped edit and improve several of my books, including this one. So Stitch, thanks for your past friendship and assistance with my business …and my books. This one is dedicated to you!

# APPENDIX A
## Locks and Dams

**Ohio River:**

| Lock & Dam | Town | River Mile | Lock Side | Lock Lift/Drop (in feet) | Pool Elev (ft. above sea level) | Pool Length (miles) |
|---|---|---|---|---|---|---|
| Emsworth Lock & Dam | Pittsburgh, PA | 6.2 | RDB | 18 | 710 | 6.2 + |
| Dashields Lock & Dam | Glenwillard, PA | 13.3 | LDB | 10 | 692 | 7.1 |
| Montgomery L&D | Shippingsport, PA | 31.7 | LDB | 18 | 682 | 18.4 |
| New Cumberland L&D | Stratton, OH | 54.3 | RDB | 21 | 664 | 22.6 |
| Pike Island L&D | Warwood, WV | 84.2 | LDB | 21 | 644 | 29.9 |
| Hannibal L&D | Hannibal OH | 126.4 | RDB | 21 | 623 | 42.2 |
| Willow Island L&D | Reno, OH | 161.7 | RDB | 20 | 602 | 35.3 |
| Belleville L&D | Reedsville, OH | 203.9 | RDB | 22 | 582 | 42.2 |
| Racine L&D | Letart, WV | 237.5 | LDB | 22 | 560 | 33.6 |
| Robert Byrd L&D | Gallipolis Fry, WV | 279.2 | LDB | 23 | 538 | 41.7 |
| Greenup L&D | Greenup, KY | 341.0 | LDB | 30 | 515 | 61.8 |
| Captain Meldahl L&D | Chilo, OH | 436.2 | RDB | 30 | 485 | 95.2 |
| Markland L&D | Warsaw, KY | 531.5 | LDB | 35 | 455 | 95.3 |
| McAlpine L&D | Louisville, KY | 606.8 | LDB | 37 | 420 | 75.3 |
| Cannelton L&D | Cannelton, IN | 720.7 | RDB | 25 | 383 | 113.9 |
| Newburgh L&D | Newburgh, IN | 776.1 | RDB | 16 | 358 | 55.4 |
| John Myers L&D | Mt. Vernon, IN | 846.0 | RDB | 18 | 342 | 69.9 |
| Smithland L&D | Hamletsburg, IL | 918.5 | RDB | 22 | 324 | 72.5 |
| Lock & Dam # 52 | Brookport, IL | 938.9 | RDB | 12 | 302 | 20.4 |
| Lock & Dam # 53 | Grand Chain, IL | 962.6 | RDB | ≤17 | 290 | 23.7 |
| Olmsted L&D | Olmsted, IL | 964.5 | RDB | ≤30 | -- | 46.0 |

**Allegheny River:**

| Lock & Dam | Town | River Mile | Lock Side | Lock Lift/Drop (in feet) | Pool Elev (ft. above sea level) | Pool Length (miles) |
|---|---|---|---|---|---|---|
| Lock and Dam # 2 | Pittsburgh, PA | 6.7 | LDB | 11 | 721 | 7.8 |
| C.W. Bill Young L&D | East Oakmont, PA | 14.5 | LDB | 14 | 735 | 9.7 |
| Lock and Dam # 4 | Natrona, PA | 24.2 | RDB | 10 | 745 | 6.2 |
| Lock and Dam # 5 | Freeport, PA | 30.4 | RDB | 12 | 757 | 5.9 |
| Lock and Dam # 6 | Clinton, PA | 36.3 | RDB | 12 | 769 | 9.4 |
| Lock and Dam # 7 | W. Kittanning, PA | 45.7 | RDB | 13 | 782 | 6.9 |
| Lock and Dam # 8 | Templeton, PA | 52.6 | LDB | 18 | 800 | 9.6 |
| Lock and Dam # 9 | Cosmus, PA | 62.2 | LDB | 22 | 822 | ≈8.0 |

**Kanawha River:**

| Lock & Dam | Town | River Mile | Lock Side | Lock Lift/Drop (in feet) | Pool Elev (ft. above sea level) | Pool Length (miles) |
|---|---|---|---|---|---|---|
| Winfield Lock & Dam | Redhouse, WV | 31.1 | RDB | 28 | 566 | 36.6 |
| Marmet Lock & Dam | Dupont City, WV | 67.7 | RDB | 24 | 590 | 15.1 |
| London Lock & Dam | London, WV | 82.8 | RDB | 24 | 614 | ≈ 8 |

**Monongahela River:**

| Lock & Dam | Town | River Mile | Lock Side | Lock Lift/Drop (in feet) | Pool Elev (ft. above sea level) | Pool Length (miles) |
|---|---|---|---|---|---|---|
| Lock & Dam # 2 | Braddock, PA | 11.2 | RDB | 9 | 719 | 12.6 |
| Lock & Dam # 3 | Elizabeth, PA | 23.8 | RDB | 8 | 727 | 17.7 |
| Lock & Dam # 4 | Monessen, PA | 41.5 | RDB | 17 | 743 | 19.7 |
| Maxwell Lock & Dam | E. Millsboro, PA | 61.2 | RDB | 20 | 763 | 20.8 |
| Grays Landing L & D | Masontown, PA | 82.0 | RDB | 15 | 778 | 8.8 |
| Point Marion L & D | Point Marion, PA | 90.8 | LDB | 19 | 797 | 11.2 |
| Morgantown L & D | Westover, WV | 102.0 | LDB | 17 | 814 | 6.0 |
| Hildebrand L&D | Hildebrand, WV | 108.0 | LDB | 21 | 835 | 7.4 |
| Opekiska L&D | Opekiska, WV | 115.4 | RDB | 22 | 857 | ≈16.0 |

**Muskingum River:**

| Lock & Dam | Town | River Mile | Lock Side | Lock Lift/Drop (in feet) | Pool Elev (ft. above sea level) | Pool Length (miles) |
|---|---|---|---|---|---|---|
| Lock and Dam # 2 | Devola, OH | 5.8 | LDB | ≈ 12 | ≈ 594 | 8.4 |
| Lock and Dam # 3 | Lowell, OH | 14.2 | LDB | ≈ 12 | ≈ 606 | 10.9 |
| Lock and Dam # 4 | Beverly, OH | 25.1 | LDB | ≈ 12 | ≈ 618 | 9.0 |
| Lock and Dam # 5 | Luke Chute, OH | 34.1 | RDB | ≈ 12 | ≈ 630 | 6.1 |
| Lock and Dam # 6 | Stockport, OH | 40.2 | LDB | ≈ 12 | ≈ 642 | 9.2 |
| Lock and Dam # 7 | McConnelsville, OH | 49.5 | LDB | ≈ 12 | ≈ 654 | 8 |
| Lock and Dam # 8 | Rokeby, OH | 57.6 | LDB | ≈ 12 | ≈ 666 | 10.9 |
| Lock and Dam # 9 | Philo, OH | 68.6 | RDB | ≈ 12 | ≈ 678 | 8.3 |
| Lock and Dam # 10 | Zanesville, OH | 76.6 | LDB | ≈ 12 | ≈ 690 | 9.3 |
| Lock and Dam # 11 | Ellis, OH | 85.9 | LDB | ≈ 12 | ≈ 702 | Unk. |

**Kentucky River:**

| Lock & Dam | Town | River Mile | Lock Side | Lock Lift/Drop (in feet) | Pool Elev (ft. above sea level) | Pool Length (miles) |
|---|---|---|---|---|---|---|
| Lock & Dam # 1 | Carrollton, KY | 4.0 | RDB | ≈ 8 | ≈ 428 | 27.0 |
| Lock & Dam #2 | Lockport, KY | 31.0 | RDB | ≈ 14 | ≈ 442 | 11.0 |
| Lock & Dam #3 | Gest, KY | 42.0 | LDB | ≈ 14 | ≈ 456 | 23.0 |
| Lock & Dam #4 | Frankford, KY | 65.0 | LDB | ≈ 14 | ≈ 470 | ≈17.0 |

**Green River:**

| Lock & Dam | Town | River Mile | Lock Side | Lock Lift/Drop (in feet) | Pool Elev (ft. above sea level) | Pool Length (miles) |
|---|---|---|---|---|---|---|
| Lock and Dam #1 | Spotsville, KY | 9.1 | RDB | 7 | 349 | 54.0 |
| Lock and Dam #2 | Calhoun, KY | 63.1 | RDB | 14 | 363 | ≈45 |

* The lockmaster's telephone numbers and more specific information concerning the locks can be found in tables within the individual regional chapters (i.e., Chapters 6 through 16).

# APPENDIX B
## Connecting Highways on Both Sides of the Ohio River

### RDB (RIGHT DESCENDING BANK):

#### In Pennsylvania:
* PA Route 65 (from Pittsburgh to E. Rochester)
* PA Route 51 (from East Rochester to Beaver)
* PA Route 68 (from Beaver to Ohio State Line)

#### In Ohio: ++
* OH Route 39 (Pa State Line to East Liverpool)
* OH Route 7 (East Liverpool to Little Hocking)
* OH Routes 124, 338 (Little Hocking to Pomeroy)
* OH Route 7 (from Pomeroy to Chesapeake)
* US Route 52 (from Chesapeake to Cincinnati)
* US Route 50 (Cincinnati to Indiana State Line)

#### In Indiana: ++
US Route 50 (from Ohio State Line to Aurora)
* IN Routes 56 and 156 (from Aurora to Hanover)
* IN Route 62 (from Hanover to Sulphur)
* IN Route 66 (from Sulphur to Evansville)
* IN Route 62 (from Evansville to Illinois St.Line)

#### In Illinois: ++
IL Route 141 (from Indiana State Line)
County roads to IL 13, (from New Haven to
        Shawneetown)
IL Routes 13, 1, (from Shawneetown to
        Cave in Rock)
* IL Route 146 (Cave in Rock to Golconda)
County roads (from Golconda to Brookport)
US Route 45, (from Brookport to near Joppa)
County roads (from Joppa to Grand Chain)
* IL Route 37 (from Grand Chain to near Cairo)

**++NOTE: The entire RDB, From the PA-OH State Line to Cairo, Illinois is "The Ohio River Scenic Byway"**

* Denotes Routes with good Ohio River vistas

### LDB (LEFT DESCENDING BANK):

#### In Pennsylvania:
* PA Route 837 and 51 (the Point to Monaca)
PA Route 18 (from Monaca to near Shippingport)
PA Route 168 (from Shippingport to near to
        US Route 30)
US Route 30 (from PA Route 168 to Chester, WV)

#### In West Virginia:
* WV Route 2 (from Chester to Huntington)
* US Route 60 (from Huntington WV to Kentucky
        State Line)

#### In Kentucky:
* US Route 23 (Catlettsburg to nr. Portsmouth OH)
* KY Route 8 (near Portsmouth OH to North Bend
        Bottom). # There's a break on Route 8
        between Concord and Maysville.
* KY Routes 20, 18, & 338 (from Petersburg to Big
        Bone Lick). # There's a break between
        KY 338 and US Route 42
* US Route 42 (from East of Warsaw to Carrollton)
* KY Route 36 (from Carrolton to Milton)
US Route 421 (from Milton to Bedford)
US Route 42 (from Bedford to Harrods Creek)
* River Road (north and east of downtown
        Louisville). # There's a break between
        Downtown Louisville and Valley Station.
US Route 60 (Valley Station to Muldraugh)
Route 1638 (Muldraugh to near Brandenburg)
Route 228 (from Brandenburg to near Andyville)
Route 144 (from near Andyville to US Route 60)
US Route 60 (from Route 144 to Hawesville)
* Route 334 (from Hawesville to US Route 60)
* US Route 60 (from Route 334 to near Henderson)
Routes 136, 359, 360, 871, 667, and 109 + (from
        outside Henderson to near Sturgis)
Routes 365, US Route 60 (from near Sturgis to
        Marion)
Routes 91, 135, 133, 137  US 60 (from Marion to
        Wickliffe)

Lock on Allegheny River, near Acmetonia, Pennsylvania

Suspension Bridge near Rockport, Indiana

# APPENDIX C
## Hospitals in the Ohio River Valley

**PITTSBURGH AND WESTERN PENNSYLVANIA---------------------------------------------------:**

Allegheny General Hos.
320 East North Avenue
Pittsburgh, PA 15203
Phone: 412-359-3061

Children's Hos. of Pgh
3705 5th Avenue
Pittsburgh, PA 15213
Phone: 724-692-5325

Magee Women's Hospital
300 Halket Street
Oakland, PA 15213
Phone: 412-641-1000

Mercy Hospital
1515 Locust
Pittsburgh, PA 15219
Phone: 412-232-8111

Ohio Valley Gen. Hospital
Heckel Road
Pittsburgh, PA 15203
Phone: 412-777-6264

University of Pittsburgh
Medical Center (UPMC)
200 Lothrop St.
Pittsburgh, PA 15203
Phone: 412-578-8436

VA Hospital
Highland Drive
Pittsburgh, PA 15203
Phone: 412-363-4900

Western PA. Hospital
4800 Friendship Avenue
Pittsburgh, PA 15224
Phone: 412-578-5000

Heritage Valley H. Sys.
1000 Dutch Ridge Road
Beaver, PA 15009
Phone: 724-728-7000

**ON THE ALLEGHENY RIVER---------------------------------------------------------:**

Allegheny Valley Hospital
Natrona Hghts., PA 15065
Phone: 724-224-5100

Armstrong County
Memorial Hospital

1 Nolte Drive
Kittanning, PA 16201
Phone: 724-543-8500

**ON THE MONONGAHELA RIVER---------------------------------------------------------:**

Monongahela Valley Hos.
1163 Country Club Rd,
Monongahela, PA 15063
Phone: 724-258-1000

West Virginia University
Hospitals/Ruby Memorial

Medical Center Drive
Morgantown, WV 26506
Phone: 304-598-4000

Monongalia General Hos.
1200 J.D. Anderson Drive
Morgantown, WV 26505

Phone: 304-598-1200

Fairmont General Hospital
1325 Locust Avenue
Fairmont, WV 26554
Phone: 304-367-1482

**NEAR THE OHIO RIVER, RDB SIDE –EAST LIVERPOOL TO CINCINNATI, OHIO---:**

East Liverpool City Hos.
425 West 5th Street
East Liverpool, OH 43920
Phone: 330-385-7200

Trinity Health System
380 Summit Avenue
Steubenville, OH 43952
Phone: 740-264-8296

East Ohio Regional Hos.

90 North 4th Street
Martins Ferry, OH 43935
Phone: 740-633-1100

Belmont Com. Hospital
4697 Harrison Street
Bellaire, OH 43906
Phone 740-671-1250

Marietta Mem. Hospital
401 Matthew Street

Marietta, OH 45750
Phone: 740-374-1400

Selby General Hospital
1106 Colegate Drive
Marietta, OH 45750
Phone: 740-373-0582

Holzer Medical Center
100 Jackson Pike
Gallipolis, OH 45631

Phone: 740-446-5000

O'Bleness Mem. Hospital
55 Hospital Drive
Athens, OH 45701
Phone: 740-592-9495

Our Lady of Bellefonte
Hospital
Ironton, OH 45638
Phone: 606-833-3745

Sou. Ohio Medical Center
8770 Ohio River Road

Portsmouth, OH 45662
Phone: 740-354-5000

Adams County Hospital
210 N. Wilson Dr.
West Union, OH 45693
Phone: 937-544-5571

**THE CINCINNATI AREA**------------------------------------------------------------------------------------:

Bethesda North Hospital
10500 Montgomery Road
Cincinnati, OH 45242
Phone: 513-745-1111

Cincinnati Children's
Hospital Medical Center
3333 Burnet Avenue
Cincinnati, OH 45229
Phone: 740-636-4200

The Christ Hospital
2139 Auburn Ave.
Cincinnati, OH 45219
Phone: 513-585-2000

Deaconess Hospital
311 Straight Street
Cincinnati, OH 45219

Phone: 513-559-2100

The Ft. Hamilton Hospital
630 Eaton Ave.
Hamilton, OH 45013
Phone: 513-867-2000

Good Samaritan Hospital
11129 Kenwood Road
Cincinnati, OH 45242
Phone: 513-872-1400

The Jewish Hospital
4777 East Galbraith Road
Cincinnati, OH 45236
Phone: 513-686-3000

Mercy Hospital, Anderson
7500 State Road

Cincinnati, OH 45230
Phone: 513-624-4500

Mercy Franciscan Hospital
3131 Queen City Ave.
Cincinnati, OH 45238
Phone: 513-389-5000

Mercy Franciscan Hospital
Mt Airy 2446 Kipling Ave
Cincinnati, OH 45239
Phone: 513-853-5000

The University Hospital
234 Goodman Street
Cincinnati, OH 45219
Phone: 513-584-1000

**NEAR OHIO RIVER, LDB SIDE –WEIRTON TO HUNTINGTON, WEST VIRGINIA---:**

Weirton Medical Center
601 Colliers Way
Weirton, WV 26062
Phone: 304-797-6000

Wheeling Hospital
Medical Park
Wheeling, WV 26003
Phone: 304-243-3000

Ohio Valley Medical Ctr.
2000 Eoff Street
Wheeling, WV 26003

Reynolds Mem. Hospital
800 Wheeling Avenue,
Glen Dale (Moundsville),
WV 26038
Phone: 304-845-3211

Wetzel County Hospital
3 E. Benjamin Drive
N. Martinsville WV 26155
Phone: 304-455-8000

Sistersville General Hos.
314 S. Wells Street
Sistersville, WV 26175
Phone: 304-652-2611

Williamson Mem. Hos.
P.O. Box 1980
Williamson, WV 25661
Phone: 304-235-2500

Camden-Clark Mem. Hos.
800 Garfield Avenue
Parkersburg, WV 26101

Phone: 304-424-2111

St Joseph's Hospital
1824 Murdoch Ave
Parkersburg, WV 26101
Phone: 304-424-4111

Jackson General Hospital
P.O. Box 720
    (near Ravenswood)
Ripley, WV 25271
Phone: 304-372-2731

Pleasant Valley Hospital
2520 Valley Drive
Pt. Pleasant, WV 25550
Phone: 304-675-4340

Cabell Huntington Hos.

1340 Hal Greer Boulevard
Huntington, WV 25701
Phone: 304-526-2000

P.O. Box 448
Huntington, WV 25709
Phone: 304-525-7801

2900 1st Avenue
Huntington, WV 25702
Phone: 304-526-1234

Cornerstone Hos. of Hunt.
2900 First Avenue
Huntington, WV 25701
Phone: 304-399-2648

River Park Hospital
1230 Sixth Avenue
Huntington, WV 25701
Phone: 304-526-9111

Huntington VA Med. Ctr.
1540 Spring Valley Drive
Huntington, WV 25704
Phone: 304-429-6741

Mildred M-Bateman Hos.

St. Marys Hospital

## ON THE KANAWHA RIVER AND CHARLESTON-----------------------------------------------:

CAMC Memorial Hospital
3200 MacCorkle Ave. SE
Charleston, WV 25304
Phone: 304-388-5432

Saint Francis Hospital
P.O. Box 471
Charleston, WV 25322
Phone: 304-347-6500

Thomas Memorial Hos.
4605 MacCorkle Ave. SW
So. Charleston, WV 25309
Phone: 304-766-3600

Highland Hospital
300 56th Street
Charleston, WV 25304
Phone: 304-926-1600

Select Specialty Hospital
501 Morris Street
Charleston, WV 25301
Phone: 304-388-6671

Montgomery General Hos.
401 6th Ave # 302B
Montgomery, WV
Phone: 304-442-5151

## OHIO RIVER, LDB, ASHLAND TO PADUCAH KENTUCKY, EXCEPT LOUISVILLE :

Ashland Community Hos.
2200 Winchester Avenue
Ashland, KY 41101
Phone: 606-325-2728

Maysville, KY 41056
Phone: 606-564-0926

Phone: 502-732-4321

Owensboro Med. H. Sys.
811 East Parrish Avenue
Owensboro, KY 42303
Phone: 270-688-2000

King's Daughters M. Ctr
480 23rd Street
Ashland, KY 41101
Phone: 606-327-4682

St. Luke Hospital, East
85 North Grand Avenue
Fort Thomas, KY 41075
Phone: 859-572-3100

Methodist Hospital
1305 North Elm Street
Henderson, KY 42420
Phone: 270-827-7140

Our Lady Bellefonte Hos.
Ashland, KY 41101
Phone: 606-836-3148

St. Luke Hospital West
7380 Turfway Road
Florence, KY 41042
Phone: 859-212-4215

Western Baptist Hospital
Paducah, KY 42003
Phone: 270-575-2180

Fleming County Hospital
920 Elizaville Avenue

Carroll County Hospital
309 11th Street,
Carrollton, KY 41008

## THE LOUISVILLE AREA-----------------------------------------------------------------:

Audubon Hospital
1 Audubon Plaza Dr.
Louisville, KY 40217
Phone: 502-636-7257

Louisville, KY 40207
Phone: 502-896-7105

Frazier Institute/
Jewish Community Center
3920 Dutchmans Ln.
Louisville, KY 40207
Phone: 502-454-7363

Baptist Hospital East
4000 Kresge Way

Caritas Medical Center
1850 Bluegrass Ave.
Louisville, KY 40215
Phone: 502-361-6000

Jewish Hospital
217 E Chestnut St.
Phone: 502-587-4011

Kindred Hospital
1313 Saint Anthony Pl.
Louisville, KY 40204
Phone: 502-587-7001

Norton Healthcare
231 E Chestnut St.
Louisville, KY 40202
Phone: 502-629-6000

Univ. of Louisville Hos.
530 South Jackson

Louisville, KY 40202
Phone: 502-562-3030

VA Medical Center
800 Zorn Ave.
Louisville, KY 40206
Phone: 502-895-3401

## NEAR THE OHIO RIVER, THE RDB SIDE IN INDIANA--------------------------------------:

Dearborn County Hospital
600 Wilson Creek Road
Lawrenceburg, IN 47025
Phone: 812-537-1010

King's Daughter's Hos.
1 Kings Daughters Drive
Madison, IN 47250
Phone: 812-285-5211

Madison State Hospital
Madison, IN 47250
Phone: 812-265-2611

Clark Memorial Hos.
11500 Highway 62
Charlestown, IN 47111
Phone: 812-256-6714

Med. Ctr. of Sou. Indiana
2200 Market Street
Charlestown, IN 47111
Phone: 812-256-3301

Clark Memorial Hospital
Jeffersonville, IN 47130
Phone: 812-283-2521

Floyd Memorial Hospital
1850 State Street
New Albany, IN 47150
Phone: 812-944-7701

Sou. Indiana Rehab. Hos.
3104 Blackiston
New Albany, IN 47150
Phone: 812-941-8300

Harrison County Hospital
Corydon, IN 47112
Phone: 812-738-4251

Perry County Mem. Hos.
1701 Hospital Road
Tell City, IN 47586
Phone: 812-547-7011

Deaconess Hospital
600 Mary Street
Evansville, IN 47710
Phone: 812-464-5970

St Mary's Medical Center
3700 Washington Avenue
Evansville, IN 47714
Phone: 812-845-4000

## NEAR THE OHIO RIVER, THE RDB SIDE IN ILLINOIS--------------------------------------:

Harrisburg Medical Center
100 Hospital Drive
Harrisburg, IL 62946
Phone: 618-253-7671

VA Hospital
2401 West Main Street
Marion, IL 62959
Phone: 618-997-5311

Massac Memorial Hospital
28 Chick Street
Metropolis, IL 62960
Phone: 618-524-4402

## ON THE MUSKINGUM, KENTUCKY AND WABASH RIVERS-----------------------------:

MUSKINGUM:
Good Samaritan Hospital
800 Forest Avenue
Zanesville, OH 43701
Phone: 740-454-4503

KENTUCKY:
Frankfort Regional
Medical Center
Frankfort, KY 40601
Phone: 502-839-5575

WABASH:
Good Samaritan Hospital
520 South 7th Street
Vincennes, IN 47591
Phone: 812-885-3336

Terre Haute Reg. Hospital
3901 South 7th Street
Terre Haute, IN 47802
Phone: 812-237-1621

Union Hospital

Terre Haute, IN 47804
Phone: 812-238-7000

# APPENDIX D
## Major Universities in the Ohio River Valley

The Pittsburgh Area
University of Pittsburgh (Pittsburgh, PA)
Duquesne University (Pittsburgh, PA)
Carnegie Mellon University
        (Pittsburgh, PA)
Robert Morris University
        (Moon Township, PA)

The Monongahela River
Fairmont State (Fairmont, WV)
West Virginia University
        (Morgantown, WV)
California University of PA (California, PA)

The Upper Ohio River
Kent State University in East Liverpool
        (East Liverpool, OH)
Franciscan University of Steubenville
        (Steubenville, OH)
Wheeling Jesuit College (Wheeling, WV)
Marietta College (Marietta, OH)
Ohio Valley College (Parkersburg, WV)
Ohio University
        (Athens, OH on Hocking River)

The Muskingum River
Ohio University at Zanesville
        (Zanesville, OH)

The Kanawha River
West Virginia State Univ (Institute, WV)
University of Charleston (Charleston, WV)
WVU Institute of Technology
        (Montgomery, WV)

The Middle Ohio River
Marshall University (Huntington, WV)
Ohio University at Ironton (Ironton, OH)
Shawnee State University (Portsmouth, OH)
Hanover College (Madison, IN)
Eleutherian College (Madison, IN)

The Cincinnati Area
Thomas More College (Fort Thomas, KY)
Xavier University (Cincinnati, OH)
University of Cincinnati (Cincinnati, OH)
Southern Ohio College (Cincinnati, OH)

The Kentucky River
Kentucky State University (Frankfort, KY)

The Louisville Area
University of Louisville (Louisville, KY)
Bellarmine College (Louisville, KY)
Indiana University –Southeast
        (New Albany, IN)

The Lowest Ohio River
Brescia University (Owensboro, KY)
Kentucky Wesleyan College
        (Owensboro, KY)
University of Evansville (Evansville, IN)
University of Southern Indiana
        (Evansville, IN)
Murray State –Henderson Campus
        (Henderson, KY)

The Green-Barren Rivers
Western Kentucky University
        (Bowling Green, KY)

The Wabash River
Vincennes University (Vincennes, IN)
Indiana State University (Terre Haute, IN)
Purdue University (West Lafayette, IN)

The Cumberland River
Austin Peay University (Clarksville, TN)
Vanderbilt University (Nashville, TN)
Fisk University (Nashville, TN)
Tennessee State University (Nashville, TN)

The Tennessee River
Murray State University (Murray, KY)
Univ. of Northern Alabama (Florence, AL)
Univ. of Tennessee-Chattanooga (Chat. TN)
University of Tennessee (Knoxville, TN)

**Spanish Caravel in Maysville, Kentucky**

**Kanawha Falls near Glen Ferris, West Virginia**

# APPENDIX E
## Some Spring-Summer-Falls Annual Festivals Along The Rivers

| Approximate Time Frame | City/Town | Event/Festival | Sponsor, Comments, other Info: |
|---|---|---|---|
| Mid-March | Marietta, OH | R. City Blues Fest. | The Lafayette Hotel, ☎ 740-373-5522 |
| Late-April | Paducah, KY | Quilters Show | ☎ 270-442-8856, www.quiltmuseum.org |
| Late-April | Louisville, KY | Thunder Over Louisville | Kicks-off Kentucky Derby Week, Waterfront Park, ☎ 502 584-6383 |
| Kentucky Derby Week | Louisville, KY | Great Steamboat Race | Belle of Louisville versus Delta Queen, ☎ 502- 584-6383 |
| 2nd wknd May | Owensboro, KY | BBQ Festival | ☎ 270-926-1100, www.visitowensboro.com |
| Mid-May | Pittsburgh, PA | V. Outdoors Fest. | Pittsburgh's North Shore, Near Heinz Field |
| Mid-May | Pittsburgh, PA | Colonial Fair | Fort Pitt Museum, Point State Park, Pittsburgh |
| Late-May | Louisville, KY | KY. Reggae Fest. | River Road & Zorn Avenue, ☎ 502-583-0333 |
| Late-May | Louisville, KY | Abbey Road Fest | Belvedere Festival Park, on River |
| Late-May | Metropolis, IL | F&I War Reenact | French & Indian War at Fort Massac |
| Memor. Day | Fairmont, WV | 3 Rivers Festival | Weekend Festival |
| June | NewMartinsville | River Herit. Days | In New Martinsville, WV |
| June | Rokeby, OH | Lock Festival | Muskingum River Parkway |
| Early-June | Pittsburgh, PA | 3 Riv. Arts Fest. | Point State Park |
| Early-June | Cincinnati, OH | Meijer's Kids Fest | at Sawyer Point & Bicentennial Commons |
| 2nd wknd June | Newburgh, IN | Summerfest | Near Ohio River |
| 2nd wknd June | Metropolis, IL | Superman Festival | In Town |
| Mid-June | Henderson, KY | WC Handy Blues/ BBQ Festival | ☎ 270-826-3128, www.hendersonky.org |
| Late-June | Wheeling, WV | African-American Jubilee | Diana, ☎ 304-232-0511, email: ywcadiana@aol.com |
| Last weekend June | St. Albans, WV | Riverfest | Port of St. Albans |
| Last weekend June | Augusta, KY | Sternwheel Regatta | Ohio River |
| Last week June | Evansville, IN | Freedom Festival | ☎812-421-1120, www.evansvillefreedomfestival.org |
| Near July 4th | Pittsburgh, PA | Pittsburgh Regatta | Point State Park |
| Near July 4th | Point Pleasant, WV | Sternwheel Regatta | And River Festival |
| Near July 4th | Frankfort, KY | KY. Riverfest | Kentucky River |
| Near July 4th | Cincinnati, OH | LaRosa's  Balloon Glow | 6201 Kellogg Ave, Coney Island |
| Early July | Gallipolis, OH | River Rec. Festival | Ohio River |
| Early-July | Cincinnati, OH | River Way Paddlefest | ☎ 513-588-6936; email: info@ohioriverway.org |
| July | Kenova, WV | Virginia Pt. Days | |
| Mid-July | Allegheny River, PA | Oakmont Yacht Club Regatta | Washington Avenue, Oakmont, PA |
| Late July | Wheeling, WV | Italian Heritage | Third largest Italian Festival in the United |

| | | Festival | States. |
|---|---|---|---|
| Late-July | Cincinnati, OH | Cin. Blues Festival | Sawyer Point in Cincinnati |
| Late-July | Paducah, KY | Summer Festival | www.paducah-tourism.org |
| August | Aurora, IN | Riverboat Regatta | |
| August | Newport, KY | Arts and Mus. Fair | ☎ 606-555-5555 |
| August | Elizabethtown, IL | Civil War Reenactment | And Heritage Festival |
| Early August | Kittanning, PA | Folk Festival | Fort Armstrong at Riverfront Park |
| 1st weekend August | N. Harmony, IN | Wabash Heritage Paddlefest | ☎ 812-682-4488, www.canoeevansville.com |
| 2nd weekend August | Ghent, KY | Riverboat Festival | Ohio River |
| Mid-August | N. Richmond, OH | River Days | ☎ 513-684-1253 |
| Mid-August | Madison, IN | Ribberfest | Ohio River |
| 3rd weekend August | Huntington, WV | Ribfest Festival | At Harris Riverfront Park, ☎ 304-696-5990 |
| Last weekend August | Ripley, OH | Ohio Tobacco Festival | Ohio River |
| Last weekend August | Livermore, KY | Livermore Boat Races | Green River |
| Late-August /Labor Day | Charleston, WV | Sternwheel Regatta | Off Haddad Park |
| Labor Day weekend | Wheeling, WV | Vintage Race Boat Regatta | Heritage Port |
| Labor Day weekend | Portsmouth, OH | River Days Festival | Ohio River |
| September | Cave-In-Rock, IL | Frontier Days | Near Ohio River |
| Early-Sept. | Cincinnati, OH | Riverfest | At Sawyer Point & Bicentennial Commons, ☎ 513-686-8597 |
| Early-mid Sept | Pittsburgh, PA | Dragon Boat Fest. | South Side Riverfront Park |
| Mid-Sept | Moundsville,WV | Riverfest | Ohio River |
| Mid-Sept | Sistersville, WV | Oil & Gas Festival | Near Ohio River |
| Mid-Sept. | Marietta, OH | Sternwheeler Fest. | Ohio River Sternwheel Festival |
| Mid-Sept. | Golconda, IL | Shrimp Festival | |
| Late-Sept. | Cincinnati, OH | Oktoberfest Zinzinnati | At Fountain Square, 5th Street from Vine to Broadway |
| Last weekend September | Pomeroy, OH | Sternwheeler Festival | Sternwheel River Festival |
| Last weekend September | Paducah, KY | Marine Industry/ Old Market Days | And BBQ on River www.paducah-tourism.org |
| Oct., every 3 or 4 years | Cincinnati, OH | Tall Stacks Festival | ☎ 513-721-0104, www.tallstacks.com |
| Early-Oct. | Pt. Pleasant, WV | Battle Days | Near Ohio River |
| 1st wknd, Oct. | Aberdeen, OH | River Festival | Ohio River |
| 3rd Sat., Oct. | New Riv. Gorge | Bridge Day | West Virginia's Largest Gorge, New River |
| 3rd wknd, Oct | Metropolis, IL | The Encampment | At Fort Massac |

# BIBLIOGRAPHY

**Books:**

Anderson, Fred, *The War that Made America*, New York, NY, Viking/Penguin Group 2005

Bigham, Darrel E, *Towns and Villages of the Lower Ohio*, Lexington, KY, University of Kentucky Press, 1998

Blockson, Charles L, '*Escape from Slavery, The Underground Railroad*' National Geographic Magazine, July 1984

Bordewich, Fergus M, *Bound for Canaan, the Underground Railroad*, New York, NY, Harper Collins Publishers, 2005

Griffler, Keith P, *Frontline of Freedom,* Lexington, KY, University of Kentucky Press, 2004

Hagedorn, Ann, *Beyond the River*, New York, NY, Simon & Schuster, 2002

Harrison, Lowell H, *George Rogers Clark and the War in the West*, Lexington KY, 1976

Hartford, John, *Steamboat in a Cornfield*, New York, NY, Crown Publishers, Inc, 1986

Newman, Clarence W, *Ohio River Navigation, Past, Present, Future,* Huntington, WV, US Army Corps of Engineers, 1979

Rhodes, Captain Rick, *The Ohio River –In American History and Voyaging On Today's River,* St. Petersburg, FL, Heron Island Guides, 2007

Spencer, H. Nelson, *The Waterways Journal*, St. Louis MO, weekly magazine

Spencer, H. Nelson, *Quimby's 2006 Cruising Guide*, St. Louis MO, annual guidebook, 2006

Swift, James V., *Backing Hard Into River History*, Florissant MO, Little River Books, 2000

Teets, Bob and Young, Shelby, *Killing Waters*, Terra Alta, WV, Cheat River Publishing, 1985

Thom, James Alexander, *Follow the River*, New York, NY, Ballantine/Random House Books, 1981

Troyanek, Captain Gerald A., *Cruising Guide for the Ohio River Valley*, LaCrosse, WI, Delivery Captains.com, 2002

**Websites:**

Encyclopedia Britannica:  http://www.britannica.com/
Indiana Historical Society: http://www.indianahistory.org/
Kentucky Historical Society: http://kentucky.gov/kyhs/hmdb/
Ohio Historical Society: http://www.ohiohistory.org/
Pennsylvania Historical and Museum Commission: http://www.phmc.state.pa.us/
West Virginia Division of Culture and History: http://www.wvculture.org/history/
Wikipedia Encyclopedia: http://en.wikipedia.org/

# COVER PHOTOGRAPHS

**Front:**
    'Pittsburgh's Point' and confluence of Allegheny and Monongahela Rivers.......upper left
    Sunset on the lower Ohio, near Brandenburg Kentucky......................................lower left
    That notorious lair –Cave-In-Rock, Illinois........................................................upper right

**Back:**
    Cincinnati Ohio, seen from across the Ohio River in Covington Kentucky.........upper third
    Along the upper Ohio River near Wellsburg, West Virginia...............................middle left
    The Allegheny and Kiskiminetas Rivers, near Schenley, Pennsylvania...............middle right
    Vibrant Audubon Park in Henderson Kentucky .................................................lower left
    Six miles from head of navigation on the Kanawha River, Smithers, WV .........lower right

# INDEX

## LST 325, Evansville, Indiana

Allegheny River, near Rimer, PA

**Other Books by Captain Rick Rhodes:**

*The Ohio River –in American History and Voyaging on Today's River,* Heron Island Guides,
    ISBN 0-9665866-33
*Discovering the Tidal Potomac, Second Edition,* Heron Island Guides, ISBN 0-9665866-2X
*Cruising Guide to Florida's Big Bend,* Pelican Publishing Company, ISBN 1-5898007-29
*Cruising Guide from Lake Michigan to Kentucky Lake--The Heartland Rivers Route,*
    Pelican Publishing Company, ISBN 1-5655499-53
*Honduras and Its Bay Islands,* 1998, Heron Island Guides, ISBN 0-9665866-11

**More Details:**

*The Ohio River, in American History –***HARDCOVER**, 224 8½" X 11" pages, including 23 river sketches with 86 black and white photographs. $29.95. 2008

*The Ohio River –in American History and Voyaging on Today's River –*320 8½" X 11" pages, including 31 river sketches with 86 black and white photographs. $35.95. 2007

*Discovering the Tidal Potomac, Second Edition –*240 8½" X 11" pages, including 35 pages of NOAA chart extracts, and 14 pages of river/town/marina plan view sketches with 88 black and white photographs. $26.95. 2003

*Cruising Guide to Florida's Big Bend, Including the Apalachicola, Chattahoochee, Flint, and Suwannee Rivers –*360 8" X9¼" pages, including 27 pages of NOAA chart extracts, and 26 pages of river/canal/town sketches with 150 black and white photographs $32.95. 2003

*Cruising Guide from Lake Michigan to Kentucky Lake –The Heartland Rivers Route –*205 8" X 9¼" pages, including five pages of NOAA chart extracts, and 19 pages of river/area/lock sketches with 70 black and white photographs. $28.95. 2002

---

### ORDER FORM

**BOOKS:**

___ books, *The Ohio River, in American History* (HARDCOVER) @ $29.95
___ books, *The Ohio River –in American History & Voyaging Today's River* @ $35.95
___ books, *Discovering The Tidal Potomac, Second Edition* @ $26.95
___ books, *Discovering The Tidal Potomac, 1st Ed.* @ $20.00 (outdated, but has color photos)
___ books, *Cruising Guide to Florida's Big Bend* @ $32.95
___ books, *Cruising Guide from Lake Michigan to Kentucky Lake* @ $28.95

**SHIPPING:**

For Shipping and Handling, please add $3.95 for one book; add $1.95 per additional book.

Florida Residents, please add a 7% sales tax.

Check or money order for book amount plus shipping, payable to 'Heron Island Guides,' should accompany your order form. Quantity discounts offered on large orders. Phone 888-459-5992. Please allow three weeks for delivery. Mail your check to 'Heron Island Guides;' #305, 2560 62nd Avenue North; St. Petersburg, Florida 33702, or Fax to 727-527-8287, or email rick@rickrhodes.com, or visit us on the web at www.heronislandguides.com.

**Please don't forget to provide us with your name, address & telephone number or email.**

# Downbound Coal Tow near Mauckport, Indiana

## Ohio River Scenic Byway in Ohio